BUFFO

The Genius of Vulgar Comedy

Frontispiece to Terence Codex, fifteenth century, Bibliothèque de l'Arsenal, Paris.

Anthony Caputi
Cornell University

The Genius of Vulgar Comedy

WAYNE STATE UNIVERSITY PRESS   DETROIT, 1978

Library of Congress Cataloging in Publication Data

Caputi, Anthony Francis, 1924-
    Buffo: the genius of vulgar comedy.

    Bibliography: p.
    Includes index.
    1.   Comedy—History and criticism.
2.   Farce. I.   Title.
PN1922.C3   809.2'52   78-15992
ISBN   0-8143-1606-9

For my father,
one of the great lovers of *buffo*

Contents

Contents

Illustrations

Illustrations

My primary interest is in the meaning of vulgar comedy and its place in human history. What explains its persistent popularity, its remarkable intensity of effect, its extraordinary power? How has it changed in the course of the centuries, and why? What does it tell us about other kinds of comedy and about comedy in general? These larger questions underlie the discussion of specific forms of comedy throughout the text.

For much of what follows I am deeply indebted to others, and those who know what has been written on the subject will readily recognize my debts to the pioneers in the field. Accordingly, I have decided to indicate these debts either in the text or in the Bibliographical Commentary to each chapter, rather than burdening the discussion with notes. The Commentary is intended as a general guide to the works which I have found important to the discussion at hand; it is supplemented by a full bibliography. But some names must be mentioned here as well, for without them this study could not exist: E. K. Chambers, A. W. Pickard-Cambridge, C. R. Baskervill, Allardyce

Nicoll, Arnold van Gennep, and, most particularly, Paolo Toschi.

There are also a great many of those ostensibly impersonal debts without which such personal commodities as time and the opportunity to travel to the sources would have been difficult to arrange. I wish to thank the American Commission for Cultural Exchanges with Italy for a Fulbright Fellowship in 1964–65; the Guggenheim Memorial Foundation for a supplementary fellowship in that same year; the Harvard University Center for Italian Renaissance Culture at I Tatti for the generous hospitality and assistance which it provided me as a fellow; the National Endowment for the Humanities for a fellowship which enabled me to return to Europe to finish my research in 1971–72; Cornell University for academic leaves in 1964–65 and 1971–72; and the Cornell Research Grants Committee for financial assistance in the preparation of the manuscript.

Finally, I wish to thank my generous and learned friends for all the help that only such friends can give. My special thanks go to Pietro Pucci, Alain Seznec, Carlo Arcangeli, Alison Lurie, James H. Clancy, and Robert M. Adams.

PART I
Origins

Introduction

Talking about comedy is a little like talking about food: all forms of it fill roughly the same need in our lives. But the general term "comedy," even if carefully defined, tells us little or nothing about its sub-types, any more then the word "alimentation" tells us about Chinese cooking. Moreover, comedy's sub-types have about as much to do with each other as Beef Wellington has to do with a Napoleon. What, after all, does Laurel and Hardy's *Night Owls* have in common with Congreve's *The Way of the World*? Or John Heywood's *John John, Tyb,* and *Sir John* with *Twelfth Night*? A definition of comedy which enbraces these plays and others would be so general that it would tell us almost nothing about particular works.

Vulgar comedy is a sub-type of comedy, persisting robustly through centuries of vicissitudes, and at the same time is the father of numerous sub-types. It is the twice-fried beans, the potatoes, the pasta of comedy, what the Italians, with more than chronological accuracy, call the "first." It is the oldest, most widespread, most durable type of comedy we know; it is widely loved and widely scorned.

We find it virtually everywhere in dramatic history: in the Dorian mime, in the farces of the Middle Ages, in the scenarios of the commedia dell'arte, in the boulevard comedies of Feydeau, and in the films of Charlie Chaplin. Despite its age, it is very spry.

Critics have called it by various names, each of which has a limited usefulness. The term "popular comedy" works perfectly well for the plays of Hans Sachs, which were comedies of the people, so to speak, but it will hardly do for the elegancies of Eugène Labiche or Tiberio Fiorilli, the favorite Scaramouche of Louis XIV. "Farce" is the term usually used for the village square comedies of the Middle Ages and for such recent work as *Charley's Aunt*, yet not all critics would accept it as a description of the Dorian mime or certain examples of English pantomime. Moreover, as a critical term it is usually applied to dramatic wholes, while I shall sometimes be concerned with bits and pieces of plays. The term "low comedy," on the other hand, frequently identifies parts of plays, particularly episodes in Elizabethan plays, but is rarely used to describe whole ones. Indeed, the problem of terminology reflects a still deeper problem of form. As we shall see, vulgar comedy frequently reveals itself in characteristic forms — that is, in characteristic dramatic structures — yet it is not primarily or essentially determined by structure: it often reveals itself in characteristic materials or as parts of plays which are not comedies at all.

Of all the descriptive terms in use, "vulgar comedy" seems the most helpful because it points a little more decisively than the term "popular comedy" to the origins of this comedy in the traditions of the *vulgus* or folk, and suggests the relative simplicity of the state of thoughts and feelings which it elicits. Although, like other kinds of comedy, vulgar comedy produces laughter and smiles and an agreeable sense of well-being in the beholder, it has little in common with the laughter heard in Milton's heaven or the serenity of the archaic smile. This laughter is explosive and frenetic; in a popular American idiom it "breaks people up." Moreover, vulgar comedy does not stimulate serenity, or a wise, sophisticated acquiescence, or an enlarged idea of life. It is unintellectual and unphilosophical. Instead of a residue of thought, it leaves a tingle in the blood.

Consider, for a moment, what we think and feel as Scapin mimics different voices in tormenting and beating on the hapless Géronte, crouched ignominiously in his sack: in each persona Scapin threatens and fulminates while the sack twitches and quivers, then he kicks and pummels. Or consider our responses as Act IV of *The Alchemist* mounts to a fine frenzy: Dapper is in a closet, his gingerbread gag in his mouth, awaiting the Queen of Fairy, Mammon is in another room with Dol Common as the mad noblewoman who can bear no talk of divinity, and Surly as a Spanish don is in yet another room with Dame Pliant. Kastril gets his lesson in swearing from Face as the Captain; Dol comes in mad as a hatter because Mammon has touched on divinity; then comes the explosion: Face, his face blackened, comes in to report that Mammon's experiments have aborted because he has had unchaste thoughts; then Surly comes back speaking in his own person, full of threats, to meet, in succession, Drugger, who accuses him of owing him money, Kastril, who is spoiling for a quarrel, and Ananias, who sees this Spaniard as a "child of perdition." Or visualize Laurel and Hardy as they struggle up that interminable stairway with the piano, only to have something go wrong at the last moment and have it clatter all the way down to the sidewalk; or all the characters in Feydeau's *La Puce à l'oreille* ("A Flea in Her Ear") as they arrive at the Hotel Minet Galant are enveloped in a series of surprise meetings, rooms with trick beds, a drunken porter who is a twin for the central figure of husband-lover-friend, and an incensed Latin husband waving a pistol as he chases all the others. Clearly there is very little in all this of a carefully articulated vision, very little of arguments or ideas or highly complex states of feelings. These passages, with their hysterical life, elicit intense laughter, robust but notably uncritical. Even in the passage from *The Alchemist*, a play in which satirical values dominate, the mind is awash with a hilarity that is scarcely intellectual. This is vulgar comedy.

We all know vulgar comedy from plays like *Room Service* or *Arsenic and Old Lace,* or from the comic "acts" of circus clowns or television comedians. Most of us know vaguely that for centuries it has been condemned by literary critics and moralists, even as its great practitioners — the *farceurs* of ancient Rome, seventeenth- and eighteenth-century France, and the present — have been the darlings of their times. We and our predecessors have acquiesced in this condemnation, though we know that nothing can elicit more intense responses — tears, convulsions of laughter, and, in the most susceptible, a loss of control which causes us to fall to the floor or thump our neighbors unmercifully.

To account for this intensity, perhaps even to explain what this pleasure has meant to audiences for so long, I propose to look at both the plays and their antecedents in folk ritual and primitive theatrical practice. For years C. L. Barber's *Shakespeare's Festive Comedies* has served as a model for such studies; certainly no one before or since has seen more deeply into the relationship between folk custom and artistic form or has written about them more imaginatively. In seeking to illuminate the form and a good deal of the detail of what he calls Shakespeare's festive comedies, Barber looks to their antecedents in holiday rituals and customs and stresses the "saturnalian pattern" of traditional festive activities, a pattern of "release through clarification" to be found both in these customs and in the comedy derived from them. While clarifying and exploring this pattern at length in the May games and the figure of the Lord of Misrule, he produces a series of extraordinarily shrewd, subtle, and judicious essays which explain the ebullience and lyricism of plays like *A Midsummer-Night's Dream, As You Like It,* and *Twelfth Night,* as well as many of the deeper ambiguities of those plays, *The Merchant of Venice,* and the Henry IV plays.

Yet the student surveying Barber's achievement must be alert to certain self-imposed limitations in his work. His decision, for example, to focus on the May games and the figure of the Lord of Misrule as paradigmatic of the full range of festive occasions and activities has the effect of collapsing, to a considerable extent, the variety inherent in the festive material and of encouraging the inference that there is a single controlling principle in these celebrations, when there may have been many. Moreover, his decision to restrict himself almost exclusively to English folklore when dealing with experiences common to most of Europe means that better preserved and more complete evidence is ignored. As Barber recognizes, the object of this kind of study is not simply to identify an underlying rhythm, or to trace fossils of character and remnants of action, or even to account for a peculiarly festive tone, but to understand the interpenetration of all these in what linguists might call the deep structure of the work. In fact, his self-imposed limitations rarely leave anything to be desired in his work because in Shakespeare's festive comedies he is dealing with a narrow body of English drama, however important that body may be, for which English backgrounds are largely sufficient, and a body of drama distinct from those backgrounds in its sophistication. Shakespeare's festive comedies can hardly be described as theatrical attempts to duplicate the emotional content of folk festivals: they are to folk festivals what Charles Ives' symphonies are to American folk songs.

My purpose is to illuminate a much less sophisticated but more fundamental species of comedy, and to do so using the extended background of European folklore as well as other evidence. I want to dig at the roots not only of Shakespeare's festive comedies but of all those highly developed comic forms (satirical comedy and the comedy of manners among them) which are elaborations of older, simpler comic models. I wish to understand those older models as they survive most clearly in the coarse-grained, knockabout plays which are usually called farces or popular comedies and which I shall call vulgar comedy.

I see the key element in both the plays and their antecedents in folk ritual and primitive theatrical practices to be a quality which I take to be central in all the dramatic structures called "farces," "popular comedies," or "low comedies," as well as in the dramatic materials designated by terms like "comic turns," *lazzi,* or "farcical elements." This quality pervades these plays and scenes, as well as the rituals, like the laughter of a drunken Silenus, dominating all other qualities so completely that it can be seen as their governing principle. Finally, I shall argue that it is fundamental to what we are stimulated to think and feel by vulgar comedy and to what vulgar comedy means. For want of a better term, I shall call it *buffo.*

Buffo is an Italian word which identifies what in English we might call the humorous, the ridiculous, the ludicrous, or the funny. Though it has a long history, it has not accumulated the secondary meanings which complicate these English words and, in fact, most words which have been much used in theoretical discussions of comedy. *Buffo* points to the comic and the laughable, but to the comic and laughable as they exist apart from such sophisticated issues as irony, satire, wit, parody, and burlesque. It designates an instinctive, uncritical, frenetic species of fun like that indicated by Joachim du Bellay when he invites us in his carnival sonnet (*Les Regrets,* cxx, 1558) to watch Zanni *bouffonner* with Pantalone, or like that personified in the mischievous figure of Buffone, the presiding devil in the Italian May plays, or *maggi.*

Because of its long history and because its vehicle, vulgar comedy, emerges from folkloric backgrounds not once but several times, I shall look carefully at the vast, complex mass of rituals, folk customs, folk plays, and primitive comedies. Next, I propose to look at the materials from which vulgar comedies are typically made, at the forms which give them shape and organic character, and at the characteristic manner of their performance by actors and entertainers. Finally, I shall look at the relevant work of comic theorists for whatever help it might supply in sifting and evaluating these multiple perspectives. My aim, of course, is to bring all these bodies of evidence to bear on *buffo.*

1

The Background of Antiquity

Virtually all who have written on the development of comedy have traced its origins to ritual revels or to parts of ritual revels. The arguments are always problematical, and there are always critics who point out that evidence of resemblances between early comedies and ritual revels is not proof of derivation. But those who have looked most closely are almost unanimous in the conclusion that some evolutionary connection there was. Aristotle, our earliest theorist, explained that comedy "was at first mere improvisation" and that it "originated with the authors . . . of the phallic songs." Writers since have followed his lead by tracing it more elaborately to various seasonal rituals celebrating the death of winter and the rebirth of spring, fertility, and health. Much of this work is highly valuable, and all of it is useful. The trouble is that none of it suggests the actual complexity of the origins of vulgar comedy because most of the theorists, at least the best of them, are dealing narrowly with Attic or Roman comedy and their origins in Dionysiac ritual revels or the Roman Saturnalia.

The first task in tracing vulgar comedy to its folkloric backgrounds is to realize that the story is extraordinarily complicated. Vulgar comedy has many origins. There is a network of continuities and discontinuities leading from antiquity to the Renaissance, or more accurately, a series of emergences and re-emergences, births and rebirths, with the dramatic forms which crystallized in antiquity exerting now a major and now a minor influence. The story of these continuities and discontinuities reveals an elusive process of syncretism in which the same, or very nearly the same, expressive impulses recur with the regularity of hunger. Sometimes what seems at first glance a new form of vulgar comedy on closer inspection suggests a consciously sustained continuity with the past; sometimes, on the other hand, a new form really seems a fresh breaking out, or at least a re-invention. As we shall see, the Dionysiac revels which doubtless lay behind the Dorian mime, the satyr play, and the *phlyax* farces in Greece are probably not as important and useful to our understanding of the French farces of the fifteenth century and the commedia dell'arte as the carnival and May Day revels of the Middle Ages. This is not to say that the Dionysiac revels do not in some measure illuminate French farce and the commedia dell'-arte; they do. More generally, they illuminate *buffo*. The need at this point is to see that *buffo* is a continuous phenomenon which can be traced to and illuminated by a great many, quite distinct revels, all roughly cognate but different. Because they are roughly cognate, the temptation to collapse them and to create a kind of master ritual revel, like Casaubon's mythology of mythologies, is great. But this is the way to lose opportunities for discriminations which may later prove important. Better to respect the outlines of history, however problematical, and to take advantage of differences which, however unimportant they seem when reflected upon in fragments, may in the end yield a deeper understanding of the whole.

The picture of folkloric backgrounds stretches from the pre-Dionysiac festivals in ancient Greece to the carnival customs surviving today, and despite many lacunae it contains sufficient detail to reveal both a linear outline and distinct strata. The signal value of the evidence from Greece is that it exemplifies the full range of evidence, enabling us at the outset to devise categories with which to proceed with a semblance of order. Other minds might perceive in this material a wholly different set of distinctions: indeed, any attempt to argue patterned organization in so vast and disorderly a body of evidence must, in some measure, be arbitrary. But I shall propose that five distinct orders or strata of evidence are identifiable and that they reflect the different stages in any single emergence of vulgar comedy. This, of course, is no more than a good evolutionist would expect. What complicates the matter is that each of these stages — after stages have been carefully marked out — is represented only in fragments, and each seems to have coexisted with all the others. Apparently the processes of folk custom were such that the more primitive practices did not necessarily wither away and disappear as more sophisticated ones developed. Some continued side by side, while others, both early and late, withered away and disappeared for reasons which appear to have nothing to do with the development of vulgar comedy.

In any event, I shall examine the evidence of origins in terms of five strata. The first is the stratum of the ritual revels themselves, that is, the religious holidays which provided the immediate contexts for dramatic or pre-dramatic activities. The second is what I shall call the dramatic rituals, the largely processional practices which occurred within the ritual revels but which were different from the eating and drinking and jesting and random marching about in that they had a prescribed, if still very elementary, dramatic form. The third stratum comprises discrete dramatic exercises, those parts of the revels which were still more highly developed in point of dramatic content than the processional dramatic rituals, yet were not really plays of even a primitive kind. The fourth is the primitive, emergent plays still locked into the revels but distinct enough to have a clear narrative structure. And the fifth is the stratum of the early, free-standing vulgar comedies in evidence in all the periods under study. (See the Appendix for a diagrammatic treatment of these categories.) Altogether, this stratified picture implies a line of development from simple to complex forms and delineates a movement toward drama which some might dispute, pointing out that for long periods the so-called strata existed side by side. Yet despite such caveats, the totality of evidence seems to indicate that from these festive activities, or from parts of them, or from festive activities very like them, the forms of vulgar comedy developed.

◇ ◇ ◇

The evidence from Greece is suggestive, and the casual observations of Aristotle are useful here. It is clear from the *Poetics* that Aristotle felt he knew less about the development of comedy than of tragedy. Although he promised to speak of comedy "hereafter" and, of course, did not, as far as we know, he admits in chapter 5 that certain details of its history — "who furnished it with masks, or prologues, or increased the number of actors" — were unknown. A further problem is that we can never be entirely certain when he uses the term "comedy" whether he intends it to mean only the Attic comedy which first flourished in the work of Cratinus, Eupolis, and Aristophanes in the fifth century B.C. and which later evolved into Middle Comedy and then into the New Comedy of his day, or whether he intends it to include the Dorian mime and the satyr play. When in chapter 3 he seems to accept the claim of the Megarians that they invented comedy and then links their comedy with the comedy of Sicily and the writer Epicharmus (*fl.* 485 B.C.), it is clear that he is speaking of the mime, that species of vulgar comedy which developed in the Peloponnesus, notably Sparta and Megara, and in Sicily. When in chapter 4 he comments specifically on the question of origins by observing that "the lampooners became writers of comedy" and, even more tantalizingly, says that comedy "originated with the authors . . . of the phallic songs, which [were] still in use in many of [their] cities," it is highly likely that he is still speaking of the mime. When in chapter 5, however, he speaks of comedy complete with chorus, prologue, and a plot derived from Sicily, he is probably not thinking of the mime, which was the Sicilian form which provided the "plot," but of Attic comedy. Aristotle, then, is a problematical commentator, but we cannot ignore what he seemed to feel reasonably sure about: comedy had something to do with the lampoon and originated with the phallic songs. With these statements he founded a long tradition which traces comedy to ritual revels, a tradition which has survived through scholars like Varro (116–28 B.C.) in Rome, Athenaeus (ca. A.D. 170–230) among the Alexandrian grammarians, Joannes Tzetzes (ca. 1160) among the late Byzantines, and the Cambridge anthropologists in the present century.

But there is a further difficulty with Aristotle's account of origins: we cannot know precisely what he intended by the terms "lampoon" and "phallic songs." "Lampoon" was generally applied to any of the short, scurrilous attacks which participants in a ritual procession made on groups and individuals in the course of a great many known festivals. The phallic songs likewise embrace a wide variety of songs sung in a great many known ritual revels, probably by participants either equipped with prop *phalloi* or taking part in a procession which served to transport a phallic image. Beyond this it is difficult to do more than look at the available detail to see what might have been intended.

Fortunately, the first stratum of evidence in Greece, the ritual revels, is extensive, and among the earliest are several in honor of Artemis, who in pre-classical times was a fertility goddess. Evidence of the Spartan festival to Artemis survives in a number of sixth- and seventh-century comic masks, interesting because they resemble so clearly

25

the later masks which survive from the mime and Old Comedy. These masks have been linked with what is, perhaps, our oldest example of transformation in dances involving men dressed as women and women, wearing *phalloi*, dressed as men. The festivals to Artemis from Megara and Athens are more shadowy, but we know generally that the Elaphebolia, as it was called in Athens, included festive processions and games. The festival celebrated in Syracuse, on the other hand, involved a procession of animal figures decked out with stag horns and included a song contest, a comic combat, and the collection of food by revelers as they went from house to house. Taken together, these ritual revels provide our first examples of activities which survived in variant form through the age of Rome and into the Middle Ages and Renaissance.

In Greece most of the older ritual revels were gradually assimilated to the worship of the "new," sensational god, Dionysus; the one notable exception was the Thargelia, a principal Athenian feast in honor of Apollo. Celebrated in late May, it began with a procession of the *eiresione*, an olive branch twined with wool and hung with figs, loaves of bread, and a small container of wine; when this emblem had been hung over the door of a house, much as the May branch would be later, the procession made its way to the temple to offer the first fruits of the year to Apollo. The second part of the festival featured the ritual execution of the *pharmakoi*, two men who were first designated male and female and then led from the city, provided with food, beaten on the genitals with leeks and branches of wild fig, and finally burned to death in a horrifying conclusion later recalled by the burning of dummies representing Carnival and Lent. After this grisly little spectacle, the Thargelia concluded with further processions and choral contests.

This combination of a ritual sacrifice and a ceremony either to secure or to give thanks for fruitfulness was constant in the Dionysiac festivals, and here the evidence testifies to contests or combats as well as the processions and phallic symbols. In the Oschophoria, celebrated in Athens in late autumn when the grapes had ripened, the key event was a race in which twenty youths carrying ripened grape shoots ran from the temple of Dionysus in Limnae, a southern suburb of Athens, to the sanctuary of Athena in the harbor town of Phalerum; then followed processions, a sacrifice, and a banquet. The Rural Dionysia, celebrated in the country districts of Attica in January, included solemn processions to the altar of the god, a goat sacrifice, and then feasting and revelry, as well as, in the fifth century and later, important productions of plays. Substantially the same program held for the Lenaea, which was also celebrated in January and which in the fifth century became associated with the contest in comedy. The Anthesteria, by contrast, was a three-day festival celebrated by the Athenians in February and largely dedicated to the new wine. On the first day the new wine was opened and tasted, and on the second it was drunk at a public banquet. During both of these days, called the Pthoigia, or "Broaching of the Jars," slaves caroused and feasted with free men much as they would later in the Roman Saturnalia and the Feast of Fools; the key event on the second day was the symbolic marriage of Basilissa, the wife of the Archon Basileus, and Dionysus. On the third day, the Feast of the Pots, offerings in the form of pulse cooked in pots were made to Hermes for the souls of the dead.

But by all odds the most elaborate of the Athenian festivals was the City Dionysia, the festival which in the fifth century devoted three days to the contest in tragedy and lasted six days in all. Celebrated in the early spring, it involved, apparently even before it had achieved its best-known form, a full range of activities: the solemn processions in which the old wooden statue of Dionysus was transported to the Lenaeum, a bull sacrifice, choruses of boys singing dithyrambs recounting the story of the god, games, contests, feasting, and revelry.

Altogether (and this recital is scarcely exhaustive),

these remnants of the ritual revels of ancient Greece con-
vey some idea of the context of feasting, revelry, and religious observance in which such dramatic rituals (as I shall
call them) as the lampoon and phallic songs were discrete
events. It would be folly to suggest that they tell us anything very precise, yet it would be an even greater mistake
to neglect what we can learn from them about the backgrounds and the values with which the lampoon and phallic songs were associated. In fact, one could look beyond
Greece to what appear to be later, cognate revels and
extrapolate from the combined evidence a rather more
detailed picture. But there is no need to do so at this point.
Spare though they are, these fragments identify moments
when the Greeks assembled to combine religious observance with merrymaking and when, among other things,
they performed lampoons and phallic songs. As we shall
see, these fragments contain details which are repeated or
echoed in later, more fully preserved revels.

The second stratum of evidence consists of certain
processional activities which can be distinguished from
the contexts of revelry on grounds of their rudimentary
dramatic character. The *ithyphalloi*, for example, were
young men in various processions who wore masks of
drunken revelers, gay tunics, and garlands and who, in the
course of escorting a phallic image into the theater — they
themselves did not wear *phalloi* — sang a song demanding
that room be made for the god. Like them, the *phallophoroi* wore garlands of pansies and ivy and attached
flowers to their clothes, much as May revelers would do
later; their leader's face was covered with soot, a detail
frequently repeated in the annals of ritual revels; and they
came into the theater proclaiming a new song for the god.
Once in the theater, they ran up to the audience and delivered lampoons attacking individuals or groups, then
danced. Still another group, the *autokabdoloi*, or "impro-
visors," wore crowns of ivy and also gave satirical
speeches, though in their case the speeches were extem-
poraneous. All these activities seem closer to vulgar com-

edy in antiquity than do the ritual revels as wholes, and they give us a sharper sense of the purposes of celebration and purgation carried out in the songs and the satirical attacks. They even adumbrate, if they do not identify, certain central themes in the satirical attacks and the suggested combat to be seen in the singers' confrontation with the audience, themes which will later prove important. Unfortunately, however, we have no texts for the lampoons, the phallic songs, or in fact any other of these dramatic rituals; indeed, there is no certain evidence to link this order of activity with that which seems to be next in point of dramatic sophistication.

The next level of evidence consists of those parts of the ritual revels which were still more dramatic than the lampoons and phallic songs and yet were not really plays; I have called them dramatic exercises. They include the *komos*, the beast mummeries, and the comic agon. Because of their resemblance to the simpler lampoon, on the one hand, and their apparent survival in ancient vulgar comedy and the Old Comedy of the fifth century B.C., on the other, they suggest a movement toward vulgar comedy. But even here the evidence is too faint for more than informed conjecture. The main value of the dramatic exercises is that they focus still more sharply the cluster of qualities and kernels of action which supply the chief continuities in this picture.

In its simplest form the *komos* (see fig. 1) entailed a procession from house to house, songs and dances, and scurrilous attacks on individuals, all reminiscent of the *phallophoroi* and *autokabdoloi*; in its more elaborate form it consisted of a structured piece performed by a group in the theater. This theatrical *komos* began when the group entered the theater singing a song; they then engaged in a comic combat — either between two of its members or between one member and someone from the audience; and, finally, they delivered a satirical attack on the audience. Like the *komos*, the beast mummeries involved much the same procession, singing, combat, and satirical

1. *Komos* of young men. Greek vase painting, ca. 500 B.C., Vatican Museum. Photo Alinari.

attack, but differed in that the participants were dressed as birds or animals in the manner preserved for us in vase paintings. The comic agon, on the other hand, consisted simply of the combats found in the *komos* and beast mummeries. Our best evidence of it is its late accommodated form in Aristophanic plays, where, typically, one member or one part of the chorus was pitted in verbal combat against an adversary, either an individual or a group. In this late form these sides sometimes took up abstract oppositions like those between Poverty and Wealth or the Just and Unjust Arguments, or even argued topical issues. With these routine exercises, in any event, we approach the threshold of drama. It remains for the primitive, emergent plays in all traditions, plays most usefully described as carnival plays, to bridge the gap to vulgar comedy.

Unfortunately, this fourth stratum of evidence survives rather messily in Greece, in texts of rudimentary folk plays not properly recorded until the nineteenth century, though probably of great antiquity. At the turn of the century R. M. Dawkins and A. J. B. Wace gathered evidence of a number of such carnival plays then still extant in communities of northern Greece. Typical is the play from Haghios Gheorghios in Thrace, which was the central portion of a day-long ceremony. The day begins with a procession in which certain set characters go from house to house begging for food and money. The chief characters are two *kalogeroi,* men with blackened hands dressed in animal skins and bells, headdresses, and masks (sometimes in place of masks their faces are blackened). One of them carries a wooden phallus; the other brandishes a mock bow and scatters ashes ahead of the procession. The other characters include two boys dressed as girls (the *koritzia*), an old woman with a doll representing a bastard child, three or four gypsies with blackened faces and hands dressed in rags and carrying young trees, and miscellaneous policemen. After a morning of going from house to house while the *koritzia* dance and the gypsies frighten people, the main characters begin the play by forging a symbolic ploughshare while the gypsies mime the growing up of the bastard child. Next, the chief *kalogeros* gives chase to one of the *koritzia*, catches her, and marries her, but after the wedding the bow-bearing *kalogeros* shoots and kills him and then flays him, as the new bride looks on and laments. Finally, the mutilated bridegroom is revived, and, after the exultant bride has drawn the ploughshare, the day ends in feasting.

This scenario was fairly widespread when Dawkins did his work, and instances of it in variant form were later found by Wace in Thessaly, Pelion, and Macedonia. Taken as a group, these plays are of extraordinary interest, both for what they pull together from the ritual revels, dramatic rituals, and dramatic exercises of ancient Greece and for their similarities — to be seen presently — to carnival plays from other parts of Europe. The purpose, securing fertility, is the same: in the carnival play it is achieved through an enactment involving death, resurrection, and a wedding; in the ancient ritual sacrifice it is achieved through a god who is worshipped in part for his capacity to be reborn. There is the same emphasis on the phallus, on the house-to-house procession, on the collection of food, on the characters with blackened faces wearing skins and bells, and on the marvelous child. The plays must be handled with great care because we can never be entirely sure of their provenance or their history, but they are nonetheless sufficiently clear to supply a plausible transition to vulgar comedy. If we put theoretical considerations aside, we see that the trouble with them is that, despite their similarities to the revels, they still seem many steps removed from what we know of the Dorian mime, the satyr play (see fig. 2), and the *phlyax* farces (see fig. 3). At this point I can only suggest that the later, more complete evidence of this movement toward drama will supply these missing links.

We have limited information about these strata in antiquity and virtually none about the actual emergence of Greek vulgar comedy. Let it suffice for the moment that all

2. Satyr chorus, perhaps from a satyr play. Greek vase painting, ca. 470 B.C., Vatican Museum. Photo Alinari.

3. *Zeus and Alcmena*, a *phylax* farce. Greek vase painting, fourth century B.C., Vatican Museum. Photo Alinari.

the pieces taken together tell us something about the cultural context in which these activities occurred, something about the purposes and values which animated them, and something about those details which survived unchanged or with only slight alterations. If we were to work backward from later evidence — either of vulgar comedy or of its origins — we would see still further points of contact between the various strata. But that would be premature. It will be far more useful to put small pieces together until the resemblances and echoes are not merely striking and interesting but overpowering.

◇   ◇   ◇

The evidence from the Italian peninsula in pre-Roman and Roman times also comprises numerous seasonal festivals, as well as such fully developed forms of vulgar comedy — more numerous in Rome than in Greece — as the Roman mime, the Atellan farces, and the plays of Plautus and Terence. We have a fair amount of general information about the ritual revels. In a famous passage in the *Epistles* (2. 1. 139–61) Horace describes the farmers of old who in the company of their families and slaves propitiated the gods of agriculture with sacrifices and offerings and as part of their revels engaged in "rustic taunts." In the *Georgics* (II. 380f.) Virgil describes much the same scene, though he speaks of "rude verses" and "joyous songs" to Bacchus; in his *History of Rome* (7. 2) Livy modifies this picture only slightly by tying his account to an urban center and a specific occasion in 364 B.C., when, to appease the gods in time of plague, Etruscan dancers were brought to Rome to give mimic entertainments. Except for such general descriptions, however, there is relatively little precise information about the planting and harvest revels in ancient Italy, and certainly nothing which adds significantly to our picture of such festivals from Greece. The Floralia is typical. Originally a country festival, it was only gradually associated with Flora, and only in 283 B.C. was it officially recognized as the occasion for obtaining her protection for the blossoms. It was extended to cover six days (April 28 to May 3) and came to include, in addition to merrymaking, drinking, and lascivious games, mimic events and, on the last day, a beast hunt.

The ritual revels from Rome for which we have considerable evidence and which add significantly to the picture from Greece are the winter festivals, including the Calends of January and the Saturnalia, and particularly the latter. Both provided periods of absolute license, and both featured prominently what seems only a casual detail in, say, the Spartan festival to Artemis: the practice of changing roles and sexes. During the Calends of January, which occupied the first three days of the year, bands of revelers dressed as women roamed the streets while the populace hoped for good luck by starting the year on a festive note. The Saturnalia, far more famous and long-ranging in its influence, commemorated the happy reign of Saturn with a season of social inversion. The length of the season varied from era to era: under the Republic it lasted throughout December, under Augustus three days — the 17th, 18th, and 19th — and under the Empire a week. But it always began with the election of a *rex saturnalis*, a mock monarch who ruled during the period of the festival and who was literally or symbolically destroyed at its end, and it always instituted an upside-down society. All normal business stopped. Slaves were given all manner of special dispensation: they were relieved of normal work; they were allowed to wear the *pilleus*, a felt hat which was the sign of enfranchisement; at banquets they wore their masters' clothes; and they were permitted complete freedom of speech. Meanwhile, everyone else wore a loose gown called a *synthesis*, thus eradicating rank, and engaged in feasting, mummers' shows, exchanging presents, etc. In short, all or virtually all social and moral restraints were removed for the duration of the festival, and Roman society became a kind of mock society, or, which is perhaps more accurate, an anti-society. This was particularly true during the festival's most intense period, the 17th, 18th, and 19th of December, a time known as the *libertas decembris* (see fig. 4).

Beyond the Saturnalia the remaining evidence of ritual revels in Rome serves to support the general picture of revel backgrounds without extending it. Relatively little is known of the other strata beyond the comments of Roman writers. What we know of the scenario for the *rex saturnalis* dimly suggests the outline of a dramatic ritual in that festival; a clearer instance is the Fescennine verses, which Horace explicitly links with the revel backgrounds. Probably so named because of their association with the Etruscan town of Fescennium (though it is also possible that the name owes something to the word *fascinum*, or phallus, and the god Fascinus), the Fescennine verses were essentially comic, abusive, doubtless obscene speeches which were widely introduced into nuptial and harvest celebrations. According to Horace, they were so crude that a law was finally passed against them, yet it is also clear that they were dramatic in the elementary fashion of the Greek lampoon. Much more elaborate was the *satura*, a form invented by the Romans which combined song, dance, and dialogue, but not (and both Livy and Valerius Maximus were careful on this point) a plot; thus they were not plays, but dramatic exercises in the manner of the Greek *komos* and beast mummeries. They possibly account for the large musical element in Roman adaptations of Greek New Comedies.

In the final analysis the evidence of origins from Rome does little more than support the pattern of evidence provided by Greece; only the Saturnalia adds materially to that pattern. Rome is most important to this study for its rich legacy of vulgar comedy. The Roman mime and pantomime, the Atellan farces, and the plays of Plautus and Terence — these, as we shall see, are the first forms to indicate the full spectrum of vulgar comedy and to supply our first extensive examples of *buffo*. Presumably these comic forms developed from ritual revels and the rudimen-

4. Roman bacchanalia. Bas-relief, third century B.C., National Museum, Naples. Photo Alinari.

tary dramatic forms within them, much as Greek vulgar comedy had, according to Aristotle. Yet it is also clear that they, and particularly the plays of Plautus and Terence, owed a great deal to Greek dramatic precedents. From this point forward, indeed, all attempts to piece together the mosaic of origins, early and late, must take into account continuities from earlier traditions. Henceforth folklore and literary influence merge with bewildering frequency.

◇ ◇ ◇

What, we might ask, has all this to do with Géronte and his sack or Laurel and Hardy and their piano or the chaos at the Hotel Minet Galant? A survey of these relationships must begin with antiquity because the story of vulgar comedy begins there, despite many lacunae. A number of themes begin to take shape: the death of the god or the destruction of a scapegoat, the combat or contentious confrontation, the miraculous mutability reflected in rebirth, sexual substitutions, and physical restorations. One can see that these themes were inseparably linked with tremendous expenditures of energy, whether in the form of merrymaking or outright violence, and that this energy was as indispensable to the total religious observance as to its separate events. All this constitutes an initial focus, more provocative than complete, but which will prove increasingly useful as detail accumulates.

2

Carnival

The general term for ritual revels in the Middle Ages and Renaissance was "carnival." Although the term was not used for all the revels of which we know, it was often applied, if rather loosely, to the most important and the most frenzied, including those at New Year's, Easter, the beginning of May, the Feast of Fools, and Christmas. Initially, the word specifically designated that elaborate and strenuous period of revels immediately preceding Lent, the period still called "carnival." This carnival period varied somewhat in length from location to location, but it was fundamentally much the same everywhere in Europe.

Its most important events were always concentrated in the week before Ash Wednesday, what the French call the *jours gras*. The relevance of the word to a preparation for an extensive fast is apparent in its derivation. The Italian form *carnevale* and the French forms *carneval* and *carnaval* probably come from the medieval Latin *carnem levare*, meaning "to put meat aside." Certainly the variants support this derivation: the Italian *carnasciale* comes from *carne lasciare,* "to quit meat," and the French *caraman-tran* from *carême entrant,* literally, the "coming in of Lent." Moreover, despite attempts to trace the German word for the period *Fastnacht* to *fassen Nacht,* "night of fooling," the more obvious derivation from *fast Nacht,* "eve of the fast," seems the right one. The word "carnival," in any event, opens the whole spectrum of ritual revels in the Middle Ages and Renaissance, all those occasions when social restraints were relaxed and the community dedicated itself to frolicking in earnest.

It would seem logical to begin a survey of these revels with the New Year's festival; however, the first day of January marked the new year for only a limited portion of Europe: the rest, including England and much of northern Europe, continued to observe March 25 as the beginning of the year until the eighteenth century. In Italy and countries influenced by Roman practice, the Roman festival of the Calends of January survived in processions, games, and feasting during the first few days of the year, though it was never one of the major festivals.

More important among what I shall call the winter revels were those associated with Epiphany or the Feast of the Three Kings, celebrated on January 6. This was a festival day everywhere in Europe, and in many places it marked the start of the carnival period, which then continued until Ash Wednesday and thereafter, intermittently, through Lent to Easter. As the first day of carnival and as the day commemorating the coming of the Three Kings, Epiphany was a perfect occasion for electing a mock king and enacting mock ceremonies, and, like most winter revels, it featured festive fires and mummings of various kinds, as well as the usual processions. In some localities, moreover, it was associated with nuptial rituals, a distinct type of revel activity to be discussed presently.

Less well known was the rustic festival celebrated in England on the first Monday after Epiphany. Called Plough Monday, this was supposed to be the day when the farmers returned to the field; in fact, the day was set aside for fires, the setting of plough lights before the images of patron saints, and the mischievous collection of money for those lights. In this last, a ceremonial procession of thirty or forty young men in company with certain fixed characters and sometimes morris dancers made the rounds of the local farms with a bedizened plough, and threatened to plough the farmyard if they were not paid. Predictably, the merrymaking culminated in feasting, and the actual ploughing began the next day.

The last and probably the best known of the winter revels was Valentine's Day (February 14). Although it was never a major revel in the Middle Ages and Renaissance, in England and France it had a special importance even then as a favorite occasion for such nuptial rites as wooings, betrothals, and weddings.

The first major ritual revel in the course of the year as we now calculate it, and the one which apparently subsumed much of the practice of the others, was carnival. Carnival was one of the two great spring festivals celebrated everywhere in Europe (the other being the May festival). Traditionally, it began with Epiphany and ran to Ash Wednesday (forty days before Easter), sometimes being revived on special days during Lent. Since the date of Ash Wednesday is determined by Easter, which is a movable feast celebrated the first Sunday after the first full moon after the spring equinox, the carnival period varied from year to year. Moreover, its duration varied from place to place; in some localities a schedule of events was worked out for the whole period, while in others the whole festival was clustered in the last days — the final Sunday, the Monday following, and Shrove Tuesday or Mardi Gras.

Our records for these events are gratifyingly rich, though, of course, not equally full for all countries or for all localities within countries. The records of urban centers in medieval and Renaissance Italy are extremely good, and they are almost as good for France. Of the countries studied in some depth they are least good for England, yet even there we find processions and ceremonies involving a carnival king and a sacrifice; games, fires, dances, and combats; and abundant eating and drinking in anticipation of the austerities of Lent. In Italy it is possible — as it is not in England — to outline not merely a rough schedule of events but a scenario, a structure which predicates a beginning, a middle, and an end and which gives some focus to this intentionally disorderly activity.

Briefly and very generally — and here I shall draw heavily on Paolo Toschi's work — the scenario of carnival embraced a number of loosely organized episodes ranging from the election of a carnival king to his death and funeral. The election, which was common to all carnivals, might occur at Epiphany or in the final important days of the season, and the king might be called by any of a variety of names, including King Carnival, Nannu, Giorgio, Harlequin, Charnage, Pansard, Jack o'Lent, Old Man, etc. Fairly soon after his election he would parade through the community with his retinue in a day of processions and street frolics, issuing burlesque laws, replacing regular officials with members of his demonic train, and generally calling for feasting and riot. The details of these processions and of the subordinate ceremonies and pranks associated with them varied from place to place, as did the special foods eaten and wines drunk. Sometimes the festivities continued for days; sometimes they were staggered over a period of weeks; often they were accompanied by special games, dances, and competitions. At some point toward the end of these activities the king would submit to a test, either in a combat or a trial, a test which he would invariably fail. When the test took the form of a combat, he would be "killed" and perhaps "destroyed" on the spot. When it took the form of a trial, it would involve an elaborate condemnation leading to a ceremonial execution. In both cases the death of the king was usually accompanied by a reading of his testament, a sometimes satirical, sometimes fanciful charge to the community, followed by a ceremonial funeral.

This concluded the scenario except in localities

where the king was accompanied by a queen or a female antagonist, usually known as Lent. In scenarios involving this figure, in addition to extra episodes treating her relationship to the king, there was usually a final episode dealing with her disposition. Characteristically, this did not take place during the carnival period but on an additional revel day at mid-Lent. Altogether, this is the most detailed evidence we have of ritual revels relevant to *buffo*. It clearly suggests continuities with the ritual revels of antiquity, and it furnishes the clearest evidence of vulgar comedy in the process of emergence. We shall return to it frequently.

Between carnival and the May festival the most important ritual revels were those celebrated at mid-Lent (mi-Carême in France and Quaresima in Italy), on the Feast of the First of March, which was a nuptial revel particularly popular in France, at the high religious feast of Easter, and on Saint George's Day (April 23) in England. Saint George's Day, like patron saints' days elsewhere, featured processions, feasting, and special entertainments and mumming shows bearing on the legend of the saint. The May festival took place on the first of May, though in fact it continued in many places for several days thereafter.

Like the New Year's revel in Italy, which descends from the Roman Calends of January, May Day has its roots in the Roman Floralia. A rustic festival with obvious references to the season and the securing of fertility, it primarily featured flower games: bringing in the "may" (*mai* in France or *maggio* in Italy) or the greenery; in England, this would be a branch of hawthorne, in Italy, a branch or young tree. The "may" would be planted before a girl's house, and there would be dancing around Maypoles trimmed elaborately with ribbons, flowers, and greenery. But typically it also included the election of a May King and May Queen, the playing out of a ceremonial scenario, processions, games, feasting, and the performance of folk dances and plays. In some places the activities gave special prominence to nuptial rituals; in others the emphasis fell on the king — the Jack in the Green or Summer King or Robin Hood in England, usually Carnevale in Italy — and on his ceremonial destruction and revival. Everywhere, in a multitude of roughly analogous practices, the May festival was a time of "all-licensed fun."

After the May festival the remaining spring revels of importance were the religious feasts of Pentecost and Corpus Chrişti, celebrated fifty and sixty-one days after Easter, respectively. Both featured, in addition to the feasting, dancing, and processions, the performance of plays, and both were elaborate holidays in many places. By and large, however, the plays performed were mystery plays and the festival activities were revivals of activities more germane to other festival occasions. Like many of the distinctly Christian feasts of the spring and summer, including Ascension, Trinity Sunday, and the Fête Dieu on June 19 in France, Pentecost and Corpus Christi often served as excuses to repeat favorite revels which were practiced more elaborately at other times.

Among the so-called summer festivals the Feast of Saint John the Baptist was the most important. In communities where Saint John was the patron saint, as in Florence, it offered still another occasion for declaring the general conditions of carnival; in northern Europe, where the day, June 24, was called Midsummer's Day, it provided the occasion for celebrating the season. Typically it began on Midsummer's Eve with fires, dancing, and the cutting and placing of boughs at the doors of young women's houses; in the north, aided by an extremely brief night, it entailed a night of feasting and carousing. Again, the revel activities were for the most part borrowed from carnival or the May festival: for example, a Summer King was frequently elected, and various ceremonial scenarios involving him were performed. But usually the festival was an extravagant one and everywhere it had roots in ancient seasonal rites.

During the remainder of the summer and through most of the autumn there was no other major revel, though there were numerous holidays, some of which were very important in particular localities. Such, for example, were the Feast of the Visitation on July 2, the Feast of the Assumption on August 15, and in England the Minstrels' Festival at Tutbury on August 17 and the Bartholomew or Smithfield Fair on Saint Bartholomew's Day, August 24. More clearly relevant to the story of *buffo*, however, were the numerous fall or harvest festivals. The English Feast of Ingathering, sometimes called Harvest Home, was typical: held in late September, it featured the election of a king and queen, the enactment of various dramatic exercises, festive fires, and banquets and carousing. Better known today through its many survivals is Halloween, on October 31. Throughout the Middle Ages and Renaissance, as now, All Hallow's Eve was consecrated to special processions featuring mummings of spirits walking abroad, pranks and mischief-making, and parties.

The final revel of major importance in the Middle Ages and Renaissance was the Feast of Fools in December. A clear survival of the Roman Saturnalia, this festival was particularly popular and highly developed in France, but it was known throughout Europe and was much the same everywhere. Typically, it began on Saint Nicholas' Day, December 6, and continued, with varying degrees of intensity depending on the locality, for some weeks, culminating on December 17, 18, and 19 in the Roman *libertas decembris*, what is still known in parts of Italy as *la libertà di Dicembre*. Just as in antiquity, when it had been a revel especially appealing to slaves, in the Middle Ages and Renaissance it was the revel of clerks and menials, especially members of the lower clergy. They elected a King of Fools or King of Asses (a Lord of Misrule in England), and he, sometimes assuming the title of bishop or even pope, named a retinue of mock officials to take the place of the regular ones. On the days of greatest activity these "officials," supported by clerks and especially members of the lower clergy, roamed the streets in wild processions, wearing hideous masks and mimicking their

superiors; enacted elaborate burlesques of official ceremonies, including grotesque travesties on the Mass, for
which quite detailed texts remain; and otherwise engaged
in a wide variety of pranks and mischievous mock ceremonies in which, for example, they captured citizens,
levied punishments and fines, and changed clothes with
churchmen and women. Altogether, it was, as in antiquity,
a time when all normal restraints were suspended to allow
for the temporary creation of a mock society and a mock
structure of authority. In the course of centuries it became
surrounded by many prohibitions, and as a result it gradually passed out of the control of subdeacons and clerks and
into the hands of the amateur organizations known variously as *sociétés joyeuses, compagnie della gioventù,* and
compagnies des fous.

Like the Feast of Fools, the Feast of the Boy Bishop,
as it was known in England, also turned on an elaborate
inversion of the conventional authority structure. Centered
largely on the Feast of the Holy Innocents or Childermas
Day, December 28, it featured the election of children to
positions of mock authority and involved a great many
mock ceremonies and burlesques. By and large less extensive and riotous than the Feast of Fools, it was chiefly
popular in England, where the Feast of Fools all but disappeared after the Reformation. But it was also known on
the Continent; in Italy it was called the Feast of the Epis-
copello. Immediately preceding the Feast of the Boy
Bishop, of course, was Christmas, which in many places,
again especially in England, was the occasion for numerous practices relevant to vulgar comedy, particularly the
performance of folk plays and folk dances. For the most
part, however, this great religious feast, like Easter and
Pentecost, was structured in terms of its Christian content
rather than in terms of older folk customs.

◇   ◇   ◇

These, then, are the principal ritual revels of the
Middle Ages and Renaissance. Apparently, they were to

vulgar comedy in these centuries what the ritual revels in Greece and Rome were to vulgar comedy in antiquity: the matrices within which *buffo* impulses clarified themselves and pre-dramatic and dramatic forms ultimately took shape. Even in this general description of carnival, the May festival, the Midsummer festival, and the Feast of Fools it is possible to see many of the key events of the revels from Greece and Rome. The destruction of a scapegoat, the wild processions dominated by masked figures who taunt bystanders and beg or steal food, the comic combat, the temporary subversion of authority and the free substitution of roles and sexes, and, of course, the many details like festive trees and blackened faces and special foods and drink — all these events and details echo the practices of antiquity, just as the scenarios for the various revel kings recapitulate the well-known myth of the dying year. The big difference now is that all this is more clearly structured by scenarios, and the underlying purpose of securing fertility and health emphasized by the Cambridge anthropologists is more distinct.

In recent years their work and that of their followers in literary criticism has been severely attacked, and it is true that they were often too ready to find a seasonal myth in almost anything. Yet it is also undeniable that their myth of the dying year is too widespread in folk custom to be ignored. The scapegoat hero who is honored, then destroyed, then reborn in ritual scenarios is omnipresent: you meet him in Dionysus and in the bridegroom *kalogeros* in Greece and in the *rex saturnalis* in Rome; you stumble over him everywhere in the Middle Ages and Renaissance as King Carnival, Jack o'Lent, the May King, Jack in the Green, the Lord of Misrule, and numerous other figures. Always he is honored in a context of frenzy and abandon, and then he is destroyed, either literally or symbolically, so as to initiate a new season or a new year with the promise of fruitfulness. Sometimes this promise is objectified in his revival; sometimes it is not. But the principle is always quite clear.

It is also clear, however, that other governing principles are equally prominent in this revel material. Many of the ritual revels of the Middle Ages and Renaissance were, essentially, nuptial revels, that is, loosely organized ceremonies designed to bring unattached men and women together and to secure fertility, not through the magic of seasonal change but through sexual union. Elaborate wooing, betrothal, and marriage rites were built into many local May festivals, and sexual coupling was often the exclusive purpose of such minor revels as Valentine's Day or the Feast of the First of March. The principle which best explains their general structure and detail is that of rite of passage, where, as Arnold van Gennep explains in *Les Rites de passage,* a crucial change in social relations is brought about within a structure of conventional procedures.

A still different, though related, principle, most clear in the Feast of Fools, as well as in carnival and various other revels, is that which substitutes a burlesque of authority for normal authority and creates a distinct revel society. Victor Turner explains this process in his *The Ritual Process: Structure and Anti-Structure* by what he calls *communitas:* almost all healthy societies try to ensure their health by permitting the development of an anti-society or of peripheral groups hostile to or profoundly critical of society. Sometimes the society permits or even encourages the creation of an anti-society for a limited period; in such cases the normal structure of authority is temporarily inverted and normal social restraints are deliberately ignored. Sometimes the society permits groups to develop on its periphery which put themselves in opposition to that society's value system without, however, actively overthrowing it; in such cases the *communitas* group coexists with the society for an indeterminate time until it either replaces the society or dies out. Either method contributes to social health by providing a relatively harmless release for tensions inevitably built up through social restraints and by accommodating hostility and criticism. In revels like the Feast of Fools, which involves the establishment of an anti-society for a definite, limited period, the goal of social purgation is most conspicuously served.

Altogether, the ritual revels from the Middle Ages and Renaissance provide an immensely rich ground in which *buffo* impulses took seed and grew. Again it is necessary to avoid the assumption that any single dramatic development leading to vulgar comedy will contain the whole of its folkloric antecedents either in material or meaning. This was the assumption of the literary critics who derived from the Cambridge anthropologists: they posited a ritual model and then proceeded to argue tragedy's direct, one-to-one derivation from that model. However, there is no solid folkloric evidence to support the model and, in fact, no extant tragedy which unequivocally reflects it. It is perhaps fairer to the evidence to admit that the process by which ritual revel was transmuted into dramatic form was probably far more intricate than critics have yet acknowledged. We are not describing a single cumulative process. As we have already seen, numerous ritual revels may conceivably have had some bearing on the development of vulgar comedy; all of them may have contributed something; none of them seems to have contributed everything. In the fullness of time these ritual revels changed: parts of them withered away, while other parts continued to exist side by side with more sophisticated elaborations. As for the purposes which apparently informed the revels, they too tell us something about the *buffo* impulses which gradually found expression in these activities. It would be convenient to demonstrate that vulgar comedy reflects the myth of the dying year, or rites of passage, or the principle of *communitas*; but these meanings have been rediscovered by relatively contemporary minds, and we have no warrant for concluding that they are the only valid ones. We can only assume that by assembling the picture of ritual backgrounds, at first fairly generally, but then with increased attention to detail, we shall be able to move toward a broadly based awareness of what at least some of the initial *buffo* impulses were.

◇ ◇ ◇

Carnival, as we have seen, embraced a period of elaborate merrymaking during which the community prepared for the austerities of Lent and, at a greater distance, the high religious feast of Easter. A king was elected (and sometimes a queen). With his retinue he paraded through the community, dispatching his followers on miscellaneous missions of deviltry, replacing regular officials with mock officers, and issuing his orders for the holiday (see fig. 5). At some point he submitted to a test, sometimes a trial, sometimes a combat, and characteristically lost it (see fig. 6). Then he read, or he had someone read, his testament to the community, and he was executed, if he had not already been killed in the combat. Sometimes he was restored; sometimes he was not.

Everything about this scenario is interesting and provocative. As a loosely orchestrated dramatic action it recapitulates the myth of the dying year and echoes earlier ritual revels. Certain of its features, like its treatment of authority figures, the combat, the testament, and the miraculous restoration, suggest links with earlier revels and with vulgar comedy. Its pervasive spirit of energetic agitation, often violence, reflects both earlier revels and the frenetic quality of vulgar comedy. Each of these lines of inquiry is complicated in its own right and will be discussed later. For the present we need further detail, so let us look first at the part of the scenario which opens up the process of carnival and most clearly suggests continuities with vulgar comedy: its characters.

Chief among the figures of the carnival revel was King Carnival himself. He was called by a wide variety of names. Sometimes he was explicitly called Winter or Death, especially in Germany; some of his names simply represented the season — Carnevale, Caramantran, or Jack o'Lent; others were cover names for the devil, like Gianni,

5. King Carnival and his retinue. Venetian print, eighteenth century, National Museum of Popular Arts and Traditions, Rome.

from Giovanni, a familiar name for the devil in Italy; still others were derivations from other ritual revels, like Re dei Saturnali (King of Saturnalia) or Abbot of Unreason. In any event, names like Nannu in Sicily, Re dei Matti (King of the Mad) in Lombardy, and Giorgio, Paulinu, and Biagio in other localities in Italy, Charnage or Père Chalende in France, and Lord of Misrule or Jack o'Lent in England all designated the same general figure. Typically, he was the mock king who, after his election, like the Re dei Matti in Lombardy, came into town on a horse, drove off the local officials, and issued orders for feasting, dancing, and merriment. Typically, he was old, or at any rate not young, and somewhat grotesque, most frequently obese, in keeping with his dedication to feasting. Sometimes he was gigantic, suggesting his association with the devil, or dressed all in white, suggesting his association with winter and death. Invariably, he was a sacrificial figure whose ecstatic career was cut short by a combat or an execution following a trial and conviction. This figure provides the chief continuity between revel activities and vulgar comedy. His excesses, his struggles, and his destruction persist in the careers of even his most modern surrogates.

The earliest and most important of his variant forms were dictated by the different ways of handling the final, violent episode in the carnival scenario, the destruction of the king. Instead of miming the event or treating it metamorphically by having him pass out from drink, many communities substituted a dummy when the moment of execution approached and then proceeded to dismember it, while many others used a dummy throughout. In such cases the dummy was still called by the usual name, but he was typically a gigantic figure adorned with flowers or fish emblems commemorative of the season. This form made possible, of course, what was entirely consonant with the carnival spirit but otherwise difficult to perform, a violent climax in King Carnival's destruction by the mob — very frequently a dismemberment accompanied by explosions and ending with a ritual fire. In his *Origini del Teatro*

Italiano Paolo Toschi gives us many instances of the practice in Italy: in Valfurva in Lombardy, for example, the community first hangs, then burns the dummy, all the while dancing and shouting, "Out with the mad one, death to Carnevale!" In England we find references in Ben Jonson, John Taylor the water poet, and others to stoning, kicking, burning, and in other ways abusing an image of Jack o'Lent, all this against the remote backdrop of human sacrifices on Midsummer Morning at Stonehenge. In volume 3 of his *Manuel* Van Gennep reports that in many of the villages of the Bouches-du-Rhone section of Provence Caramantran as *mannequin* continues to be led to the town square by a crowd of revelers, is tried, stoned, and then thrown into the sea.

Still other communities used an animal as the scapegoat figure. Sometimes, as with the dummy, a real animal was substituted for the king at the moment of execution and then slaughtered; at Monferrato the king brought a turkey to his "confession" and then offered it up to expiate his sins. Sometimes a real animal served as a variant king through the entire holiday season. In communities where this practice obtained, the scenario was invariably modified to include an elaborate hunt culminating in an execution. All kinds of animals were used: horses, cocks, turkeys, and bulls; in Italy goats were the most common, and in France bears. Yet sometimes the animal figure was impersonated by a man, with the result that the hunt and the execution were again mimed. Toschi, in *Origini,* has preserved a number of scenarios from Italy in which men wearing goat skins and often accompanied by "she goats" (men dressed as nanny goats, complete with udders) were hunted and "killed." Van Gennep has described a scenario from Arles-sur-Tech so full of detail that we might almost call it a primitive play. Entitled *Rosetta*, it opens with an elaborate communal dance which lasts all morning; then in the afternoon a young girl (Rosetta), played by a young man, ventures into the woods, crosses a stream, and meets a bear, also played by a young man.

When the bear attacks and abducts her, the hunters from the town track him down, rescue Rosetta, and take the bear back to the town. The bear resists, however, and continues to try to attack Rosetta, until the hunters are forced to kill him. The episode concludes with another dance.

Of the remaining variant forms of King Carnival, only two or three are important enough to mention here. Clearly suggestive of the animal variant was the use in some communities of a savage man. In Trentino and Savoy in Italy this figure was usually dressed in goat- or bearskins and often accompanied by a savage woman; in France, especially in Languedoc, he was often dressed in feathers. Whatever his form, he was hunted and captured, and then subjected to a mock execution. Still closer in form and spirit to the original figure of King Carnival were all those figures which emerged from his retine to assume his role, Harlequin, Pulcinella, and others. In all these variants, of course, the outline of the central scenario becomes dimmer. Yet they are useful in that they represent extensions of the carnival figure and the scenario.

Next in importance to King Carnival was the female figure who, under various guises, complemented him and occasionally substituted for him. Sometimes she was his wife, sometimes his antagonist, sometimes, more vaguely, his alter ego. In Italy she was called Quaresima (Lent), la Vecchia, or la Befana (this last name is still associated with Epiphany), and usually she was Carnival's wife. In France she was less common but was also well known under the names of Dame Blanche, la Vieille, and la Grandmère. In England and Germany, where evidence survives, she was more simply the Old Woman or the Witch. Her functions in the carnival scenario differed from place to place and depended on whether she was a substitute for King Carnival, his wife, or a female who appeared at some point in the latter half of the scenario to oppose him, literally or symbolically. As his wife she would attack him verbally, or physically, or both, and play an important part in bringing about his destruction. In any of her more abstract guises, as

Lent or as any of the figures which are variants on Lent, she would appear at some point late in the scenario to indicate the arrival of the time of abstinence. Yet she frequently comprehended much more than simple austerity. As an extension of her femaleness, though hardly of her age and characteristic ugliness, she was often associated with fertility and the promise of plenty. In many localities this aspect was elaborated in a separate holiday at mid-Lent, when her destruction was accompanied by feasting. For such purposes she was usually represented by a dummy and dismembered or burned; quite often she was sawed up in a ceremony called in Italy the Segavecchia (the "Sawing of the Old Woman") but also known in France, Spain, and Portugal. In Florence, for example, we learn from Toschi's *Origini,* the dummy was filled with candies and fruits of all kinds, which spilled out when it was sawed. At Harfleur the practice of sawing the Grandmere was so popular that a Confrèrie de la Scie ("Brotherhood of the Saw") was organized; it arranged a festive procession featuring a bedizened saw for chastizing sinners. Altogether, then, the female figure varied widely from place to place, when she appeared at all, but as Lent she served consistently to oppose King Carnival and much that he embodied (see the forlorn female figure on the drawn platform in fig. 6). A spirit of austerity and self-deprivation, in contrast to King Carnival's carnal extravagance, she was the embodiment of the discipline which would eliminate carnival and bring on Easter.

The remaining figures in the scenario were for the most part the numerous, diversified attendants who made up King Carnival's retinue. The history of this mischievous crew is profoundly, if sometimes obscurely, involved in the story of *buffo,* and the earliest information that we have about them — that they were initially and basically devil or spirit figures — could well be the most important. Carnival himself, as I have indicated, often had demonic aspects in certain of his names and in his frequent monstrousness and grotesqueness. But his followers, particularly in their ear-

6. *The Fight between Carnival and Lent*, detail. Pieter Breugel the Elder, 1559, Kunsthistorisches Museum, Vienna.

liest form, were literally devils, or spirits of the dead, or creatures from under the earth. These figures always wore masks, and the oldest of the masks to survive are distinctly demonic. Colored black, made of leather or sometimes wood, they suggest malign creatures and occasionally, even more interesting, faces in the process of decaying. In the Middle Ages this retinue was so closely associated with demons or spirits of the dead that they were called "masks" (*maschere*), a term which probably traces to the medieval Latin *masca*, "ignoble spirit," and which Dante twice linked with *larvae*, meaning "the dead." (As late as 1851, when Rigoletto calls for a *larva*, he means a mask.) Moreover, the later generic name for Carnival's crew, *zanni*, has been traced, though not without difficulties, to Gianni, a familiar name in Italy for the devil. Certainly what we know of the crew's dress confirms these associations. The earliest evidence, from northeast Italy, indicates that their costume was loose and white, which is even today the appropriate garb for a ghost or spirit; this all-white costume survived in the characteristic dress of the later *zanni* of the commedia troupes and of Pulcinella. The other well-known costume, though it apparently emerged somewhat later, was the tattered or patchwork suit suggestive of grave clothes or, more remotely, of leaves or foliage; this was the dress, of course, that ultimately became stylized in the parti-colored costume of Harlequin and the English Patch (see fig. 7).

The characterization of the retinue of Carnival as devils or spirits of the dead is a matter of great importance in the story of *buffo*. It is fundamental to the rationale of a long tradition among carnival entertainers, clowns, and comic actors. Certainly Carnival's retinue were the figures "in disguise as devils" described by Giovanni Villani in his *Cronica* for May 1, 1304, when the carnival festivities resulted in the collapse of the Ponte alla Carraia in Florence. But then we also meet them in rather more abstract form as late as 1732 in the engraving by Hogarth, which shows seven devils drawing the famous pantomimist John

O la belle chanfon, Pantalon chantons bien, | Accordons nous tous trois, fi bien & proprement | Courage (mes amis) ie chante le deffus,
Si voulez efgayer voftre maiftreffe belle, | Que puiffions t'endormir au doux fon de ma lire, | De ce plaifant trio, compofé pour madame,
C'eft le moyen certain pour en fin iouïr d'elle, | Encor que comme vous ie n'aye apris à lire, | La douceur de ma voix luy penetrera l'ame:
Qu'eftre mufeau de chien, dy-ie muficien. | Ie ne laifferay pas de iouër brauement. | Mes paffages ne font ni tortus ni boffus.   J.

7. (*Above*) Sixteenth-century Harlequin with non-symmetrical patches. From Plate 20 of *Receuil de plusieurs fragments de premières comédies italiennes ... representées en France ... dit de Fossard* (ca. 1577), Drottingholm Theater Museum, Stockholm. (*Right*) Seventeenth-century Harlequin with symmetrical patches. French print by Jean Dolivar, Cabinet des Éstampes, Bibliothèque Nationale, Paris. Photo Giraudon.

Rich, dressed as Harlequin, into the new Covent Garden. Literature, too, contains many references to them. Boccaccio cuts across the tradition in his tale of Bruno and Buffalmacco (novella 9a, VIII day, *Decameron*), in which Buffalmacco dresses as a bear-devil to take part, as Boccaccio puts it, in the ancient "game" no longer practiced in his time; Machiavelli addresses the tradition head-on in his *Canto de' diavoli,* in which he says that the devils have come from hell to enter the life of the city by way of carnival; and as late as 1761 Charles Churchill uses the line from Milton in his satiric *Rosciad* to describe Harlequin in company with "Gorgons, and Hydras, and Chimaeras dire."

Carnival's retainers suggest continuities with both earlier and later times. It is but a short step, for example, from the demonic masks and blackened faces of Carnival's train — masks and faces, it should be remembered, appropriate to creatures from the world of the dead — to the grotesque masks of commedia dell'arte performers and the sometimes blackened, sometimes whitened faces of clowns and *farceurs* like the famous Gros-Guillaume of the Troupe Royale in seventeenth-century Paris and the Emmett Kelly of our own day. They may also be connected with the blackened face of the leader of the *phallophoroi* and the grotesque, if not notably demonic, masks of ancient comedy. As we have seen, moreover, the white or patched grave clothes of Carnival's retainers survived in stylized form in the clothes of the *zanni*, Pulcinella, and Harlequin, while parti-colored suits were characteristic of minstrels and jesters from the tenth century on. Chambers tells us (*Medieval Stage,* vol. 1) that the Roman mimes also wore a parti-colored *centunculus,* and the history of fools, minstrels, and comic actors in all ages suggests other points of contact. The bells worn by Carnival's retainers to warn householders as they scoured from house to house in search of food are met again on jongleurs and court jesters. The animal figures of certain carnival festivities are echoed in the asses' ears of the medieval fool's costume and are seen in the animal features of some ancient masks, perhaps

even in the ancient animal choruses and the beast mummeries.

Yet in a general way all these figures, as they partici-
pate in revels rather than in any of the dramatic exercises
which apparently grew out of the revels, had the common
function of stirring things up, of creating agitation, of
generating noise and hilarity. This was true of the
ithyphalloi, the *phallophoroi,* and the members of the
komoi in Greece; it was true of the singers of the Fescennine verses in Rome; it was true of Carnival's retinue and
of the professional fools in the Middle Ages; it is still true
of the troupes of clowns in contemporary circuses. All
these figures perform in groups; they do not constitute the
main event, but they contribute to it by preparing for it,
building toward it, "assisting" it. Of Carnival's retainers it
is possible to say that by cavorting, making noise, and
playing pranks, they were carrying out the orders of Carnival, furthering the scenario as a rite of passage by commit-
ting the "crimes" for which Carnival would be tried and
executed. According to the magico-religious interpretation
of the ritual, they were, as spirits from the earth, assisting
in the process of rebirth, helping the old year, with all its
sins on its head, toward death and a new beginning. Still
more obviously, they served as stimulators of agitation,
hilarity, and joy, demonstrating the capacity for renewal
through energy and animal spirit. What clearer proof of the
promise of abundance and health than an exhibition that
the earth and nature, as prefigured in these spirits from
under the earth, and men, as seen in the persons provoked
by them, are full of life? In any event, this is the argument
which has in various ways been made for the attendants of
Carnival. It is tempting to conclude that what seem to be
cognate figures in other folk traditions were, very generally
at least, playing the same game.

In time, certain members of this retinue developed
distinctive and even celebrated characters. Toschi and
others have traced all the servant and support figures in the
commedia troupes to Carnival's crew; despite the

obscurities in the history of any one of them, clearly the commedia figures owe a good deal to carnival tradition. The term *zanni*, for example, was originally used in northeast Italy for one of the carnival figures; he dressed all in white, wore low felt shoes and a bell behind, and often substituted for Carnival in that region. Sometimes this *zanni* was animal-like, especially like a bear; frequently he behaved like a madman; always he roamed around and, holding his bell in his hand, quietly entered houses to steal food or to frighten women. Later, of course, *zanni* became a general term for all carnival mischiefmakers not otherwise notable.

Harlequin, on the other hand, apparently achieved definition first in France, though traces of him as a chief devil are found widely in Europe. He may owe something to the Hellequin (Erlkönig) of German myth; he probably owes something to Hennequin, a chief hunter in the ritual carnival hunt in parts of France. By the ninth century he was, according to the English chronicler Odericus Vitalis (d. 1143), the chief devil in New Year's festivities in Normandy, and by the twelfth and thirteenth centuries he was met all over Europe. Harlequin, too, frequently substituted for Carnival, but usually he led the troupe of demons in playing pranks and creating confusion. Wearing a black, diabolical mask, a hat with bells, a suit at first white and then later parti-colored, he carried a wooden sword or stick as a sign of his leadership, the one detail perhaps suggestive of the prop phallus of ancient ritual.

In southern Italy, Pulcinella was supreme among the carnival demons. His characteristic dress consisted of a black, long-nosed mask, a conical hat, white clothes, and a stick, and he had a distinctively shrill voice thought appropriate to the dead. Like Harlequin and Zanni, he typically led the carnival rout, and in Calabria he frequently was Carnival. We hear of him early as a carnival figure in the verses of Giovanni de' Boni in the twelfth century; gradually he came to be associated more and more closely with

Naples, until he came to be thought distinctively Neapolitan.

These, then, are the most celebrated members of Carnival's crew. They are by no means the only ones — we hear, as well, of Brighellas, Buffones, Tom Fools, Hanswursts, and others — and they were not necessarily the most important in particular localities. But they exemplify the movement toward drama and embody one of the chief continuities with later plays.

◇　◇　◇

Like the carnival figures, however, the loose scenario of carnival also gradually acquired dramatic definition. Even as it was attenuated over several days or more, lending a faint focus to the revel as a whole, it had a distinct beginning, middle, and end and a number of discrete episodes. Once Carnival had been elected, had made his triumphal entry in company with his hellish crew, and, with their help, had transformed the community into a scene of hilarity and riot, he was invariably accused of egregious crimes and either brought to trial or forced to fight a combat. In time, the combat, the trial, the reading of the testament, and the execution were refined upon until they passed into dramatic exercise and even into primitive plays. These episodes have especially intricate affinities with the materials and forms of vulgar comedy.

An essential episode in the carnival scenario, the trial or combat, provides the model for most of the struggles found in other ritual revels and for a good many of those found in elaborated form in vulgar comedy (fig. 6). I use the term "model" here rather than some other word more clearly suggestive of influences and continuities because the task of tracing influences and continuities is treacherous. Yet just as the trial or combat in the carnival scenario embodies a struggle between the old year or winter or age and all that wants fructification and rebirth, so the combats, or agons, or contentions met in other revels and in vulgar comedy frequently embody a cognate struggle. It is easiest to trace this model in certain dramatic exercises which early became part of the scenario. Dramatic confrontations between Carnival and Lent, for example, were widespread: called *contrasti* in Italy and *débats* in France, they represent the simplest and most elementary drama to develop within the carnival framework. We have thirteenth-century texts from Italy with titles like *Contrasto fra Carnevale e Quaresima* or *La horrenda et mortal battaglia fra Carnevale e Quaresima;* from France, we have a *Conflit de Carême et de Carnaige* and a *Bataille de Karesme et Charnage;* from Spain, we have a *Pelea que hobo Don Carnval con la Quaresma.* Although it is probable that none of these texts reproduces precisely what was said in a specific carnival, all reflect the gist of the exercise. Moreover, where we do not have texts, we have descriptive accounts. In some communities, however, the elaboration of the episode took a heroic direction as attention focused on the actual combat. The "combat" described by Sabatino degli Arienti in a letter to Isabella Gonzaga, which took place on February 24, 1506, in Bologna, suggests the epic battles of the May festivities. It is likely that in many communities such events contributed importantly to the violent competitions and games which developed within the carnival framework. In still other places a literary emphasis developed, and *contrasti* and *débats* became recognized literary forms, though sometimes even these retained characters like Morto and Vivo or Acqua and Vino. But what is most interesting is that frequently these simple dramatic exercises shaded into a more sophisticated order of activity, the primitive plays, which typically embraced several episodes from the scenario, including the combat.

The next episode in the temporal sequence of the scenario was the reading of the testament of Carnival. Once Carnival had been either killed in combat or tried and condemned, he often reads — or, if he is represented by a dummy or an animal, someone reads for him — a testament to the community. All kinds of such testaments survive: testaments of Carnival, of the animals which substituted for Carnival, and of various other substitute figures like Harlequin and Befana; all are dominantly satiric in tone and content. Sometimes the recitals consist of a catalogue of Carnival's sins, but more typically they involve a lengthy denunciation of the sinners and sins of the community. By either technique the elaborated episode serves to invoke, so that they might be eliminated, the weaknesses and sicknesses of the community; the whole episode becomes a kind of public confession culminating in the sacrificial and penitential execution of Carnival, which is always a heavily satiric, gaily grotesque, if sometimes brutal, exercise.

In *Origini* Toschi has preserved a good many such *testamenti* from Italy. Typical is the one from Staffolo, near Ancona, in which (in a version only recently recorded) a dummy representing the dying Carnival is exhibited, attended by a Doctor and a Notary; after the Doctor has "operated" by cutting open the dummy's stomach and removing a salted fish and a flask of wine and, according to the familiar formula, has pronounced the surgery a success and the patient dead, the Notary reads the testament. The testament consists of a good-humored attack on the notables and citizens of the community. It illustrates the mechanism by which the scenario and its purposes are at this point related explicitly not only to the community but to specific individuals within it.

In France and Germany, where testaments were not frequent, individuals were accused and ridiculed in various other ways. Such exercises were often part of the extended procession and took the form of satiric mimings of the persons to be denounced. In France the ridiculed might be, among others, newly married young folk who had had no child, couples living in concubinage, or newly married old folks. In Haute-Savoie, for example, where becoming pregnant, or winning one's *alouilles*, was a matter of great moment, the insult recited was "La femme est stérile, le mari est mulet." Inevitably (though again we are dealing with what look like recurrences rather than continuous traditions) one is reminded of the similar exercises in antiquity: the lampoon, the *komos,* and the Fescennine verses, in all of which individuals or groups in the audience were attacked verbally. All these exercises served, among other purposes, to relate the broader ritual to the specific social context and suggest some rationale for *buffo's* persistent connection with the commonplace stuff of life.

The final episode from the carnival scenario which took on enough in the way of dramatic form to qualify as dramatic exercise was the death of Carnival. In its most fully articulated form this episode consisted of two parts, Carnival's execution or expulsion and his funeral. Again, practice varied widely from community to community. The evidence from France indicates that Caramantran was regularly burned, drowned, shot, stoned, impaled, decapitated, or hanged, or any combination of these, and then buried. The evidence from Italy indicates no less variety. These events were frequently accompanied by a burlesque funeral cortege. The evidence for all this is the set practices handed down for use at festival time in various communities (see especially Toschi, *Origini,* and Van Gennep, *Manuel*) rather than texts of any kind, but these practices are sufficiently uniform to indicate the salient features of the episode.

It is not surprising that texts of the episode have not survived: what was most important in the Middle Ages and Renaissance, and what is still most important, was not the words which might have been part of the episode, but the fact of execution and the violence with which it was typically carried out. The elaborated episode as it survived into the nineteenth century and down to the present is useful not for the links which it provides with more sophisticated dramatic developments, as, say, the trial and testament do, but for the way in which it clarifies the meanings which pervade the whole. The screaming, the frenzy, the savage brutality of so much of the carnival season are especially easy to understand in terms of this episode: the more violent the execution, the more effectively the episode is consummated. The elaborated episode of the death of Carnival will take us part of the way toward understanding the violence and brutality so frequently met in vulgar comedy.

To summarize, then: in carnival, a key ritual revel in the Middle Ages and Renaissance, more and more sophisticated strata can be seen within the revel materials. In the scenario, and particularly in those of its episodes which reflect dramatic amplification and definition, like the trial, testament, and death of Carnival, dramatic rituals imperceptibly become dramatic exercises as they are elaborated and refined. In the *contrasti, débats,* and combats featuring the opposition of Carnival and Lent or of cognate figures we see the more sophisticated order which I have been calling dramatic exercise. What is unique and especially exciting about carnival is that the picture does not break off here. It also includes emergent or primitive plays, plays with clear continuities with the dramatic exercises, and dramatic rituals. The picture of graduated forms, in fact, continues up to the very threshold of vulgar comedy.

◇　◇　◇

The folkloric backgrounds from antiquity are like a vast but highly incomplete mosaic. Some parts seem to antedate and to have influenced the shape and character of others. Yet all we know is that they are parts of the same mosaic, and we can hope that the ensemble will illuminate in a general way the forms and materials of vulgar comedy which derived from it.

Fortunately, the picture provided by carnival is more complete. Here it is possible to construct a model of graduated dramatic activity which indicates how the materials, forms, purposes, and meanings of the revels fed into the mainstream of the *buffo* tradition. This model is made possible by the excellent condition of numerous emergent plays in the carnival tradition (for a visual example see fig. 8). Although these plays are only a small part of the canvas, they constitute a unique and highly useful kind of evidence.

Italy provides the best examples of primitive plays. From Tuscany we have one entitled *La Rappresentazione e festa di Carnasciale e della Quaresima,* which descends from a text printed in Florence in 1568 and consists of a simple dramatic amplification of the combat and destruction of Carnival. As Carnival eats and drinks, he is first warned that he is about to fall, and is then sent for by Lent (Quaresima). When he ignores her and continues his carousing, she mobilizes an army and lays siege to his castle. Throughout the battle which ensues, Carnival continues to eat, drink, and make merry, until finally the castle is taken, he is burned, and his soul is carried off by the devil. The great value of this "play" is that it represents a direct and straightforward use of carnival materials in an action which clearly seeks to preserve and even intensify their playfulness and hilarity. Unlike the many folk plays in which these same materials have been adapted to quasi-heroic ends, the Tuscan play extends the ritual base by prolonging and amplifying an essentially comic struggle between Carnival and Lent. The result is a primitive play which was apparently substituted for one part of the ritual and was performed in the public place normally used for that ritual.

The other examples from Italy include treatments of the combat-death episode, or of other episodes, all in texts established in the nineteenth century. From Siena we have a loosely derived action which goes under the title of *Bruscello sulla caccia* ("Play of the Hunt"), *bruscello* being another term for "carnival play." This "play" consists simply of a speech by an Old Man (the Vecchio) inviting everyone to hunt in celebration of the carnival season, followed by speeches assigned to hunters, cooks, and personified cooking implements, and then the feast (prepared earlier) which follows when the hunters return without game. Altogether, the action represents a simple,

8. Street production of a carnival play. Detail of *The Fight between Carnival and Lent*.

yet clearly festive, dramatization — again for the purposes of advancing the ritual — of a part of a scenario in which a hunt has come to replace the combat. The combat itself appears in other *farse di Carnevale* from Calabria and Sicily; a trial and execution are met in *Il Processo e la condanna di Arlecchino* from Vicoforte, near Mondovì, and in another Tuscan play called *La Condanna della Vecchiacia* ("The Condemnation of the Old Woman").

Most elaborate of all, perhaps, is the remarkable Tuscan piece *Befanata drammatica profana: scherzo campagnolo*, *befanata* being still another term for carnival play. In this case the play features the Befana, or Old Woman. In the *Befanata* a chorus announces the arrival of the executioners (*segatori*, literally, "sawers") who have come to saw up the Old Woman (the Vecchia) at the request of the Old Man (Vecchio); the Old Man, her husband, gleefully prepares for the task because, as he says, she has grown old and ugly and he wants to marry a younger woman. When she pleads with him, pointing out that he had loved her once, he turns a deaf ear; and when his son tries to stop him, he argues that the Old Woman has dishonored them. Together, then, the Old Man, his son, and the *segatori* saw up the Old Woman, singing as they work. When they have finished, two carabinieri arrive and arrest them, but before they are taken off, they discover the Old Woman's testament, and a Notary reads it, after which, with a toast all around, the *Befanata* ends. The adaptation made of the carnival materials is straightforward and clear, yet sufficiently sophisticated to qualify as a play, if a rough-hewn one. Moreover, the qualitative emphasis is unmistakably comic, as the term *scherzo* implies.

Altogether, this group of primitive plays constitutes only part of the evidence from Italy; the quasi-heroic plays and wooing plays associated with carnival are actually more numerous and come closer to being bona fide plays. The special importance of this first group is that, in addition to remaining close to the carnival scenario, it demon-

strates how the carnival materials were adapted to intensify a spirit of wild, rather grotesque, exhilaration.

Unfortunately, the evidence of emergent drama is
somewhat less good in England than in Italy, and is still
worse in France. Despite the richness of French farce in
the Middle Ages, I have found only one example of this
kind of carnival play, the piece described by Baron de
Rothschild under the title *La Dure et cruelle bataille et
paix du glorieulx sainct Pensard alencontre de Caresme.*
Printed about 1535, this piece is, according to Rothschild, a
"mascarade à grand spectacle." It includes a great many
characters, including Charnau, Caresme, and several *cap-
pitaines,* and the action apparently consisted of elaborate
preparations for battle, the battle itself, and then the peace.
Since I have not seen the text, however, I cannot be more
precise. Clearly it reflected a dramatic adaptation of the
combat episode from carnival; apparently, despite its
length (at a rough estimate, 750 lines), it was insufficiently
dramatic to be unmistakably a play. Although it doubtless
occupied the ground between the *débats* and early vulgar
comedy in France, it is impossible to be more explicit.

From England we have numerous folk plays which
derive from the scenario of carnival, but they are complicated for our purposes because they combine and collapse
quasi-heroic and comic treatments of scenario episodes
within single plays. Most common are the morris dances,
mummers' plays, and Saint George plays. Usually they
were not associated with the carnival season but with one
of the other revel occasions, and they frequently included,
in addition to the "heroic" episode, a wooing and, what is
more relevant here, a series of grotesque characters who
entered in varying degrees into all episodes.

The Plough plays were linked with the traditional
carnival season by Plough Monday, in many places the first
day of carnival. Although the texts which survive, typically
from the eighteenth and nineteenth centuries, never reflect a simple, straightforward treatment of the carnival

scenario, they have enough points of contact to justify our attention. E. K. Chambers' reconstruction of the *Bassingham Plough Play*, for example, unites two early nineteenth-century texts and comprises a confused action in which the Fool by turns opposes the Old Witch (at one point she is his wife, who is trying to foist a bastard child off on him), fights and loses to Saint George, and successfully woos a "Lady." Of most interest to us here is the short but unmistakably high-spirited struggle between the Fool and the Old Witch. The *Revesby Plough Play*, on the other hand, which survives in a good text from 1779, combines burlesque combats between the Fool and a Hobbyhorse and then the Fool and a dragon. The Fool kneels and makes his will, suffers death at his sons' hands, and revives when "cured" by Pickleherring. The play then concludes with a wooing episode. Altogether, the *Revesby Play* is the clearest English example of a primitive play which reflects a comic elaboration of portions of the carnival scenario. Moreover, it is clear that in England, as in France and Italy, such pieces were performed in public, in the open, probably taking the place of the revel ritual.

From Germany the evidence of emergent drama is again reasonably abundant but is different in that, though the "plays" were clearly performed at carnival, they were apparently presented in inns and private homes; they retained the characters of Carnival and Lent and the idea of carnival but little of the scenario. Indeed, the whole of this order of revel activity in Germany apparently took place at a greater distance from the revel than elsewhere. The pieces in question are exceedingly simple in form, consisting typically of comic arguments between husband and wife and the speeches of advisers seeking to reconcile them. Play 29 in Adelbert von Keller's collection of *fastnachtspiele* ("carnival plays") is, perhaps, typical: a complaining wife asks how she and her husband might live in harmony and twelve waiters offer advice and prescribe a regimen for them; the piece concludes with the Ausschreier's hope that they keep Lent happily. Still closer to the ritual backgrounds are nos. 72 and 73, in both of which the relative merits of *Fastnacht* and *Fast* are debated. In no. 73, for example, five waiters enumerate the blessings brought by *Fast,* especially Easter, and conclude that *Fastnacht* brings only harm.

Yet despite these points of contact with carnival, none of these primitive *fastnachtspiele* is actually close to it: though they are simpler than the plays found in, say, Italy, they are also less firmly grounded in the revel backgrounds. Moreover, to the extent that fun can be found in them, it is rather to be found in the wildness and humor of individual arguments than in the action; indeed, they can scarcely be said to have an action. Yet their intention is clear: like the other carnival plays, they represent attempts to adapt the materials of the carnival scenario to a dramatic form which enhances the comic values implicit in the materials. It should be no surprise that these adaptations differ from country to country. What is remarkable is that in so many respects the plays are the same, in purpose, if not method, over a geographical area too vast for much collaboration to have occurred.

◇　◇　◇

The picture of carnival thus reconstructed is our best source of insight into the origins of vulgar comedy. Having seen what we have seen of the combat, the test, and the destruction of carnival, as well as of the frenzy which usually characterized these episodes, it does not now seem far-fetched to ask what all this has to do with Géronte and his sack, Laurel and Hardy and their piano, and the chaos at the Hotel Minet Galant.

3

The May Festival, Wooing Revels, and the Feast of Fools

Carnival is the key revel in the Middle Ages and the Renaissance because its scenario subsumes whatever we find of scenario in the other revels and its pattern of graduated activities illuminates the more fragmentary patterns of other revels. There we see something more of the diffusion of these activities throughout the year and can identify and explore the differences between carnival and the other revels.

In northerly countries the May festival was often more important than carnival, probably because it took place in better weather. In most respects it retained the seasonal emphasis of its Roman antecedent, the Floralia, as other ritual revels in the Middle Ages did not: moreover, it never acquired the superstructure of Christian materials found in carnival, and it always emphasized greenery, flowers, and sex in a relatively straightforward celebration of fertility. It was common practice at Maytime to decorate virtually anything with flowers and foliage, from the humblest domestic animals to whole towns. Key activities were dancing around the Maypole or bringing in the "may." When the revel had the loose structure of a scenario, its chief characters were often called Jack in the Green, le Feuillu, or Verde Giorgio, as well as the King and Queen of May; apparently at the time of his importation into England the French Robin à Wood was confused with the Robin Hood of balladry, with the result that by the sixteenth century Robin Hood and Maid Marian were frequently the king and queen of the season in England. At the very least, the May festival consisted of the election of such a king and queen and of processions, games, dancing, and feasting. At its most sophisticated it included dramatic rituals, dramatic exercises, and simple plays.

Where it can be traced, the scenario of the May King comes closest to illustrating what I have been calling dramatic ritual. Again it is Italy, with its relatively well-preserved urban records, which provides the most detail. Very briefly, the Re di Maggio, or Verde Giorgio, or Arlecchino (the name varied with the community) opened the festival season with a procession, gave orders concerning the games, competitions, and dances which were to be parts of the revel, engaged in a combat with a devil or some other black-faced adversary (usually accompanied by a clownish devil called Buffone), and was killed, to be revived shortly afterward by a comic doctor. With this scenario as a loose framework, the community apparently gave most of its energy and attention to the games, competitions, and dances.

In fact, the bulk of our evidence from the May festivals relates not so much to the scenario as to elaborations of specific parts of it and to games, competitions, and wooing ceremonies. Most of the dramatic exercises and emergent plays cluster around two motifs, love and war, and consist of activities structured to bring the sexes together or of quasi-heroic amplifications of the combat-death-revival episodes.

Among these dramatic exercises which derive from the combat-death-revival episodes are a few *contrasti* and *débats,* but chiefly a number of dances entailing a simple dramatic action. The basic type was the sword dance, a type known virtually everywhere in Europe and of great antiquity. Tacitus mentions seeing such a dance among the Germanic tribes in the first century A.D. (*Germania*, 24), and occasional references to others crop up among widely disparate peoples in the early Middle Ages. These dances combined dancing and an expert and highly athletic use of the sword with a simple dramatization of the death by combat and the revival of the May King. The proportions of dancing, swordwork, and dramatization varied from place to place, yet in their most dramatic form certain of the sword dances unmistakably qualify as emergent plays. Their basic cast included the May King or his substitute, attendant grotesques such as Buffone in Italy or Tom Fool and Dame Bessy in England, and the dancers.

Rather more elaborate than the sword dances were the related morris dances, called *moresca* in Italy, *morisque* in France, and *moreskatanz* in Germany. These dances comprised essentially the same materials found in the sword dances, without the swordwork, but added an overlay of references to Christian struggles with the Moors, hence the reference to them in the title. The morris dancers usually wore white costumes and bells, as did the early attendants of King Carnival, and the principals frequently had blackened faces like Moors but also like the demonic attendants of the seasonal king. In England the comic characters in blackface were sometimes known as King Coffee or Dirty Bet. Everywhere the dramatic content was more elaborate than that of the sword dances, though still more heroic than comic.

This quasi-heroic emphasis persisted in the emergent plays. The *maggio* from Italy and the Saint George plays, mummers' plays, and some of the Robin Hood plays from England all involve quite elaborate treatments of the combat-death-revival episode. Despite their great importance in the history of the drama, however, they seem to have little connection with the development of vulgar comedy. In the Saint George plays, Saint George is the seasonal hero and his adversaries are a Turkish knight with a blackened face and/or a captain with a name like Slasher or Bold Slasher. The action is usually divided in two parts, the combat and the revival, and includes, in addition to the combatants, a comic doctor and a group of comic grotesques who sometimes had minor parts. The mummers' plays covered substantially the same ground, but did so still more elaborately. Saint George was usually replaced as the protagonist by a local hero of the season — a Tom Fool or Lord of Misrule; the comic characters were usually more prominent than in the Saint George plays; and the action usually included, in addition to the central combat-death-revival episode, a wooing episode of the sort we shall take up presently. The Robin Hood plays, in their simplest form at least, constituted a simple variation on all this by substituting Robin, the sheriff of Nottingham, and the other characters from the Robin Hood cast for the characters usual in the Saint George and mummers' plays. In this form the Robin Hood plays were apparently popular fixtures at a good many May festivals in England. In their more elaborate form, as more complete, self-conscious dramatizations of episodes from the Robin Hood legend, they are probably not usefully thought of as folk plays at all. Finally, the *maggio* in Italy is a perfect parallel to these plays except for the fact, of course, that it uses the Re di Maggio or his substitute as the seasonal hero and adds his comic attendants, including Buffone, Corriere, and Paggio. It differs from the English examples chiefly in that during the Renaissance its most highly developed forms were overlaid with characters and details from Tasso and Ariosto. Some of these "literary" *maggi* are still performed each year in communities like Montepulciano in Tuscany.

The combat-death-revival episodes in the May festival are of marginal importance to the story of *buffo*: the more completely they achieved dramatic form, the more they acquired a distinct heroic emphasis. Yet they fill out the general picture, if only to the extent of linking the heroic with the comic by way of common sources. There have always been profound affinities between the exalted and the absurd. The Olympian religion itself emphasized burlesque and parody of its gods, and the treatment of the gods and mythic heroes in ancient vulgar comedy shows how the magnificent often contains the ridiculous. In the May festival it is possible to read the evidence the other way: if the heroic can contain *buffo*, *buffo* can also contain the heroic — Hercules as fool is nonetheless still Hercules. In other words, the linkage goes deep: there is something heroic about the purposes of *buffo*, both as we meet them in pre-dramatic form and as we shall meet them in vulgar comedy.

Of much greater relevance to the story of *buffo* than these quasi-heroic activities, however, are those which clustered around the motif of love — the various wooing ceremonies and wooing plays. Sex had been an important part of seasonal revels since antiquity, and of course Maytime was not the only occasion for wooing and nuptial rites. Epiphany was important in Italy; Valentine's Day — when it was believed that birds mated — was especially popular in France and England; New Year's Day, patron saints' days, and the first of March were often the occasion for special rituals and weddings everywhere. Moreover, it is clear from the wooing rituals themselves that the celebration of fertility was scarcely their only purpose, though always an important one. Most of the wooing and nuptial rituals from the Middle Ages and Renaissance were unmistakably rites of passage, that is, rituals designed to bridge a crucial change in social relations, in this case to bring men and women together and formalize "couplings" or marriages.

The wooing and nuptial rituals embraced a wide variety of activities. Many were simple ceremonies for blessing newly married couples. Troupes of revelers would assemble and sing a traditional song in front of the house of such a couple, or they might shower the house or the couple with pieces of candy or cake. This practice, known in France as *semer les épousés*, survives in our custom of throwing rice at newlyweds. More important to the story of *buffo,* however, were those rituals designed to bring men and women together and to declare engagements but which were also sufficiently dramatic to qualify as dramatic rituals; it was from these that the wooing plays developed. The most common and widespread of these dramatic rituals turned on the fetching of a tree or branch — variously called, as indicated earlier, a *maggio,* or *mai,* or may — and planting it by the house or placing it over the door or on the roof of the house of the desired young woman. This custom frequently involved, in addition to the suitor and the young lady and her family, a considerable entourage of supporters for the suitor and a variety of fairly standard practices. In Italy the entourage often served as a chorus which assisted the suitor in a serenade; in many places the young woman or her father had some standardized way of responding which indicated her acceptance of the match and amounted to a public engagement. In England we see a variation in the custom preserved in Robert Herrick's *Corinna's going a-Maying:* there, apparently, the young man awakened the young woman on May morning and together they went to cut down a bough of hawthorne; then, after a round of love-play in the woods, they went to the country priest and declared themselves.

These activities, numerous and diverse but always simple and clearly expressing the joint purposes of celebrating the season and formalizing engagements, in some localities ultimately yielded to more sophisticated practices featuring set dialogue and a cast of characters, as well as a formulaic action. The evidence for the dramatic exercises which doubtless preceded the wooing plays is rather scant; most of it comes from Italy and related territories. From Sardinia we have an exceedingly simple exercise in the *Pricunta,* a structured episode in which a band of sheepherders rides up to a farmhouse, reports the loss of a beautiful sheep in set dialogue, and, while searching for it with the father of the family, "finds" the young woman they have come to ask in marriage. From Naples there is

79

the rather famous *Canzone della Zeza*, a street entertainment which was partly sung and partly acted until the eighteenth century: Pulcinella and Zeza, his wife, deal with the problem of a Calabrese student's suit to their daughter Tolla. Pulcinella resists the match while Zeza encourages it, until finally Zeza wins out and the match is made. From northern Italy, particularly from Veneto, we have numerous exercises which go by the generic names *mogliazzi, mariazi,* and *maritazi.* Typically devised for wedding celebrations (which, it is worth noticing, were usually held on the occasion of one of the revels), they consisted of broad and in part improvised parodies and burlesques of a wooing or of a country wedding and featured as performers members of the comic crew of King Carnival — Arlecchino, Brighella, the Vecchia, and others. All these activities reflect an accommodation of the materials of the wooing rituals to forms more dramatic than the rituals themselves, yet none quite qualify as even primitive plays. Limited geographically to Italy and Sardinia, they furnish valuable information about the evolution of wooing plays in that important region but offer only the broadest hints concerning the way in which the transition from dramatic ritual to emergent plays was made elsewhere.

The scarcity of this material is all the more unfortunate since our evidence of wooing plays is so very good, especially in Italy and England. From both countries we have numerous examples, ranging from quite primitive episodes, still linked with the quasi-heroic action and the season, to more sophisticated plays which can stand alone and which could have been part of a specific wedding celebration as well as of a revel. In these plays we can see two distinct formulaic actions. What might be called the English action, since it is more common to the English plays than to the Italian, consists of a parade of wooers who one by one sue for the hand of the Lady; she rejects them all in favor of the Fool, though she may reject him too before accepting him. The group of wooers typically includes a number of authority figures such as the Lawyer (*The Bassingham Men's Play*) or the Sergeant (*The Recruiting Sergeant's Play*), as well as certain comic characters like Fool and his sons Pickleherring, Allspice, and Blue Britches. This is the pattern of the plays preserved by E. K. Chambers and of those reprinted by C. R. Baskervill from versions mostly recorded in the early nineteenth century. Among the Baskervill texts *The Broughton Christmas Play*, *The Recruiting Sergeant's Play*, and *The Swinderby Play* are free of elements from the quasi-heroic scenario.

The action of most of the Italian wooing plays is basically simpler, but it took on more intricate elaborations. There is a suit by two young men or by a young man and an old one for the hand of a young lady, a rivalry which sometimes takes the form of a fight (a survival, surely, from the quasi-heroic action), sometimes the form of a dispute which is resolved before a judge or a mayor, and a final dance and/or supper. In northern Italy such a play was usually called a *bruscello*, a term derived from one of the Tuscan words for the May tree and ultimately used to designate virtually any revel play. Examples are relatively numerous, though again mostly preserved in nineteenth-century versions. From Lucca we have a text entitled *Rondone e Rosalba*, which treats of the rivalry of Rondone, an old suitor, and Gianello, a young one, for the hand of the lovely Rosalba, a prize which Gianello finally wins; other characters include Arlecchino, here Rondone's servant, Rosalba's father, and Paggio, who serves as a prologue. From the south we have a parallel example in *Il Vignarolo e l'ortolano* ("The Vinetender and the Orchard-Keeper"); in this case the characters of the title are the rival suitors.

What is important about the wooing plays from Italy is that, in addition to suggesting continuities with the simpler wooing rituals, they trace a nicely graduated scale of increasingly sophisticated forms. Most of these pieces survive in Renaissance or seventeenth-century texts, probably because even in their time they had the status of plays rather than of revel entertainments. *Il Mercato* ("The Mar-ket"), for example, treats of the rivalry between a knife-grinder and an old doctor named Laterna for the hand of the merchant's daughter Beppina. The action is complicated, somewhat in the manner of the English plays, by several other characters — a haberdasher, a seller of almanacs, and a tinsmith — but is happily resolved through the contrivances of the servant Brighella, and ends in the wedding of Beppina and the knife-grinder.

With *Il Mercato* the dividing line between revel backgrounds and a bona fide, if very simple, vulgar comedy begins to be difficult to draw. The line is still hazier in a play like *Gli Amori di Belinda e Milene*, which survives in a nineteenth-century text. Here two hunters, Milene and Gerano, love Belinda; Belinda prefers Milene, but her father, aided by his cowardly servant Brighella, favors Gerano. Complications, protests, and lamentations ensue until Belinda flatly rejects Gerano and he and her father scheme to ambush and kill Milene. But Brighella, now the lovers' ally, prevents this disaster by engaging a magician to charm the villains while the lovers are safely married. The *bruscello* concludes with the promise of a feast.

There are numerous plays of this order of complexity. Some of them are not explicitly associated with the May festival, though most are clearly related to revels, as *Gli Amori di Belinda e Milene* is with carnival. Many of the more polished pieces are linked with the names of writers like Marcello Roncaglia da Sarteano (fl. 1520) or Leonardo di Ser Ambroglio Maestrelli (fl. 1513), Renaissance humanists who elevated the wooing plays to the status of a rude literary form and wrote them for such amateur troupes of farceurs as the Rozzi of Siena. With works like Roncaglia's *Commedia di Maggio*, Leonardo's *Farsetta di Maggio*, the anonymous *Ragazza canzonata* ("The Mocked Mistress") and *Liberatione d'amore*, and Fumoso's *Batecchio* and *Panecchio*, we have the rare opportunity of observing the wooing scenario assume the status of a simple play. Yet many of these pieces are still identified with Maytime or one of the other revels by their titles, by allusions within them to the season, or by the May songs sung in the course of the performance, and all retain clear traces of the scenario of the simpler wooing plays and wooing rituals. As a group, moreover, they throw light on one of the ways in which more and more domestic rather than quasi-heroic detail came to be introduced into vulgar comedy.

The whole question of *buffo*'s affinity for commonplace, largely domestic materials is very important and will be treated at greater length later.

◇　◇　◇

Unlike carnival, the May festival, the Midsummer festival, and many of the secondary revels, the Feast of Fools and the related Feast of the Boy Bishop did not have a standard scenario. Many commentators have argued that the King of the Fools, the Lord of Misrule, the Boy Bishop, and the other leaders of these revels were cognate to King Carnival, and they are probably correct. Like Carnival and his many substitutes, these figures were elected mock rulers, and they too led elaborate processions through the community. Unlike King Carnival, however, these figures had virtually no other function. We have no evidence that the Feast of Fools or the Feast of the Boy Bishop ever involved a test or a combat, a death or an execution — anything, in other words, suggestive of the full scenario of carnival. The emphasis in these revels was entirely on the subversive, burlesque aspect of the mock king and the activities which he and his lieutenants generated; the general thrust was to define and establish an anti-society. We have a vivid picture of such a society in a letter from the Faculty of Theology in Paris to the bishops and chapters of France, dated March 12, 1444/5 and translated and quoted in part by E. K. Chambers (*The Medieval Stage,* I, 293):

Priests and clerks may be seen wearing masks and monstrous visages at the hours of the office. They dance in the choir dressed as women, pandars or minstrels. They sing wanton songs. They eat black puddings at the horn of the altar while the celebrant is saying Mass. They play at dice there. They run and leap through the church, without a blush at their own shame. Finally they drive about the town and its theatres in shabby traps and carts; and rouse the laughter of their fellows and the bystanders in infamous performances, with indecent gestures and verses scurrilous and unchaste.

In this we come closest to a structured episode in all the many burlesques of specific official ceremonies. Toschi has recorded and reprinted several descriptions of such ceremonies from Italy, and Chambers has done the same for England. Records and even texts survive from virtually every part of France, ranging from the extremely full scenario of the *festa asinaria* from Beauvais to the *Missel des Fous* from Sens, a missal which is really a collection of the special chants used in the course of the burlesque of the Mass. Since most of the burlesque turns on the substitution of nonsense or improvisation for the actual words of the service, however, it is not surprising that complete texts are rare. We hear of the *Messe liesse*, the nonsense Mass, which was widely known, and of the *sermones fatui*, the equally popular mock sermons, but they had no fixed form. It is tempting to think of them as dramatic rituals of a sort, or even as dramatic exercises, though it is not especially useful to do so. In the Feast of Fools and the Feast of the Boy Bishop we find something like an encompassing scenario, chiefly focused on the idea of an anti-society. It is this idea which provides the common ground for the diverse activities of these revels.

The Feast of Fools and the Feast of the Boy Bishop, accordingly, do not provide us with even a fragmentary version of the graduated activities found in the other festivals from the Middle Ages and Renaissance. They are chiefly important to the story of *buffo* for their satiric impersonations, their numerous burlesques, their many forms of mockery — and for the idea of a world turned upside down and the wild, destructive spirit which informs it. Some of these materials are clearly reminiscent of other revels. The election of the mock ruler, the procession through the streets, the games, the burlesque impersonation — all these had clear counterparts in carnival. Even more interesting, the practice of wearing costumes decked with leaves or flowers, women's clothes, or hideous masks — apparently even beast masks — suggest ritual origins still more clearly. But in these emphatically urban festivals all this is subordinate to the self-conscious expression of an impulse to tear down and somehow — by this destruction — to reinvigorate.

A definite connection between the Feast of Fools and the Feast of the Boy Bishop and the tradition of *buffo* was established when the performance of these December festivals passed from the lower clergy and clerks to the amateur lay societies which developed as the revels were expelled from the churches. This expulsion took place in most areas during the thirteenth and fourteenth centuries; numerous decretals, ordinances, and semi-official letters attacking, condemning, and banishing these activities survive from this period. In France the movement resulted in the creation of numerous *compagnies des fous* or *sociétés joyeuses*, among the most famous of which were the Infanterie of Dijon and the Enfants sans souci of Paris; in Italy in the establishment of numerous *associazioni giovanili* with names like the Abbazia degli Stolti ("Brotherhood of Idiots") or Società della Gioventù ("Society of Youth"). Such societies did not develop in England, apparently because of controls on these revels there, or in Germany or Spain, where these particular revels were never very important. Once the transition was complete in France and Italy, however, the *compagnies des fous* assumed responsibility not only for the Feast of Fools and the Feast of the Boy Bishop but, in time, for the supervision of all revels throughout the year. Gradually they de-emphasized the December and other winter festivals in favor of the spring and summer festivals, when the weather was better. Increasingly, they produced plays as part of the revels, until by the fifteenth and sixteenth centuries — when many of

85

the forms of vulgar comedy had already crystallized — they had become the principal presenters of primitive plays.

Unfortunately, a great many questions about the *compagnies des fous* must remain unanswered. Each organization had its own history, and each confronted the tasks of mounting revels and producing plays in a somewhat different way. It is clear, however, that the development of these organizations represents a major phase in the story of *buffo*. For one thing, after concentrating the presentation of a full year's program of revels in the hands of a relatively few people, these societies undoubtedly took the next, quite natural step of editing, collapsing, and combining practices from the different revels, and it is highly probable that this process was favorable to the development of vulgar comedy. Moreover, in producing primitive plays year after year they very probably not only polished and embellished them but encouraged their treatment as plays, works to be performed by a special group in a special way.

The example of the *basochiens* in France is instructive even if not especially typical, since the *basoches* were specialized societies of law students and lawyers' clerks. Organized early in the fifteenth century, these societies (there were several in Paris) took a prominent part in most of the ritual revels and even in certain private entertainments. Whatever the occasion, their special contribution, in addition to the usual parades and merrymaking, was a mock court before which they performed a variety of burlesque lawsuits ranging in complexity from a few comic speeches to pieces of considerable intricacy. Called, among other things, *causes grasses* because they were given at carnival, these primitive plays turned on some comic complaint, such as a wife's dissatisfaction with her husband as a lover or a comic episode involving judges or lawyers. The fifty-third *arretz* pleaded before the *basoche* in Rouen and preserved in Martial d'Auvergne's *Les Arretz d'amour* (ca. 1500) is typical: the whole action consists of the arguments which are generated when wives bring a suit against their husbands for their arrears in love. Also reasonably typical is the eighth plaidoyé contained in *Les Plaidoyez de M. C. Expilly, Président de Parlement de Grenoble* (1605) on the question of whether a child is legitimate if born six months after the marriage has been consummated. Of course students of the *basochiens* have always recognized the relevance of such performances to the development of French farce during the fifteenth and sixteenth centuries, particularly in those plays, like *La Farce de Maître Pathelin,* which feature lawyers, judges, and trials. What has not been emphasized sufficiently is that in the work of the *basochiens* we have clear traces of the full line of development: from the Feast of Fools, to the *société joyeuse,* to the specialized *société,* to the primitive plays contributed by the society to the year's revels, and finally to fully developed vulgar comedies. Not the least important feature of this progression is that the primitive plays are clear outgrowths of the earliest activities associated with the Feast of Fools, the burlesques of official ceremonies.

◇   ◇   ◇

To this picture of ritual revels in the Middle Ages and Renaissance one final, quite different element must be added: the elusive but probably extensive contribution made by dramatic materials surviving from antiquity. By the time of the Roman empire the classical world had developed a considerable wealth of vulgar comedy. We shall look at this material more carefully in the next chapter, but it is useful to remember here the Dorian mime from the Peloponessus, the satyr plays, the *phlyax* farces from Sicily and the Greek colonies in Italy, the Atellan farces from Campania, the Roman mime, and, finally, the achievement of Plautus and Terence. This large corpus of characters, standard actions, principles of organization, and conventions of costuming and acting was all, along with the hardiest of the ritual revels, passed on to later ages.

Although the process of this transmission is mysterious in the extreme, it is perfectly clear that, just as the Floralia survived to influence the May festival, and the Saturnalia to influence the Feast of Fools, so these materials and forms made their way into the Middle Ages to influence the forms and materials of vulgar comedy then in the process of emerging.

It is probably safe to assume that some of these materials were preserved by the folk and transmitted by way of the dramatic rituals, dramatic exercises, and primitive plays which were part of their revels. Just as certain revels (like the Floralia), or certain features of them (such as bearing the symbolic phallus or tree in procession), were apparently passed from generation to generation, so also dramatic rituals and exercises like the lampoon or the comic combat were doubtless transmitted. It is easy to imagine that highly popular materials, successful characters, and details of costuming and behavior would survive in the revels, as they do in the work of professional clowns today, even after the dramatic exercises in which they originated had disappeared. Much the same argument has been made for a variety of materials from antiquity. In *Masks, Mimes, and Miracles* Allardyce Nicoll traces the fool with shaven head from Rome to the Middle Ages, the pilos worn by Odysseus in one of the vase paintings of a *phlyax* farce to the conical hat worn by Pulcinella, and the patchwork suit of the Roman mime actors to the *jongleurs* of the Middle Ages and the Harlequin of the Renaissance. Eighteenth- and nineteenth-century scholars found a direct line of descent from the Atellan farces and its four famous characters, Pappus, Dossenus, Bucco, and Maccus to the commedia dell'arte. All such connections are highly problematical, but the difficulty of proving them does not mean that they did not exist.

Nicoll and others most often assume an unbroken line of professional entertainers extending from the Roman mime actors to the minstrels of the Middle Ages and argue that materials were simply passed from generation to generation. The history of the Roman mime actors after their final expulsion by the Christian church in the sixth century is obscure. Occasional references to them in far-flung locations in Europe suggest that they first were wandering entertainers and then gradually merged with local entertainers to become the minstrels and jesters of the Middle Ages. By the time of Charlemagne they had apparently united with the Germanic *scop* in the territories under study to become the jugglers, dancers, and reciters of tales known by such names as *ioculatores, jongleurs,* and *giullari.* But the fusion seems never to have been complete or uniform. E. K. Chambers reminds us that even at the end of the thirteenth century Thomas de Cabham distinguished three groups of such entertainers in his *Penitential:* (1) "those who wear horrible masks, or entertain by indecent dance and gesture," (2) "those who follow the court and amuse by satire and raillery," and (3) "those who sing of the deeds of princes and the lives of saints" (*Medieval Stage,* I, 59).

Yet despite confusion and diversity there is enough material to suggest continuities with the Roman mime actors and to support the theory that, in addition to retaining the patchwork suit and "horrible masks," entertainers also preserved in the minstrel repertory a fragmentary tradition of *buffo.* Certainly among the more literary of their specialities were a number of dramatic exercises relevant to its development. Debates like *Le Débat de l'hiver et de l'été,* wit combats like *Le Roi d'Angleterre et le jongleur d'Ely,* and a flyting like that in Rutebeuf's *Charlot et le barbier* probably owed more to contemporary folk tradition than to the comic agon of antiquity. Such *parades, dits,* and *fabliaux dialogués* as we have, on the other hand, often suggest survivals of an earlier dramatic tradition. Miscellaneous evidence like the frontispiece of the Terence Codex in Paris, showing a medieval mime production of Terence by masked actors and a reader, clearly confirms dramatic continuities (see fig. 9). For Allardyce Nicoll the assumption of such continuities best explains such

9. Medieval production of Terence. Detail of frontispiece to Terence
Codex ("Le Terence des ducs"), French or Italian, fifteenth century,
Bibliothèque de l'Arsenal, Paris. Photo Giraudon.

medieval phenomena as the reappearance of certain figures like the bald fool with large ears and the hunchback, the character of the masks and certain details of costumes, and plays such as the curiously mime-like *Comedia Bile*, a dramatic dialogue from the early fifteenth century in which a *jongleur* named Episcopus outwits his stingy host. At present there is no better explanation for these matters.

The last important way in which the traditions of antiquity were passed on to later ages was the more conventional method of scholarship. We know that various monastic communities sustained an interest in the classical dramatists, most notably in Plautus and Terence; they read and copied plays and, in the Benedictine community at least, occasionally performed them. This activity led to the remarkable appearance in tenth-century Saxony of Hrosvitha, the nun who wrote six plays in the manner of Terence. Moreover, it accounts for the survival of Plautus and Terence and for their reappearance at odd moments and in unexpected contexts during these centuries; it also supplies a connection with the classical past for the so-called Elegiac Comedies, those semi-dramatic tales in Latin, so much like the vulgar comedy of antiquity, which are found in considerable numbers from the fourth to the twelfth centuries. Yet it is clear that the total contribution of these medieval scholars to the fresh emergence of vulgar comedy in the Middle Ages was probably negligible by comparison with that made by the folk or the minstrelsy. Certainly their influence was very small when compared with the later influence of the Renaissance humanists.

Looking back over the total picture of revel backgrounds and of the various developments within them which appear to have some bearing on vulgar comedy is a little like assembling fragments of ancient spring songs from all over Europe with a view toward inferring from them something of the history and meaning of the spring song. It is trying work; too often it only reinforces existing knowledge: in the spring people all over Europe sang spring songs, for example. With care, however, the evidence of origins can tell us a good deal about vulgar comedy and *buffo*. It is reasonably clear that vulgar comedy as we have known it for the last several hundred years did not develop in a single cumulative process by which one body of ritual led to one body of drama, but from a far messier process by which revel activities flourished and fostered dramatic activities of varying orders of sophistication, then partially withered away, with what survived influencing later revel and dramatic activities. The story of *buffo*'s progress from antiquity to the Renaissance is a story of repeated emergences. Some of the revel activities along the line are similar; some are not so much similar as cognate; some are clearly different from all others. Moreover, much the same is true of the respective forms of vulgar comedy which emerged.

The chief advantage of this approach is that it enables us to skirt what could be thorny problems in a rigorously chronological treatment of origins and to get at what is important. For example, it is impossible to determine when these plays were felt to be separate from ritual by those who performed and experienced them, that is, when they were no longer close enough to ritual to depend on its power and meaning. It is clear that this process of individuation occurred often and in different ways. But what is far more important than having precise knowledge about that is that by assuming a continuous ritual base — a base structured at all points by similar if not identical principles — and numerous cognate emergences, we make available a great deal of evidence with which to explain the plays and their relations to the ritual backgrounds. It is clear, for example, that the primitive plays which represent the opposition of Carnival and Lent originate in that part of the carnival scenario in which King Carnival was tested. We can learn something about these plays from the part of the scenario from which they derive, from the total context of that part, and from cognate parts — in this instance tests or trials — in other scenarios or rituals. Such elements from the primitive plays as the characters, their typical behavior, their dress, and their frequent ugliness and violence, on the other hand, can be best understood in terms of the whole ritual context.

Looked at in this way, the revel backgrounds shed a good deal of light on *buffo*. Perhaps most important, the most persistent patterns of organization in the revels and in the pre-dramatic activities which developed within them tell us a good deal about the dominant patterns of organization in vulgar comedy. Even now it is clear that the combat in all its forms, the opposition of youth and age, the destruction of authority figures, and the achievement of sexual union are all patterns of action which reverberate through both the ritual revels and the plays, expressing an impulse to celebrate fertility and creativeness and to destroy all that inhibits them. Moreover, the detail of these backgrounds explains a great deal about the details of vulgar comedy — the masks, the costumes, and important aspects of characterization. Finally, the revel backgrounds are crucial in explaining the frenzy, energy, violence, and ugliness of vulgar comedy. These features have a far clearer basis in the revel backgrounds than in any literary evidence that might be adduced and, accordingly, can best be explained in terms of those backgrounds.

Our picture of the revel backgrounds is rather like the view of a quite elaborate city seen only through clouds and mists. The terrain of that city is man's creation, devised to make life more endurable, more secure, more enjoyable. Like all great old cities, it has system and pattern, but not one system or one pattern, and we can see it only in part, and then not always clearly. My aim has been to clarify as much as I can of the system and pattern, and of the detail, and from this evidence to develop a sense of the whole which will make one of the many important developments from that whole easier to understand. I take vulgar comedy to be a creation, like the city, designed to make life more endurable, more secure, more enjoyable. Vulgar comedy, like its origins, embraces an intricate set of conventions for releasing within those experiencing it a sense that they have dominated all that opposes fruitfulness and health, an exhilaration which, even if only temporary, makes life tolerable. This quality, as it appears in the comedy and in the beholder, is *buffo*.

PART II
Materials and Forms

4

From Revel to Play

The second important body of evidence
to be examined is the plays which constitute the tradition
of *buffo*, and here we appear to be on safer, more familiar
ground. Unlike the ritual revels and many of the pre-
dramatic forms, the plays usually survive in complete form
and in an abundance which makes selectivity necessary.
Typically, they speak loudly and distinctly, contributing to
the accumulating evidence a boldness of outline frequently lacking in perspectives obtained from a study of
origins. Yet they continue the story begun in that study,
and one of the chief problems will be to consolidate the
evidence of continuities among them as full-scale expressions of *buffo* and the problematical anticipations of
it in the evidence of origins.

As I have tried to show in earlier chapters, the
emergence of *buffo* is apparently a story of multiple
emergences. To oversimplify somewhat, the evidence of
antiquity indicates that the phallic songs, the lampoon, and
the Fescennine verses mark an early stage in a development which led to finished forms of vulgar comedy like the

Dorian mime, the satyr play, the *phlyax* farces, the Roman mime, the Atellan farces, and ultimately the plays of Plautus and Terence. The evidence of later ages suggests that this process, or something like it, was in time repeated in a number of different places. All these reinventions are problematical: they had relatively little to do with each other, or with the achievement of antiquity; most contain gaps in what appears to be the evolutionary pattern. Only for the wooing play do we seem to have documentary proof of every step in the movement from revel to free-standing play.

The initial problem in attempting to deal with the literary evidence is to see what more can be learned about the process of vulgar comedy's emergence by looking at fully developed plays. The vulgar comedies of greatest relevance here are, of course, the simplest and most primitive. Fortunately, many of these simple, transitional plays have survived.

◇   ◇   ◇

The juxtaposition of transitional plays with the prior evidence of revels and pre-dramatic forms makes one general conclusion inescapable: the key principle in the movement from revel to play was one of gradual concretization. Despite all the lacunae, the process seems to have been the same everywhere. As the ritual revel, or part of it, gradually became dramatic ritual, then dramatic exercise, then emergent play, and then, finally, free-standing vulgar comedy, the relatively abstract kernel of action from the ritual was gradually supplanted by particularized forms of it. Among the first elements with a dramatic quality to emerge from the ritual revels of Greece and Rome were the abusive speeches directed at individual members of the crowd in the lampoon in Greece and the Fescennine verses in Rome. Although we do not know which specific individuals were attacked, the very fact that the earliest dramatic developments involved attacks on particular persons anticipates strikingly the tendency of later, more sophisticated forms to use commonplace figures and events. The parallel development in carnival, in which members of Carnival's demonic retinue taunt and prey upon individuals in the community or Carnival himself denounces them in his testament, permits a further conjecture. Since such attacks were often directed at officials, old husbands with young wives, and newly married but childless couples, we might speculate that the underlying purpose of the revel, the celebration of renewal and rebirth, was expressed in these attacks on individuals or types who were felt to inhibit or deny life.

Certainly something very like concretization is suggested by the rest of the movement from revel to play. An inspection of any two stages in the movement will indicate that the later, more sophisticated stage — the primitive carnival play as compared with the *débat* or *contrasto*, for example — is always more abundant in commonplace characters and detail. There are not only more characters — in even the earliest plays there are at least three, four, or five — but they have, like their immediate contexts (the shoemaker's shop, the wine shop), a detailed particularity. Still more conclusive is the evidence provided by the Schembart carnival in Nuremberg, a celebrated feast for which a guild of butchers had the privilege and responsibility of producing new tableaux each year. A selection of 867 miniatures of *Schembartlauf* tableaux and characters has been reprinted by Sumberg in his *Nuremberg Schembart Carnival* and testifies to the industry and pride of the guild during the fifteenth and sixteenth centuries. Faced with the task of discovering new ideas year after year, the good butchers were inevitably moved, however gradually, to accommodate the scenario to domestic and civic materials. Where the earliest tableau, from 1475, simply shows a dragon on a sleigh, by 1518 the tableau for the Arbor of Love depicts a highly complex scene involving several pairs of lovers, a lute player, and a Fool, and mentions still other characters who are not shown. In all this

99

the process is uniform: the ritual, abstract and fabulous, was gradually translated into the materials of everyday life. Concretization seems to have involved both elaboration, in the sense of the proliferation of detail, and "vulgarization," in the sense of a movement toward the experience of the *vulgus* or folk.

Once this principle has been recognized, we can theorize further. We shall probably never know as much as we would like about the process by which vulgar comedy became character-centered comedy; yet it did, and apparently rather quickly. From antiquity we know little beyond what has already been said about the development of abusive speeches; the *komos*, the comic agon, and the beast mummery are too poorly documented to permit more than general speculation. We do know, however, that all the evidence of vulgar comedy from antiquity points to plays dominated by characters of commonplace dimensions. The earliest Dorian mimes — the recited mimes of Sophron of Syracuse (fifth century B.C.) — were monologues presenting a short scene from ordinary life and bore titles like *The Needlewoman, The Sorceress,* and *The Mother-in-Law;* in the same period the performed mimes of Epicharmus (fl. 485–67 B.C.) apparently attracted later scholars because of their celebrated treatment of character. Our evidence of the satyr play, consisting chiefly of Euripides' *Cyclops* (ca. 410 B.C.) and the long fragment of Sophocles' *Ichneutae* ("The Trackers," ca. 460 B.C.), suggests that, in addition to burlesque figures from legend, a well-defined Silenus was always central to the plot. What survives from Rome in the way of titles and fragmentary accounts of the work of Catullus the mime-writer (ca. 50 B.C.) and Decimus Laberius (ca. 106–43 B.C.) confirms the primacy of character there; in fact, the many surviving terracotta figures of Roman mime characters (see fig. 13) suggest that they were fairly well known throughout the Roman world. The marvelous vase paintings of the *phlyax* farces, the fourth-century B.C. mime form from Sicily and southern Italy, indicate not only well-defined characters but characters sufficiently distinctive and popular to have appeared in play after play (see fig. 3). Allardyce Nicoll, in *Masks, Mimes, and Miracles*, who has identified some eight or nine such figures, does not include Hercules, the heroic buffoon so frequently robbed of his dinner in these plays.

But the form of ancient vulgar comedy which most clearly documents the rapid development of character-centered drama is the Atellan farce, a species of short comedy dealing with ordinary life which developed in Campania in the third century B.C. and later enjoyed such a vogue in republican Rome that it was taken up as a literary form. Our knowledge of the *atellanae* comes chiefly from such late literary practitioners of it as L. Pomponius Bononiensus (fl. 100–85 B.C.), of whose work many titles but only a few fragments of text survive. However, the evidence is sufficient to establish that, in addition to its burlesques of myth and legend and of episodes from ordinary life, the form produced four characters of tremendous popularity: Bucco, a fool with puffed-out cheeks; Dossenus, a sharp-witted, rather terrifying hunchback; Maccus, a stupid, awkward fool; and Pappus, a distracted, rather dull old man. The appeal of these characters survived to the eighteenth century, when scholars traced certain characters of the early commedia dell'arte troupes directly to them. Although that theory is now discredited, it calls attention to a key feature of the characterization in vulgar comedy: over several centuries it evolved a kind of archetypal cast of characters, one aspect of which first achieved definition in the *atellanae*.

Precisely how the movement from abusive speeches, the *komos*, the comic agon, and the beast mummery to these short rowdy plays featuring grotesquely masked figures and bearing titles like *Pappus' Marriage* and *Maccus the Soldier* was accomplished we do not know. We are certain only that with the first fully developed vulgar comedies we are confronted with the outsized, grotesque masks of Pappus, Dossenus, Hercules the heroic buffoon, the quack Doctor, the braggart Soldier, and others, all staring at us across the centuries as if to announce that some-how, very early in the history of vulgar comedy, a decision was taken to construct plays around boldly drawn charac-ters. This decision means that the makers of these plays assumed that man is the prime mover of events and that human character is the first cause in the human scene. This assumption was to become one of the basic premises of vulgar comedy, as well as of a good many other kinds of comedy derived from it.

In the Middle Ages and early Renaissance the prog-ress of revel materials through stages in which definite characters first appear separated from dramatic contexts and then pass into fully developed dramatic form is clear. The figures of Carnival and Lent can be traced from the simplest, most abstract rituals through intermediate forms like the *contrasti* and *débats*, primitive carnival plays like the Tuscan *Befanata drammatica profana: scherzo cam-pagnolo* and simple *fastnachtspiele* like *Fastnacht und Fasten* right down to the threshold of fully developed vul-gar comedies. Each in his way is an authority figure par excellence — the Old Man and the Old Woman in various guises — and together they exemplify the eternal couple and the eternal strife of domesticity. They appear everywhere, but their origins are most clear, of course, when there is continuity of detail, as in the late fifteenth-century French play *La Farce du Pont aux Ânes* ("The Farce of the Bridge of Asses"), in which the wife is called the Old Woman. Much the same movement toward in-creasingly well-defined characters is also evident in other parts of the carnival scenario. Paolo Toschi has shown in great detail in the last few pages of *Origini,* how members of King Carnival's demonic retinue gradually became the fools and pranksters of the later commedia dell'arte casts — the *zannis,* Arlecchino, Scaramuccia, Pulcinella, and others — while the Doctor and Notary of the carnival ritual survived unchanged in the comic doctors and notaries who appear everywhere in early vulgar comedies.

The line of development from the Feast of Fools to

the vulgar comedies is more difficult to document because so little drama of a conventional sort came out of these revels. Yet everything we know of the Feast of Fools indicates that even in its earliest stages it focused on character in the figures of the religious and civic officials which it regularly debunked, and it is clear that as its management passed into the hands of the *sociétés joyeuses*, these figures gained in definition, depending on the special concerns of the producing organizations. In the hands of the *basochiens*, for example, figures of judges, lawyers, and policemen were as popular as those of contending husbands and wives and, accordingly, were given a high order of definition.

But the clearest example of the movement toward character-centered plays appears in the wooing rituals and wooing plays, which move from simple betrothal rites to plays sufficiently sophisticated in treatment to be indistinguishable from fully developed vulgar comedies. Here we find first a young couple and their parents; then a young couple, a rival, a servant, and parents; then a young couple, a more distinctive rival, a more distinctive servant, and more distinctive parents; and finally several young couples, several servants, and so on. The process by which this cast was gradually defined and domesticized is unmistakable, especially in Italy in the nicely graduated *bruscelli* leading to fully developed plays like *Il Mercato*.

One final example of this type of concretization is seen in the divine or mythic figures of the ritual revels: these figures were increasingly scaled down to the dimensions of everyday life and ultimately translated into commonplace authority figures. In antiquity the process is traceable in what we know of the popular burlesques of myth and legend. The celebrated mime-writer Epicharmus apparently excelled in this kind of burlesque, as did Rhinthon of Tarentum in his *phlyax* farces; though only fragments and titles of their plays remain, it is clear that they turned on god-like or heroic figures reduced to human size. Euripides' *Cyclops*, the long fragment of Sophocles'

Ichneutae, and the other extant fragments of the satyr plays leave no room for doubt that divine and heroic figures were regularly "vulgarized": Polyphemus becomes a pederast, and Old Silenus, the father of the satyrs and their leader, becomes a cringing illustration of the flesh.

In the Middle Ages and Renaissance much the same process is evident in the gradual substitutions of commonplace figures for the mythic figures of the carnival scenario or the officials of the Feast of Fools. King Carnival — tyrant, soldier, spiritual father, husband — almost imperceptibly yields to a host of domestic tyrants, soldiers, fathers, and husbands. We meet him in uncomplicated form in the impotent husband of *La Farsa del Baglivo* ("The Farce of the Judge," ca. 1510); most of the fun in that play proceeds from the discussion of the husband's sexual failings. We see him in subtler form in the figure of the old blind beggar in the well-known early farce *Le Garçon et l'aveugle* ("The Boy and the Blind Man", ca. 1270). Here the whole question of what is pleasurable about young Jeahannot's deception of his helpless old master by means of ventriloquism and beating him can best be resolved by referring the characters and the action to the carnival scenario.

◇   ◇   ◇

This provides an outline of one way in which concretization worked in the history of *buffo:* ritual revels or parts of them were converted into dramatic equivalents dominated by characters which were progressively elaborated in detail and were gradually yoked to everyday life. This principle also accounts for the direction taken by episodic elements in the transitional plays, those formulaic actions from the ritual revels which also indicate a movement toward familiar, pedestrian surfaces. This evidence of concretization is extensive but tricky. There is, for example, no firm historical link between the widespread food-stealing pranks of the processional revels and the many little plays dealing with thefts of food, yet the similarities between them are too striking to be accidental. We know that the acquisition of food by theft or begging was a standard activity of the revelers both in antiquity and in the Middle Ages (it is most clearly seen in the mischievous thievery of Carnival's retainers); we know, too, that these "episodes" frequently involved beatings and that they contributed to the frenzy generated by the revel as a whole. The similarities between this and such early fragments of evidence as the reference in Aristophanes' *Sphekes* ("The Wasps", 422 B.C.) to a mime in which Hercules is defrauded of his dinner, or the vase painting in the Louvre depicting a scene from a mime in which slaves have apparently stolen wine from Dionysus, point to very early dramatic accommodations of ritual practice. Gradually, food, thefts of food, the beatings which frequently attended these thefts, and the almost metaphysical hunger that prompted them became constant subjects in vulgar comedy, particularly in its early forms.

It is but a short step from these dimly perceived links to a fully developed play like the late fifteenth-century *La Farce du pasté et de la tarte* ("The Farce of the Meat Pie and the Tart"). In this play two rogues bemoan the cold, their hunger, and the thin pickings to be had by begging. Then the first of them overhears a pastry cook taking leave of his wife and telling her that he will send someone to her to fetch a meat pie; his instructions are that she should give the pie to whoever comes and takes her by the finger. The first rogue quickly confides this to the second, who, of course, gets the pie; when the pastry cook returns and learns of the loss, he beats his wife. Next, the first rogue goes to the shop and himself tries to get a tart, but this time the wife traps him and the pastry cook beats him. To equalize matters, the first rogue then sends the second to the shop, telling him that the wife wants him, and the second rogue is also beaten. The play ends with the rogues taking solace in what is left of the meat pie and the first rogue explaining that, after all, they had agreed to share everything. In these events the continuities between revel and play are reasonably clear: in the rogues, the theft of food, the beatings, the attention to moments of frenzy, the absence of anything like a moral point of view. Altogether, the play preserves these elements from the revels even as it exemplifies the movement from revel to a conspicuously commonplace, "vulgarized" action.

Such continuities are almost as clear in other accommodations of events from the ritual revels. The combat which was so constant a feature in the ritual struggles between Winter and Spring, the Old Year and the New, and Carnival and Lent is traceable at various stages of development. The movement toward an increasingly concrete form is evident in the simple *contrasti* and *débats*, pieces like *Il Contrasto fra Carnevale e Quaresima* and *La Horrenda e mortal battaglia fra Carnevale e Quaresima,* and it is even clearer in more sophisticated pieces like *Il Contrasto di Brighinol e Tonin,* where the combat is still central but the content has been "vulgarized" so as to set peasants against each other. As this revel episode was repeatedly adapted to dramatic form, it apparently split into two kinds, both implicit, if largely unseparated, in the revel materials: one a struggle between male and female, Carnival and Lent, the other a struggle between youth and age.

A good example of the male-female contention is to be seen in *La Farce du Pont aux Ânes.* Against a background of carnival, a husband and wife quarrel, and she refuses to do anything for him. Baffled by her stubbornness, he wanders through the town until he meets a Friar, who, when asked for advice, tells him in a kind of pig Latin to go to the Bridge of Asses for an answer. There the husband sees that the Boskeron is having trouble with his ass, but that when he beats it, he gets results. Armed with this solution, the husband goes home and beats his wife with the same happy results while singing the Boskeron's refrain: "Trottez, vieille, trottez, trottez." Although it would be difficult to find a more straightforward adaptation of the Carnival-Lent struggle, many other versions of it only slightly less direct are in fact to be found in early vulgar comedy: in Italy, in *La Farsa del Baglivo,* mentioned earlier, in Germany, in the mid-sixteenth-century *fastnachtspiel* no. 29 in Keller's collection, and in England, in plays like *Tom Tyler and His Wife* (ca. 1575).

Good examples of the combat as a struggle between youth and age are also abundant. Apart from all the plays dealing with the defeat of old husbands by young lovers, like Francesco Mariano Trinci's *Il Bichiere* ("The Beaker"), written for the Rozzi in Siena in the middle of the sixteenth century (here the old husband is appropriately named "Senile"), there are many early plays in which the young defeat the old without sexual profit. Niccolò Campani's *Strascino* (ca. 1519), also for the Rozzi, is typical: in it four peasant brothers, led by Strascino, pay back Old Dolovico the money they owe him with a beating. A more brutal example is the student play in Latin which we know to have been presented on the first of May in 1497 in Pavia, the *Janus Sacerdos:* here young Sacuvius, posing as a woman-hater, lures Janus, a kindly old pederast-priest, into his house with the promise of a boy; once there, Janus is beaten and robbed by Sacuvius' young friends, who then spend the money on a banquet. In all these plays almost as important as the straightforward treatment of the combat and defeat of the old is the persistent indifference to humanity and morality. Like Carnival, the old struggle and lose, and humane or moral considerations have no place in the process. This feature of *buffo,* everywhere evident in early vulgar comedy, can best be understood by referring to their sources.

◇ ◇ ◇

Yet this picture of the movement from revel to play permits still further observations. Once the numerous lines leading from the revels to the early plays have been drawn, it becomes apparent that fully developed vulgar comedies are more often dramatic equivalents for discrete parts of the ritual revels than recapitulations of entire revels. This is rather remarkable. Most of the anthropologists who have tried to explain drama in terms of its ritual origins — the Cambridge anthropologists and their followers — believe that the plays which stand at the end of the supposed evolutionary process constitute something like recapitulations of the whole purpose and meaning of the rituals to which they trace. Such is patently the case in the work of Gilbert Murray and his followers on Greek tragedy and the myth of the dying year. But the evidence of early vulgar comedy appears to lead to a quite different conclusion. Many of these plays, rather than embodying anything like the total outline of the carnival scenario or of any of the ritual revels, trace to single episodes or to selected elements in the revels, hence the large number of plays which deal with food-stealing episodes, with attacks on authority figures, with a struggle between a surrogate Carnival and a surrogate Lent, or with the destruction of a surrogate Carnival. A good case in point is the early seventeenth-century *singspiel* by Jan Van Arp entitled *Van Droncke Goosen* ("Drunken Goosen"). (Like the English song-plays of the sixteenth century, the Dutch *singspiele* were little musical farces; the text of this one has been reprinted by Baskervill in *The Elizabethan Jig.*) The play opens with Goosen, dead drunk, being dragged from a tavern by a Host and Hostess; they knock him about, blacken his hands and face, steal his money, and go off. When he awakens, he recoils in terror because he has turned black, at first thinks himself a devil and tries to fly, and then, failing that, tries to conjure up a devil. At this the Host and Hostess return, now disguised as devils, drive him about again, and attach a rocket to his breech so that, finally, he flees in panic. In addition to preserving from the revels such details as the blackening of hands and face and the mischievous "devils," this play quite clearly turns on the purpose of dramatizing the destruction of Goosen, a figure like King Carnival in that he is drunk and intractably immoral. Here Goosen is pure victim, a scapegoat borne away by a rocket, even as Carnival as dummy was frequently blown up by firecrackers. In other words, the play looks neither to earlier nor to later events in the carnival scenario; it is strictly limited to the execution episode.

We see much the same thing in plays like *La Farce du gouteux* ("The Farce about the Man with the Gout," 1534), in which Maître Minim, suffering from a painful case of gout, is tormented by his deaf servant, or *La Farce d'un chaudronnier* ("The Farce of a Tinker," ca. 1530). In this latter piece a man and his wife quarrel and, to settle the question of sovereignty, each bets that the other will speak first. Into the silence of this combat comes a tinker, who, when he gets no answers to his questions, decks the husband out like a fool and fondles his wife. Outraged, the husband finally flies out at him and drives him off, but in the process loses his bet with his wife. Here, too, the plays echo discrete parts of the carnival scenario: the execution episode in *La Farce du gouteux* and the contention between Carnival and Lent in *La Farce d'un chaudronnier*.

Still other fully developed vulgar comedies embody several episodes from the revel scenario. In the Elizabethan song-play *The Black Man*, for example, Thumpkin, an old man, makes a match with Susan, only to be thwarted and driven off by two gentlemen. But he returns, persuades them to fight among themselves for her, and while they are fighting makes off with her. When they catch him, they tie him to a stool and drape him with a sheet. Brush, a brush salesman who comes in next, mistakes him for a ghost and refuses to release him. But later, when a black man appears, Thumpkin promises him Susan's maidenhead if he will release him, and together they — they are called "devils" in the play — terrorize the gentlemen. This play, too, is easy to see as an adaptation of the execution episode from the carnival scenario: clearly enough the Old Man is "killed" when old Thumpkin is tied to a stool and draped with a sheet. But the play also includes a wooing episode in the first part and a "resurrection" toward the end. In fact, here we find a very rough outline of the whole death-resurrection pattern basic to many of the ritual revels, as well as a number of ritual details like the black man and, again, the terrorizing by "devils."

The value of recognizing that some plays derive from the whole, some from several episodes, and some from a discrete part of the revels is that plays can be traced to their sources more accurately and plays virtually impossible to understand without help from their sources can be comprehended. Plays like *Van Droncke Goosen* or *Le Garçon et l'aveugle* seem to be little more than wanton and rather irrational exercises in cruelty unless we recognize that they stem from the execution episode. We can imagine that a play like *Le Garçon et l'aveugle* fell into a familiar pattern for contemporary audiences, the pattern in which the old master, ailing — in this case blind — is destroyed by a younger man. The pattern has a long history in the Middle Ages and is readily referable to the carnival scenario. The scenario, much more clearly than the play itself, clarifies for us how that pattern embodied a happy or fortunate knowledge.

Yet these critical distinctions do not enable us to understand, for example, that small group of plays from antiquity and the Middle Ages which consist of a tradesman hawking his wares or an artisan proclaiming the glories of his craft in the manner of Simon Eyre from Dekker's *The Shoemaker's Holiday*. What such plays meant, why they were pleasurable — here we confront a sensitivity to ritual which now entirely eludes us. What the surviving evidence does tell us (and it is a great deal) is that the movement from revel to play consisted essentially of a process of concretization, a process by which ritual revels, or parts of them, evolved through pre-dramatic forms to increasingly commonplace, domestic dramatic equivalents. Along the way a group of characters, a selection of formulaic actions, and a body of conventional detail were defined which became the substance of vulgar comedy. We shall meet these characters, episodes, and details again and again, and they will change under cultural pressure, though never so much that we lose sight of their origins.

Concretization as a principle is indispensable both for what it explains of the complex and discontinuous historical process by which revel materials passed into vulgar comedy and for the way it adjusts our view of familiar, pedestrian materials so that we can see pattern and idea beneath the skin. Moreover, it continues to apply even later, where dramatic materials which have already been concretized themselves undergo changes. Perhaps the biggest problem in reading vulgar comedies critically is in reading them as structures of transposed signs. I am not proposing that vulgar comedies be read as symbolic plays; however, the failure to see a structure in vulgar comedy deeper than anything that first meets the eye is to oversimplify dangerously. Finally, only this structure can account satisfactorily for vulgar comedy's persistent power to elicit intense, if largely uncritical, responses.

5

The Revue Play

We are now in a position to survey the
range of vulgar comedy. For the moment I shall continue to
concentrate on transitional plays, those relatively close to
the pre-dramatic forms considered in previous chapters.
They add still further detail to the picture of the development of vulgar comedy since many of the early plays retain
clear continuities with the revels; more important, this will
enable us to deal with vulgar comedy in a relatively pure
form, before the cultural pressures of later ages modified it.
There is no lack of material at what might be called the
threshold of *buffo*. Although the texts from antiquity are
fragmentary, we know more than enough about ancient
vulgar comedy to indicate its prevailing character. From
the thirteenth to the sixteenth century we have such an
abundance of superior work that we shall be forced to view
it as one of the great periods of *buffo*.

For clarity's sake it will be useful to survey this transitional work under two headings. The first I shall call the
"revue play," a term first proposed by Walter French in his
monograph on Hans Sachs (pp. 1–7) and then used by Leo

Hughes in the first chapter of *A Century of English Farce*, where he distinguishes between the short play, which strings what he calls "farce materials" on a thread, like a revue, and the longer play of elaborate intrigue. Unfortunately, the distinction must remain rough, even arbitrary, because of the variability of the plays in question: they embody so many combinations of materials and are so full of elaborated intrigues that any attempt to categorize them inevitably results in some overlapping. Yet the categories will prove helpful if, in general, we understand by the revue play the short play designed to exhibit selected materials from the tradition of *buffo* and by the second type, which I shall call the Plautine play, the longer play of more sophisticated structure. Some such distinction was understood in eighteenth-century England: writing for the *London Journal* on April 3, 1725, one "Momus" differentiated in his discussion of the rise of pantomime between the "short Interludes, and *Antick Dances*, between Acts" and "long *Farces*." Indeed, any attempt to survey work as different in point of complexity as the farces of Samuel Foote, David Garrick, and George Colman, on the one hand, and the afterpieces of that century, on the other — or the immensely sophisticated structures of Georges Feydeau and the farces of medieval France — makes the distinction inescapable.

The typical structure of the revue play consists of a fairly straightforward treatment of one or at most two or three units of material from the revel scenario. We have already seen that simple plays like *Van Droncke Goosen* or *La Farce du pasté et de la tarte* look like dramatic adaptations of discrete parts of the carnival scenario, while a somewhat more complex play like *The Black Man* accommodates several such parts. The plays dramatize these units of material and simple combinations of them as if the unit or units were sufficient unto themselves — as if, so to speak, any of a number of separate melodic statements carried with them enough of the whole cantata to be complete and meaningful. We find one that treats a struggle

113

between a husband and wife, another that presents the destruction of the Old Man, another that turns on a theft of food and beatings, another that treats a rivalry between suitors, and still another that combines two or three of these actions. Each revue play recapitulates a unit of material or a simple combination of units, and each does so without reference to the contextual scenario. For these reasons it seems appropriate to speak of the "exhibition" of *buffo* materials: these plays do not interpret, or transform, or reintegrate these materials so much as they simply present them.

But the relations between the parts and the vestigial whole is more complex than my musical metaphor suggests. We cannot know how much of the whole scenario was conveyed through effective recapitulation of one part for audiences still aware of the ritual background. We can only observe that the playwrights were often content to limit the plays to a single unit of material and that, thus limited, the plays do not make sense to us without reference to the backgrounds. We can further observe that the makers of these plays clearly exercised selection, with the result that some units of material appear far more frequently than others. I shall focus on those which occur most frequently, alone or in combination; it seems likely that in them we shall find further evidence of what *buffo* is.

◇ ◇ ◇

The first and perhaps the most obvious of these is the dramatic combat, or agon, a central episode in all the ritual revels. This combat takes two principal forms: struggles between husband and wife and struggles between youth and age. In the earliest plays the struggle between husband and wife consists of little more than uncomplicated domestic warfare. A husband and wife quarrel, one beats the other — sometimes each beats the other — and domestic peace is restored. A good example of the type is *La Farce du Pont aux Ânes*; another is *Tom Tyler and His Wife* (ca. 1575), a relatively late work, but still a primitive one. Tom Tyler, called Patch, is married to a shrew named Strife, who, after he goes off to work, joins her neighbors in the alehouse. When Tom happens in, thirsty too, she accuses him of loafing, beats him, and drives him off. Tom then goes to his friend Tom Tailor and asks him to help "put her in hell." Tom Tailor agrees, and they change clothes and plot to lure Strife out of doors so that Tom Tailor can beat her. The plan works, and Strife is duly beaten by one she takes to be her husband; she is even forced to kneel, beg forgiveness, and promise to be good. But when Tom Tyler returns to take over and she moans, he confesses the plot to her, and she again beats him. The play concludes with all the characters assembling; Patience urges them to reform, and they sing a song. In this rowdy, rather brutal little play, reminders of the Carnival-Lent struggle are obvious: in the wife's name, Strife, in the drinking, in Tom Tailor's association with the devil ("Am I a devil?" he asks, when Tom Tyler talks of putting his wife in hell), and in Tom Tyler's association with Patch, the English fool whose tattered costume can be traced to the graveclothes of carnival figures. But even more notable here is that, as so often in carnival, it is the struggle and not its outcome which is important. It doesn't matter who beats whom, or who finally wins; it matters only that there is a struggle.

A subtler, far more artful version of the same combat is to be seen in *La Farce de Calbain* (ca. 1485). Calbain's wife complains that she needs a dress, that she's *toute nue*, while he ignores her, responding to everything she says with songs; to her plea that he desist in his songs he replies with still more songs. Finally, she asks a friend for help, and he advises her to give Calbain a good meal and then drug him. She does, and while Calbain is sleeping, she steals his purse. When he awakens, he of course descends on her to get his purse back. But now it is she who sings, and the song is, appropriately, one which recalls his former "barking": "Maudit soit le petit chien / Qui aboye, aboye, aboye" ("Cursed be the little dog / That barks and barks and barks"). He strikes her; she threatens to leave him; he then repents and accepts his fate as a cheater cheated (*trompeur trompé*). The subject is essentially that of *Tom Tyler*, but its treatment is distinctly more sophisticated. The struggle is far less a matter of blows in the style of Punch and Judy than of the noiseless thrust and parry of words and feigned indifference. Moreover, the deception and the subsequent reversal which it produces are beautifully stylized by the symmetries of the songs and the wit of the final irony.

Deception is unmistakably important in these plays, not only in those dealing with the male-female struggle, but in the dramatic adaptations of virtually all the units of material under study. Yet deception is not so much a unit of material in its own right as a device which proved highly effective in the dramatic elaboration of *buffo*. It could be argued that as a dramatic device — as a way, that is, of spinning out and opening up these *materia* — deception can be traced to the pranks of the merrymakers in virtually all the revels. Certainly there is a line of development from this source to the primitive plays which turn on thefts of food, and certainly in the plays deception is often practiced by cunning servants and dependants, figures like those in Carnival's retinue.

In any event, deception's immense usefulness is abundantly clear in the plays in which the male-female struggle turns on adultery or attempted adultery. These plays typically convert the male-female combat into an intrigue by which either the husband or the wife seeks to cuckold the other (again, it does not seem to matter which is the schemer and which the victim, though the husband is the more frequent victim); in the course of the action the schemer and his or her companion are forced by the cuckold-to-be to adopt some stratagem or other. We have numerous examples of the type, all somewhat different in detail. The fact of sex may be thinly disguised in the act of eating, usually in the form of a meal eaten by the wife and her lover during the husband's absence. In Giovan Giorgio Alione's *La Farsa de Zohan* (ca. 1520), during Zohan's absence his wife entertains a priest with dinner; in Hans Sachs' *Der farend Schüler mit dem Deufel pannen* ("The Wandering Scholar Who Raised the Devil," 1551), the peasant's wife does the same with a crippled, hunch-back priest; in John Heywood's *John John, Tyb, and Sir John* (ca. 1520), John John's wife and the parish priest Sir John eat a special eel pie, in this instance in the presence of John John, who is made to run errands for them. In some of these plays the struggle leads to actual combat, as in *John John,* in which John John drives Tyb and Sir John off and then fears that they are cuckolding him. In some it leads to a beating or beatings: in *La Farsa de Zohan* Zohan returns, discovers the priest hiding in a basket, and beats him, then worries about how he will explain the priest's presence in the house to his neighbors. In some plays, on the other hand, the lover is entirely victorious, as in *Der farend Schüler mit dem Deufel pannen,* in which the hunchback priest, having had his face blackened, is passed off on the peasant husband as a devil summoned out of hell.

Some of the plays increase the number of essential characters to four as the deception becomes increasingly intricate. The wandering scholar of Sachs' play, for exam-ple, is added to the triangle of woman, lover, and husband. He is first repulsed by the priest and the peasant's wife when he comes to them asking for alms; later he performs the trick by which the husband is duped, staging the "magic" invocation which calls the black-faced priest from the hell of the stove where he is hiding. In *The Humours of Simpkin,* an Elizabethan song-play of uncertain date, Simpkin and the Old Man's wife are interrupted by one Bluster, another wooer, as they take advantage of the Old Man's absence, and Simpkin hides; then Bluster and the wife are interrupted by the husband. The wife concocts the explanation that Bluster, with sword drawn, chased some-one into the house, a story which, after Bluster's departure, enables her to explain Simpkin's presence in a chest and to win the husband's consent that he remain.

Altogether, the plays which treat the male-female struggle in terms of an adultery or an attempted adultery reveal numerous variations in detail, but the differences are of marginal importance. It apparently does not matter whether the lover is successful or beaten or both, whether the husband learns the truth or not, whether the adultery promises future pleasures or not. What is important is the struggle between male and female. The adultery or attempted adultery and the deception which it provokes are accidental incidents in a dramatic articulation which derives its primary power from that struggle.

This is not to suggest that these plays do not vary tremendously in quality, that there is not a great distance between a little romp like *Der Pferdekauf des Edelmannes* ("The Aristocrat Buys a Horse," ca. 1615), a German version of an Elizabethan song-play, and a play like *La Farce du savetier* ("The Shoemaker's Farce," ca. 1500). In the first the aristocrat enjoys his new mistress, the "horse" of the title, in an outhouse while her ignorant husband stands outside the door jingling keys to assure her that he has not moved. The play's comic power derives almost entirely from the adultery and the witty stratagem by which it is brought off; as if to sharpen this focus, the figure of the husband gets all the final emphasis as he stands at the end, baffled, jingling his keys, and protesting that he too must use the "facilities." In *La Farce du savetier,* on the other hand, the subject is still adultery, but its achievement is complicated and extended. Audin, a shoemaker, and his wife, Audette, quarrel: he complains about domestic life in general; she complains that he neglects her and nags all the time. Each asserts his sovereignty, and quickly they fall to insulting each other. Then a priest comes in, lamenting that he loves Audette and praying to the Virgin Mary for help. When Audin goes off to drum up business, the priest goes to the house and begs her to come away with him. Alas, Audin has locked her in. But she has an idea. When Audin returns, she insults him again and strikes him, and in response he cries, "The Devil take you!" At this the priest, disguised as a devil, comes in and in fact carries her away. The lovers rejoice, but so does the shoemaker, who advises men at large to get rid of their wives by giving them to the devil. In many respects this is the best example of an early play of this type. It preserves echoes of the revel background in the directness, length, and violence of the opening quarrel and in the detail of the "devil" who carries off the wife, but it also shows how art, in this case in the form of calculated ironies, surprises, and symmetries, can intensify the native power of the materials.

It is not surprising, of course, that a number of the early plays which turn on the combat do so in such a way as to embrace both the struggle between male and female and the struggle between youth and age. It is possible to see a modified version of the Carnival-Lent model in old Lucas and his young wife, Ameline, in *Le Bon payeur et le sergent boiteux et borgne* ("The Good Creditor and the One-eyed, Crippled Justice of the Peace," ca. 1518) and in the old husband and young wife of *Der Monch im Sacke* ("The Monk in the Bag," ca. 1615), still another German version of an earlier English play, yet both plays also deal with the broader issue of youth versus age. As we have seen in *Strascino* and *Il Bichiere,* there is no want of early plays in which the conflict is unmistakably between youth and age. Frequently the problem is sex; sometimes it is simply power; but it is always treated so that the old person — usually an old man — is defeated or shown to deserve defeat. One of the most delightful plays of this type is *La Farce d'un ramonneur* ("The Chimneysweep's Farce," ca. 1520), in which the whole action turns on the use of chimneysweeping as a metaphor for making love. As the play begins, the sweep and his young helper are in the streets soliciting work; the sweep confesses that he is now too old and fat to work very much. Wishing to save face with his wife, he asks his helper to support him in the lie that he has had a good day and has cleaned his usual eight or ten chimneys. As they tell this story to the wife, however, they fall out, and the helper accuses his master of incompetence. The wife's response to this is to lament her case to her neighbor (nothing for three months), while the sweep's is to urge everyone to clean while he can. The emphasis in all this salaciousness is not on youth triumphant, but on the failing energy of age. Thus the play makes no attempt to resolve the struggle between youth and age (see fig. 10).

By contrast, Anton Francesco Grazzini's *La Giostra* ("The Trick," ca. 1556), a play which has not survived but which is known from an adaptation in the last two acts of another, *L'Arzigogolo* ("The Quibbler," ca. 1560), carries the struggle to the expected resolution. Here the miserly old lawyer Alesso, who wishes to marry an heiress, is persuaded by his servant, secretly acting for his son, to drink a draught which costs 100 *scudi* and which presumably has the power of making him young. Then, when the heiress pretends she cannot recognize him as a young man, he pays another 100 *scudi* for a draught to restore him to his real age. In this context, clearly, money is power which ought to be in the hands of the young, and the old man is an impediment which must be cleared out of the way.

◇ ◇ ◇

The second unit of material prominent enough in the revue plays to require extended discussion can best be described as the destruction of the Old Man — all those actions which turn on the destruction or defeat of authority figures cognate to the spirit of the old year or King Carnival. Occasionally, of course, it is difficult to distinguish between this action and the struggle between youth and age, since attention may be equally divided between the young characters' efforts to trick the oldster and the destruction of the oldster. In Anton Francesco Grazzini's *Il Frate* ("The Friar") — first performed on the revel occasion of the night of Epiphany in 1540 — emphasis is divided between Fra Alberigo's plan to cuckold the old Florentine Amerigo and Amerigo's entrapment and humiliation. But usually, as in *Le Garçon et l'aveugle*, interest is focused on

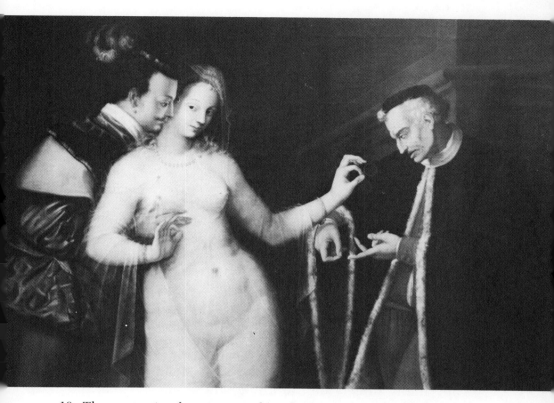

10. The contention between youth and age: a wooing. Anonymous French, *La Femme entre les Deux Âges*, ca. 1575, Museum of Fine Arts, Rennes.

the defeat of an old man or his equivalent, in actions reminiscent either of the Feast of Fools and its treatment of authority or of the execution episode from the carnival scenario.

The surrogate for the Old Man with the richest and most painful record in the history of vulgar comedy is doubtless the husband. Although he is not necessarily old, he is never young. Although he does not appear to have been highly popular in antiquity, when old men and ridiculous gods seem to have filled this role, by the late Middle Ages and early Renaissance he had been given sufficient impetus by the model of King Carnival to become the favorite butt in the plays (see fig. 11). Some of these plays consist simply of an action in which the husband is undone. A splendid example is Hans Sachs' *Der farend Schüler im Paradeis* ("The Wandering Scholar from Paradise," 1550), in which a simple-minded wife believes that a wandering scholar who is begging alms has said that he has just come from paradise, when actually he said that he had just come from Paris. Having recently made a bad second marriage to a miserly farmer, she eagerly asks for news of her dead first husband; when the scholar tells her that the deceased is hard up, she gives him money, food, and clothes. When the farmer returns and learns all this, he sets out on horseback after the scholar but overtakes, instead, an "idiot," who is actually the scholar in disguise. The "idiot" directs him to a bog where he says that the scholar is hiding, holds his horse while he goes in after him, then steals the horse. Late that night the farmer returns home and tells his wife that he has also given the horse to the scholar for the dead husband; overjoyed, she tells him that she has already told the neighbors about it, while he dissolves in anguish. The purpose in all this is reasonably clear: although we might see a struggle between youth and age or wit and stupidity, the main emphasis of the action is on the husband's descent into frustration and mortification. He does not die, it should be noted — he rarely does in any but the most primitive plays — but he suffers a conspicuous loss of power.

This loss of power, this defeat, is crucial to all the plays in which this unit of material is primary. Sometimes the surrogate for the Old Man is a father; sometimes he is an authority figure — judge, lawyer, policeman, soldier — sometimes he is an authority figure in addition to being a husband. But whatever his precise character, the action is essentially the same. In *La Farce de Mestre Trubert et d'Antrongnart* by Eustace Deschamps (late fourteenth century), Master Trubert, a lawyer, pleads to recover damages for Antrongnart and ends by losing not only Antrongnart's money but his own. In *La Farce des deux savetiers* ("The Farce of the Two Shoemakers," ca. 1506) a poor cobbler and a rich one live side by side, and the poor one annoys the rich one with his wailing but refuses to desist for less than a hundred crowns. In the battle of wits which follows le Pauvre successively wins ninety-nine crowns, a fine robe, and a trial, as le Riche is progressively humbled. In *Thersites* (ca. 1537) Thersites, the soldier-bully, is reduced to the familiar outline of the braggart, and in keeping with the tradition he is routed by a broken-down soldier from Calais, himself no hero.

Of course not all the plays which feature the destruction of the Old Man do so with such convenient simplicity. Some also embrace other interests; indeed some retain the Old Man and his defeat while deriving, structurally, from one of the other key units of material from the revels. *Thersites,* for example, deals primarily with the defeat of the military bully, but it also includes an episode in which Telemachus comes to Thersites' mother to be cured of worms. The play as a whole, then, represents not only the destruction of the authority figure but also a miraculous cure. *The Humour of John Swabber*, which was called at the time of its publication in 1655–66 an ancient farce, also has a multiple emphasis. Swabber is both a husband and a braggart captain (actually a seaman), and he rants and raves

a

b

d

11. "Old Men." (*a*) Silenus drunk. Roman bronze statue, ca. first century B.C., National Museum, Naples. Photo Alinari. (*b*) Papposilenus with the infant Dionysus. Greek terracotta statuette from Melos, middle of the fourth century B.C., British Museum. Photo courtesy British Library Board. (*c*) Polichinelle and Pantalone. French print by P. Mariette, seventeenth century, Cabinet des Éstampes, Bibliothèque Nationale, Paris. Photo Giraudon. (*d*) Harpagon instructing Maître Jacques. Frontispiece to Molière's *L'Avare* (Paris, 1682).

that he is going to destroy Cutbeard, a barber, for seducing his wife. When Cutbeard comes on like a "windmill," however, Swabber quails, confesses that "his brains are fallen into his britches," and humbly accepts Cutbeard's friendship. To prove his friendship, Cutbeard offers to beautify Swabber; then, instead of powdering him, he blackens his face (like the carnival figures, Swabber is called "Fool"). Finally, Swabber's wife reveals what has happened, and he goes off to fetch his "devils," once more to exact his revenge. In the final episode Swabber's wife first disguises Cutbeard as an infant to save him from Swabber and then substitutes a real infant for him; the play concludes with a reconciliation and a dance. Again, as with *Thersites*, the primary interest of the play is the discomfiture of the husband-braggart, and again this defeat is complemented by a rebirth. In this case the context is rich in such detail from the revel backgrounds as the blackened face and the crew of "devils."

The destruction of the Old Man is not difficult to identify if we are prepared for varying degrees of emphasis and ready to distinguish between plays in which this unit of material is primary and those in which the familiar surrogates appear and are defeated but which are actually constructed in terms of another basic action. By the end of the sixteenth century, with the development of the commedia dell'arte troupes, the chief figures stand out with brilliant clarity: in Pantalone, the old Venetian business man; in Doctor Graziano, the pedant from Bologna who unites in a single figure all the pedants, schoolteachers, and quack doctors tracing back to antiquity; in Capitano Spavento dell' Vall'Inferno, the braggart in love and war who epitomizes the type begun in Plautus' braggart captain and often repeated; and, finally, in a whole crew of professional types, policemen, and burghers — virtually anybody who stands for authority and hence, potentially, for tyranny. But these figures, though they are usually defeated, are not restricted to plays which turn primarily on their defeat; they also appear in plays based on another unit of material, like the combat, in which their defeat always contributes to the basic interest. Like the Old man or King Carnival or any of the scapegoat figures which people the ritual past of these characters, they are, whatever the particular focus of the play, never far from its center.

It is important to be aware, moreover, that these authority figures change as society and its ideas of authority change. The military bully was apparently a painful reality from antiquity through the Renaissance — in Italy in the sixteenth century he was frequently a Spanish military bully — but by the eighteenth century he was distinctly less in evidence. In plays dealing with student life in the fifteenth and sixteenth centuries, oddly enough, prostitutes frequently played this role. In the eighteenth century rich businessmen or land owners, usually fathers, were the favorite scapegoats; in the twentieth century, in silent film comedies especially, policemen, among others, become prominent. Certain characters persist, of course: husbands and fathers have never gone out of style as figures of fun, and the descendants of the pedants and quack doctors of antiquity can be traced through the famous doctors and savants of Molière to the mad scientists of our time. All these figures embody authority — what we fear and what we grudgingly respect; in a world dominated by *buffo* they must be destroyed.

◇ ◇ ◇

The third unit of material met regularly in the revue play is the wooing which leads to sexual union or the promise of it. As we have seen, the continuities between wooing rituals, especially in the May festival, and the so-called wooing plays are unusually clear. There is a step-by-step progression from simple ritual practices like planting the May tree or "Maying," through emergent plays like *The Bassingham Men's Play* in England and the *bruscelli* in Italy, to plays like *Il Mercato*, still simple yet sufficiently sophisticated to qualify as free-standing works. The essential action of these plays is, of course, most familiar in Western drama: an attractive young man and woman overcome obstacles so that they can be united sexually. Sometimes the obstacle is a parent, sometimes it is a rival or rivals, sometimes, in recent centuries, when marriage is the form of union desired, it is money or social position. But the invariable pattern is to move the lovers through the obstacles to union, in the process recapitulating something like the ancient celebration of spring, greenery, and fertility.

A simple example of this kind of play will indicate their nature. In *The Jig between Simon and Susan* (ca. 1600) Simon and Susan wish to marry but do not have Susan's father's consent, so they go first to her mother, who agrees to support their plea, then to her father, whom ultimately they win over. Another play of this elementary order is *The Wooing of Nan* (ca. 1600), in which Nan's hand is sought by several suitors. At a country dance she announces that she will marry whoever dances best, and in a scene remarkably close to the dancing competition of the revels everyone dances, including, finally, a Gentleman and a Fool. As always in the revels, the Fool wins. More complex than these examples, in that it involves a deception and a suggestion, at least, of rebirth, is *Rowland* — a popular Elizabethan song-play, according to Baskervill (*The Elizabethan Jig*), though now extant only in a seventeenth-century German version. In this play Rowland complains to his friend Robert that his Peggie is being wooed by the Sexton and that even now they are "juggling" in the churchyard, and Robert agrees to help him. When Peggie and the Sexton approach, he has Rowland lie down and then tells them that he has died. Peggie seems grieved, while the Sexton is delighted. When Rowland suddenly springs up, however, she eagerly returns to him and together drive the Sexton off.

One final example, still more complex, is Silvestro Cartaio's *Panecchio* (ca. 1549), another of the plays for the

Rozzi of Siena. Panecchio, a peasant, sues with characteristic coarseness for the hand of the nymph Britia, who in turn loves the shepherd Coridio. When Panecchio is rebuffed by Britia, he ignores it until he is also beaten physically; when his scheme to ambush Coridio fails, he is beaten a second time. The play concludes, as any of these examples easily could, with a song to May.

In all of these relatively simple treatments of the wooing nucleus what is crucial is the process by which the lovers win through against odds. Sometimes the obstacle is a father or a gentleman — a figure, that is, of authority or convention; sometimes he is not characterized by a social role at all. Sometimes the "hero" is a poor but attractive young man; sometimes he is a gentleman; sometimes he is literally the Fool. Again, these details are accidentals, always subordinate to the process by which the lovers are united and through which the instinctive forces driving them are celebrated. Even the denouement in marriage is inessential. In Cartaio's *Capotondo* (ca. 1550), a three-act play for the Rozzi, sexual union is achieved through adultery and the defeat of the husband; yet *Capotondo* is best explained as a wooing play because it gives primary attention to the young Gentleman's wooing of Meia and working out a future arrangement with her husband. Here conventional morality and marriage are irrelevant; the action emphasizes other sources of energy and vitality in the process of achieving union. Even a lengthy commedia scenario like *L'Amore e lo sdegno del Dottore Graziano* ("The Love and Indignation of Doctor Graziano," ca. 1600), with its complicated maneuverings by Graziano, the Capitano, and Rosmiro for the hand of Stella, remains in its general outline a straightforward elaboration of the wooing action.

◇   ◇   ◇

The fourth unit of material prominent in the revue play lacks the clear continuities with the revels to be seen in the wooing actions but asserts itself clearly in a great many simple, transitional plays in which stupidity, animality, or amorality, or of a combination of these, are treated to exhibit a resolute intractability in nature and human nature. Here nature reveals its stubbornness, chiefly in actions which turn on characters mired in a sovereign stupidity, or driven by monumental lusts or hungers, or blissfully unaware of moral imperatives of any kind — characters who not only will not but cannot conform to the dictates of law, morality, or reason. Nature or human nature as we meet them in these plays is a nature which will not yield, will not take the imprint of civilization; it is a nature which mindlessly resists everything but the impulse to be itself.

Why the celebration of this stubbornness has been pleasurable since antiquity is not immediately clear. Moreover, the evidence of origins is of doubtful help here. Perhaps the attacks on individuals in the lampoon and kindred dramatic rituals, where stupidity, animality, and amorality must have been issues, are the source, or possibly it is the crew of demoniac revelers found in virtually all the revels. As we saw earlier, these figures were initially spirits of the dead come from their graves to assist in the rebirth of the year; as such they were reminders of the dead who would not stay dead, or of a nature that would not die, and perhaps their stubbornness was the source of the stubbornness in the plays. In either case this stubbornness consists of a toughness or resilience which worked to affirm life regardless of what anything or anyone, even death, might say.

Despite the mystery of its origins, however, this stubbornness appears at all points in the history of vulgar comedy. Perhaps it is clearest in the many early plays which deal with stupidity, especially in the classroom plays. Among the mimes of the Alexandrian Herodes (ca. 290–250 B.C.), the third, entitled *Didaskolos* ("The Schoolmaster"), provides a simple example of the type: a mother brings her unteachable son to a schoolmaster, complains that even beatings do not help, and then, after the schoolmaster has failed and himself beaten the boy, goes to tell her husband how well the beating went. The plays of Vincenzo Braca of Salerno, *Della scola* (ca. 1585) and *De la maestra* (ca. 1586), are also simple, though richer in detail. In the first a stupid, uncultivated teacher attempts to lead a class of rowdy boys, only to have it collapse into a shambles; in the second a group of equally rowdy girls tease, trick, and then beat the schoolmistress until she finally dismisses them. They go off, singing that they are going to throw water on passers-by because it is carnival time ("Corrimo a fare ad aqua, ch'è carnovale").

The most skillfully made of the classroom plays are French. *La Farce de Pernet* (ca. 1525) duplicates the situation of the Herodan mime in that it has a mother bring her extremely dense son, Pernet, to a teacher to study to be a priest and then a bishop. When the Maître tries to teach him his ABC's, however, Pernet continually confuses the letters with things — *ashe* (the letter h) for *hache* ("hatchet"). In *La Farce d'un qui se fait examiner* ("The Farce of the Examinee," ca. 1525) much the same mother presents much the same son to the priest; when the priest examines him, he responds to questions he cannot answer — anticipating Eugène Ionesco's *La Leçon* — by protesting that he is thirsty or needs to urinate. These plays, of course, begin a long tradition of classroom comedy in which unteachable students' minds and spirits instinctively refuse the harnesses of discipline and teachers' small learning makes them mechanical men. The situation is ideally suited to provide images of nature in revolt against man and civilization.

Even more common than the classroom play as a vehicle for the peculiar triumph of stupidity in early drama were the countless plays about doltish peasants. Maccus, the awkward, usually hungry rustic from the *atellanae* is an example of the kind of character central to this work. Such figures, blessed with a simplicity of mind which sometimes amounts to saintly innocence, have been favorites with *farceurs* throughout the entire history of *buffo,* from Maccus through the early Pulcinella Cetrulo to the bulbous-nosed Auguste of the brothers Fratellini. To take but one example, *La Farce de Mahuet Badin* (ca. 1500) does not redeem stupidity by gilding it with saintliness; it uses it simply to compound disaster. Mahuet is sent to Paris by his mother to sell their cream, cheese, eggs, and bread "au prix du marché." He gets lost, wanders through the marvelous city, and meets a woman who wishes to buy his wares but whom he refuses because, as he explains, he must sell them "au prix du marché." The woman then tells Gaultier, who comes to Mahuet and tells him that he *is* "le prix du marché," whereupon Mahuet gives him everything. Still lost, he gets his hand caught in a jar, and Gaultier tells him he must break the jar over his head. When he does, he is so besmirched that even his mother does not recognize him when he finally staggers home.

As in the classroom plays, the central quality defined here is a kind of sovereign stupidity. But it would be a mistake to conclude that our pleasure consists in anything so simple as feeling superior to poor Mahuet. On the contrary, we can follow his disasters with pleasure because something about stupidity as we meet it here and in the classroom plays is affirmative, expressive of a kind of stubbornness in nature which represents life, or which, at any rate, resists the defeat of life.

Like stupidity, animality too is frequently used to define the kind of humanity which instinctively resists civilization. A common feature of vulgar comedy, animality appears in the obesity of some characters and in the epic lusts and appetites of others; it is evident at those moments when the flesh becomes supreme, as in *La Farce d'un qui se fait examiner*, when the examinee protests that he is thirsty and has to urinate, or in Niccolò Campani's *Il Coltellino* ("The Little Knife," ca. 1525), when the clown who tries to commit suicide for love finds he cannot. But in some plays, especially early transitional ones, animality is the central quality, the key unit of material in actions which seem designed to confirm man's bestiality. We meet it in all the *fastnachtspiele* which turn on extended scatological jokes and in a play like *La Farce du pect* ("The Farce of the Fart," ca. 1476). In this play (a version exists in Italian as well) Hubert is awaiting his supper when Jehannette, who is preparing it for him, lifts a basket and breaks wind. They quarrel, they go to the Procurer, and at last to court, where everyone talks at once until the Judge decides that both are responsible because man and wife are one. The play has a good deal of the interest of the *causes grasses* in its ridicule of lawyers and jurists, but its representation of how natural man demolishes civilized forms is even more prominent.

Finally, just as stupidity often shades into animality, animality oftens shades into amorality — amorality in the sense of an inveterate incapacity for moral behavior. Many characters are either totally oblivious to the dictates of morality and polite society or are so tenuously committed to them that they inevitably drift toward the amorality which is the true center of their being. The action of a play from Italy like *Conquestio uxoris Cavichioli papiensis* ("The Complaint of Cavichiolo's Wife"), a student play in Latin from the early fifteenth century, is typical. Cavichiolo's wife complains that, though he is generous and kind, he neglects her sexually and prefers boys. When she threatens to disgrace him by going home to her mother, he agrees to let her have his boys; and as the play ends, he leaves her with a boy who has just arrived.

This quietly rebellious amorality explains a great many simple, transitional plays which are otherwise rather puzzling. Herodes' fourth mime, for example, presents two women who come to the temple to make offerings to Asclepius. We hear their conversation — their thanks, their sacrifice (a modest chicken, not a steer), then gradually their admiration of the temple and especially of the statues of naked young men on all sides. The play concludes when a Verger appears and in his homely way thanks them for their offerings. Crucial here, of course, is the contrast between the temple, with its ritual, and the women, whose conversation inevitably drifts from professed interests to real interests, but the contrast is handled with so light a touch that it could easily be missed. *La Commedia di più frate* ("The Comedy of More Brothers," ca. 1520) presents a group of friars some of whom determine to leave the monastery so that they can chase women. Their superior argues that the monastery itself is the best place for that, but they go off anyhow. *La Farce des chambrières* ("The Chambérmaids' Farce," ca. 1530) deals with three serving women who go to Mass at 5:00 A.M. hoping to be blessed with holy water. As they talk about their domestic situations — really a question of who is sleeping with whom — it becomes clear that by being blessed they mean fornication; in fact, they debate the advantages of being "blessed" in various parishes. Finally, they go to Domine Johannes and ask for his blessing, but he tells them he does not have enough for all. He does "bless" two of them, however, and then tells them to come back on Sunday, when he will "bless" them again. In all these figures, of course, we have the spiritual forebears of Pompey Bum and the thieving Pierrot who steals even his own head from the guillotine scaffold. They are no more wicked than a dog tipping over a garbage can is wicked; they are unself-conscious embodiments of a nature which refuses, to use Pompey Bum's words, to be "geld[ed] and splay[ed]."

In all these examples nature reveals its stubbornness in character traits which resist civilized control. Moreover, it is possible to describe these traits, especially if one takes a civilized point of view, as mental deficiencies or deformities — as evidence of an insufficiently developed mind, when stupidity or animality are at issue, or of a mind somehow lacking one or more of its faculties, when amorality is at issue. These mental deficiencies are often linked with physical disabilities. Although we usually think of lameness, blindness, or other physical defects as a failure of nature and regard those afflicted as objects of compassion, in these plays physical disabilities are so often yoked with stupidity, animality, or amorality that they too become expressions of nature's unwillingness to conform to human expectations. The familiar hunchback, which goes back to the Dossenus of the *atellanae,* for example, is not a figure of pathos like Hugo's hunchback of Notre Dame but an ambling, scrambling proof that nature is often intractable. The stutter which was natural to Raymond Poisson, the most famous Crispin, and was retained in the role by his son and grandson; the long, thin legs and great pimply face of Hugues Guéru, the Hôtel de Bourgogne's Gaultier Garguille; the barrel-like figure of Robert Guérin, the Gros-Guillaume: such details became indispensable facets of these famous characters, continuous reminders of nature's stubbornness.

Yet physical deformity, though common, is never, as far as I know, the key material in a play. In *Le Miracle de l'aveugle et du boiteux* ("The Miracle of the Blind Man and the Cripple," 1496), by Andrieu de la Vigne, the fact of deformity is omnipresent in the two characters who team up to move about and beg on the blind man's legs while using the cripple's eyes, but the main emphasis is on the amorality with which these scoundrels resist being cured by the relics of Saint Martin because then they would have to abandon their profession. By this strange chain of associations physical deformity, a frequent, ugly reality in vulgar comedy, becomes a part of a celebrative effort, a process which moves us to a happy knowledge. One may recall that court jesters, who stood outside the confines of conventional social orders mocking everyone and everything with their jibes, were frequently deformed.

◇ ◇ ◇

The fifth category of material from the revue play also reveals properties of nature; it is different in that it exemplifies not nature's power of resistance but its power of change. In English pantomimes of the nineteenth century actions in which things, places, or most frequently people change into something or someone else were routinely called "transformations." Transformation can be traced to a variety of elements in the revels. It may be seen in the attention to rebirth and restoration in various rituals, but only plays which turn on resurrections or miraculous cures — though they are numerous — suggest that indebtedness. It could also owe something to the widespread use of masquerade in revels, especially the Feast of Fools; masquerades and disguisings, after all, call attention to the unstable character of surfaces. It might be traced to the practice from earliest times of sexual substitutions. The truth is that tracing continuities from the revels is complicated by the fact that transformation as a key unit of material in plays emerged fairly late. We find anticipations of it in antiquity in scattered references to Miraculous Child and comic Doctor episodes, and in the Middle Ages and Renaissance in plays constructed in terms of other *materia*. *La Farce de Mahuet Badin,* for example, which concentrates primarily on nature's stubbornness in the form of Mahuet's stupidity, concludes with something approaching a transformation when Mahuet so besmirches himself that his own mother does not recognize him. *The Humour of John Swabber,* in which the destruction of Swabber is the central interest, concludes with a scene in which Cutbeard, Swabber's enemy, is first placed in a cradle and passed off by Swabber's wife as her child, and then is replaced by a real baby, all of this to Swabber's great confusion. But very few of the early, relatively simple plays use transformation as a basic subject. Such plays did not appear in great number until well into the sixteenth century, and then usually as part of relatively sophisticated dramatic structures; only in the seventeenth and eighteenth centuries did transformation gradually become a highly popular device among writers of vulgar comedy.

Most early instances of transformation, or, to be more precise, of the sense of variability which in a heightened form becomes transformation, are the uses of disguise in plays dominated by one of the other units of material. Disguise is always vaguely suggestive of the uncertainty of surfaces; when it is widely used, the whole world of the play can take on a chameleon-like quality. In the early plays, however, it is rarely prominent enough to perform this function: it may give the play a sense of variability, but it rarely endows it with a sense that the world is teetering on the brink of a metamorphosis. Hans Sachs' *Der farend Schüler mit dem Deufel pannen* comes near to this in its climactic scene, when, as the scholar "raises the devil," the hunchback priest rises in blackface from the stove where he has been hiding. It is perfectly clear in *La Farce de Maître Minim* (ca. 1485), one of the few early plays in which transformation is the primary material; here the whole play moves toward a marvelous, magical sense of reality. Minim's parents have heard that, while studying astrology, he has learned Latin but forgotten how to speak French, and they, along with Minim's fiancée and her father, go to the school to see what can be done. When their worst fears have been confirmed, they agree with the Magister that Minim should have his head caged so that, like a bird, he can be taught French anew by the fiancée, since it is women who teach birds. The experiment succeeds, but to everyone's surprise Minim speaks like a woman and, like a bird, wants to sing continuously. When, at the last, he amazes everyone again by carrying his fiancée off on his shoulders, his action is sufficiently close to normality that the play concludes happily for everyone. Altogether, this play provides a good example of the use of transformation to demonstrate the metamorphic potential of nature, the wonderful capacity of things and people to become something else. This metamorphic sense of reality is not the only effect achieved by transformation, but it is probably basic.

This is also the sense of the world conveyed by all those later vulgar comedies which, with some debt to the aristocratic pastoral, use magic extensively. Most important here is the widespread use of magic places — woods, grottoes, dens, etc. — places in which anything is possible, where people change appearance and identity and objects become people, where, in a word, a wholly new set of natural principles obtains. In the plays, of course, such places manufacture complications and possibilities for complication at an incredible rate, generate tremendous activity and confusion, and then provide miraculous denouements. The commedia dell'arte scenario *Il Creduto Principe* ("The Impostor Prince," ca. 1633), associated with the second Confidenti troupe, is a good case in point. In it Trivellino is transformed by a magician who lives in a nearby magic wood into the figure of his absent prince, and for a time he rules, in Feast of Fools fashion, by his own rather than by the restrictive Pantalone's laws. The primary thrust of the work is to suggest a world marvelously variable, literally magical in its capacity for change and alternative modes of life.

Something like this metamorphic sense also obtains in those plays which betray their revel origins by emphasizing rebirth and renewal. There are fewer plays which turn on rebirth, or a renewal sufficiently impressive to suggest rebirth, than there are plays containing details and episodes which merely touch on these matters, but there are some early ones, many of which center on the paradox of the living dead. In Annibale Caro's *Gli Straccioni* ("The Ragged Rascals," 1544), a young man and woman both presumed dead return to complicate an already complex situation involving the girl's sweetheart and the man's "widow." There are also a great many plays in which the characters, usually young men or young women, are enabled to "find" their families, thus discovering a new identity. Plautus abounds in this sort of thing; a later, simpler example is the Elizabethan jig *The Cheaters Cheated*, in which the baby handed around by Moll ultimately "finds" his family when Moll confesses to Filcher that he is their child. An exceedingly complex instance of rebirth through the discovery of a family is Pietro Aretino's *Lo Ipocrito* ("The Hypocrite," 1545), a long, self-conscious, humanistic tale of the return of a long-lost twin brother. Toward the end of the play death is explicitly associated

with a loss of personal identity, and rebirth with the discovery of one's family and position in the world. One
character, Brizio, says, "Whoever has no relatives has no
blood. . . . And whoever has no blood is not alive" ("Chi
non ha parenti non ha sangue. . . . Chi non ha sangue,
non è vivo").

In all these examples, rebirth, whether literal or
metaphorical, becomes a proof of the world's capacity to
change unexpectedly for the better. If prominent enough,
rebirth, miraculous cures, and other types of unexpected
renewal, like wholesale transformations, beget a metamorphic sense of reality, a sense of a world not merely unstable
and unfixed but seething with creative forces for change.

◇   ◇   ◇

The sixth and final type of revue play is unlike the
others in that it is not defined by a characteristic episodic
content, like the combat or the destruction of the Old Man,
but by a characteristic organization. Where the other types
of revue play declare themselves and the *buffo* impulses
which they express by way of their materials, this type
does so by way of a structure designed to generate a frenzy,
both in the world of the play and in the beholder. A wide
range of highly variable materials are used, often drawn
from the other *materia*, often, in early plays especially,
from the food-stealing pranks and beatings of the revels.
But whatever the materials, the crucial variable is the
compounding of comic suspense, of piling surprise on surprise in such a way as to intensify hilarity. This purpose
cannot be traced to any particular part of the revels, though
it probably owes most to the pranks and antics of the
revelers; rather, it reflects the pervasive purpose of the
revels: to stir up and create agitation, to prompt the revelers to lavish expenditures of energy — energy which itself
becomes proof of the capacity of the revel to renew life.

The simplest examples of plays of this type are probably those which use deception to create suspense and

hence to heighten the frenzy, and simplest among these, surely, are the food-stealing plays. As we have seen in *La Farce du pasté et de la tarte* (ca. 1470), one of the strategies of such works is not merely to have a character trick someone, usually an authority figure, out of food, but to have him outwit him or try to outwit him a second and a third time. Such repetition, especially when the victim is the same and the probabilities of success become fewer with each attempt, intensifies the comic excitement.

A very good example of this structural strategy is the sub-plot of John Marston's *Dutch Courtezan* (1604), a comic action which has a hazy history before Marston but which was adapted by numerous hands in the seventeenth and eighteenth centuries. A rascal named Cockledemoy literally destroys by stages a vintner named Mulligrub. Through a series of disguises and craftily contrived messages he first cheats him out of a supper and a goblet, then out of some money, then out of an ornate cup, and then out of a piece of salmon. After manipulating Mulligrub's arrest for theft, he disguises himself and accompanies him to the gallows, where he makes an assignation with his wife for after the hanging. The fact that Marston's and subsequent versions of the action end in forgiveness and reprieve should not obscure the intended effect: the intense hilarity which results from a series of deceptions carried out against mounting odds. In the final scene the outrageousness of Mulligrub's situation is perfectly consonant with the frenzy achieved.

Another strategy of these plays is to pit the deceiver against a knave, someone whose recognized rascality diminishes the probability of a successful deception. In *La Farce du cousturier* ("The Dressmaker's Farce," ca. 1500), the dressmaker combines cleverness with a niggardliness which causes his apprentice Esopet to complain that he does not get enough to eat and drink. When a Gentilhomme and a chambermaid come in to order a dress and give the dressmaker a capon and a partridge in part payment, telling him to be sure to give some to the apprentice, he cunningly replies that Esopet does not like these meats. On learning this, Esopet counters with the story that the dressmaker is mad and that when he shows certain symptoms, like turning his head, he must be bound and beaten. The next time the Gentilhomme sees the dressmaker, he of course shows these symptoms, and, to his amazement, the Gentilhomme binds and beats him. The familiar pattern of the knave outwitted is found in variant versions in the other units of material. In *La Farce du cousturier*, however, the emphasis is not on the knave or his victim, or on the fact of the victim's destruction, but on the peculiar tensions given the action through the notably suspenseful treatment of the deception.

Still another strategy of these plays is to intensify suspense by having the schemer carry out a deception so difficult that the probability that it will not succeed is overwhelming. In a play like *Le Chaudronnier, le savetier, et le tavernier* ("The Tinker, the Shoemaker, and the Tavernkeeper," ca. 1510), comic excitement is generated by the tinkers' trick of disguising himself as the shoemaker's wife as part of a plan to cheat the tavernkeeper, then pretending to be mad, beating the tavernkeeper, and finally driving him away. An even better example, perhaps, is *The Interlude of Jack Juggler* (ca. 1555), in which the knave Jack Juggler determines to avenge himself and his master on a varlet named Jenkin Careaway by persuading Jenkin that he is not himself. Having learned the details of Jenkin's normal day, Jack intercepts him at the door of his master's house and in a kind of reverse recognition scene gradually overpowers him with the argument that he, Jack Juggler, is in fact Jenkin Careaway. He then beats him and leaves him to try to explain all this to his master and mistress, who also beat him.

In all these examples deception is used not as part of a combat or an attack on an authority figure but as a structural device to produce the comic excitement which is itself the key variable in this kind of play. The distinction is elusive, admittedly, but it is necessarily so because we are here turning from plays in which characteristic actions or patterns of action are of primary importance to plays in which an inner structural dynamic is primary.

Deception is not the only means by which this comic frenzy may be generated, however. Comparable in purpose and effect are all those plays which create what might be called a comic disaster *à outrance*, plays in which comic catastrophe is piled on comic catastrophe in such a way as to test probability to the limit while leading to a climactic disaster. Again, although details from other units of material occur frequently in these plays, the governing principle is to generate a frenzy. In *La Farce de Colin, fils de Thévot le maire* ("The Farce of Colin, Son of Thévot the Mayor," ca. 1525), Thévot anxiously awaits his son Colin, who went off with the family mare six months earlier to fight the Turks. His return touches off a series of disasters. Before he arrives, a woman comes in protesting that he has stolen her chickens and abused her. When he appears, he reveals that he has lost the mare, though he tries to offset that news by claiming that he has brought back a bound prisoner, who turns out to be only a bound pilgrim. Finally, he tells Thévot that he wishes to marry Gaultier Garguille's lame daughter. All in all, his return is a mounting series of catastrophes so compounded that the skies appear to be falling in Thévot's world.

La Ricevuta dell'Imperatore alla Cava ("The Reception for the Emperor in Cava," ca. 1536), an early play among many developed in Salerno in the sixteenth century to make fun of the rival city of Cava, is more satiric in purpose but also works toward an explosion of outrageousness. The citizens of Cava learn that the Emperor Charles V is to pass through their city, and accordingly they embark upon frenetic preparations for his stay — they expect him to be there for a month. In the midst of their heated arguments about a gift of money, ceremonies, documents, food, and the rest of it, the emperor passes through without stopping. Appalled — he has not even worshipped the local relics — the community leaders send a message of protest; when the messenger returns with emperor's regrets and his acceptance of the gift of money, the community turns on its leaders. One final example: The Elizabethan jig *The Cheaters Cheated* combines the outwitting of knaves with multiple disasters, as Filcher and Nim are twice foiled in their attempts to rob the bumpkin Wat, and Filcher is finally finessed into marrying Moll. It differs from the others in that its "build" toward the final comic disaster is accompanied by the discovery of a child, the immediate cause of Filcher's marriage to Moll and an unexpected proof, amid mounting evidence of chaos, of the possibility of renewal.

In these plays the piling up of catastrophes has the effect — like the deceptions repeated or carried out in the face of great odds — of suggesting a world astonishingly rich in surprises. As these surprises rush in upon the beholder, they generate a state of excitement not unfairly, if a bit hyperbolically, described as a frenzy. It is tempting to go even farther and to argue that such plays are designed to celebrate anarchistic principles, that the frenzy they generate is attuned to the impulse toward disorder in the world. Certainly we find more than just a trace of this linkage in the revel backgrounds, in the mischief-making in all the revels, and unmistakably in the subversiveness of the Feast of Fools. But the argument is difficult to sustain for all plays of this type. Distinctly more basic to the group than the celebration of anarchic principles is the frenzy produced.

◇ ◇ ◇

These, then, are the nuclei of action which most frequently govern the structure of what are, for the most part, relatively simple expressions of *buffo*. I have used the term "material" and variations on it in an effort to suggest to how large an extent the revue plays seem constructed to exhibit certain episodes like the combat or the destruction of the Old Man or a transformation. But since these episodes are inherently dramatic, I might also have used the term "exercise." In a sense these units of material are like dramatic exercises which the writers of vulgar comedy perform again and again: the plays might be described as a variety of attempts to render the combat, to destroy the Old Man, to contrive a sexual union against odds, to illustrate the innate stubbornness of nature, to display a transformation, or to generate a frenzy.

In the hundreds of short plays which have come down to us, these patterns persist. Something like a sifting, or sorting out, or boiling down apparently took place; somewhere in the centuries which saw the mime, the satyr play, and the *phlyax* farces develop from Greek ritual revels and in the more recent but still hazy period in which the farces, jigs, and interludes developed from carnival, a discontinuous and ill-coordinated process of selection occurred. By the end of the Middle Ages — by the time, that is, when revue plays begin to survive in numbers — these units of material had been fixed upon. That fact is of singular importance not only in any attempt to describe and classify the immense body of plays in question but also, which is more to the point, in any attempt to describe and understand *buffo*. More than any other piece of evidence to be abstracted from the long story of *buffo*, these *materia* establish that vulgar comedy, despite its abundance, consists essentially of the same small number of plays worked up again and again. In all the variety a limited number of formulaic actions stand out; in those limited actions one quality, one genius, dominates — *buffo*.

6

The Plautine Play

Even a cursory comparison of the revue plays and the extant plays of Plautus reveals that the materials basic to the former are everywhere in evidence in the latter. The combats between husbands and wives (*Asinaria*) and between young folk and old (*Casina*); the destruction of the Old Man in the shape of the old miser Euclio (*Aulularia)* or the braggart Captain (*Miles Gloriosus*); the wooings leading to sexual union in virtually all the plays; the stupidity, animality, and amorality expressive of nature's resistance to civilized demands; and the transformations in the form of numerous discoveries of parents by their long-lost children and vice versa — all these can be traced to Plautus with the greatest ease. Moreover, Plautus' skill with structural strategies calculated to generate a frenzy was so great that this interest came to dominate the others. In other words, the common substance of the revue and the Plautine play are easily demonstrated.

Difficulties arise only when we look for differences, and even then only when an attempt is made to explain the differences by putting the plays into some sort of historical relationship. As I have said before, a strictly historical approach to vulgar comedy will invariably be frustrated by the fact that the early evidence is so fragmentary. What we have been looking at is a little like a damaged mosaic; some parts stand out in brilliant detail, while others survive only in bits and pieces. Yet an overall pattern can be discerned, though it is extremely faint in places.

Any attempt to relate the Plautine to the revue plays inevitably runs afoul of the paradox that the Plautine plays are both earlier and more sophisticated than the revue plays which supply most of our evidence of the *materials* of *buffo*. This is not to say that we have no evidence of the revue play before Plautus: we have a great deal, and much of it indicates that the materials identified in the revue plays of the Middle Ages and Renaissance are also to be found in antiquity. But the evidence of the revue play in antiquity is far too fragmentary to allow the conclusions which have been drawn from the numerous complete texts of later plays. What we know of the Greek and Roman mimes, the satyr play, the *phlyax* farces, and the *atellanae* is sufficient only to indicate that Plautus owed something to them and to the ritual revels which lay behind them. We must extrapolate from later evidence to flesh out the historical outline and to account for the achievement of Plautus.

This procedure is not as irresponsible as it may sound because in the few complete texts which survive and in the numerous titles, pieces of plays, comments, vase paintings, and other fragments which complete our evidence of the revue play in antiquity there is enough to confirm that the *materia* which crystallized in the revue plays of the Middle Ages and Renaissance had taken shape in Greece and Rome. From the evidence assembled by Allardyce Nicoll in *Masks, Mimes, and Miracles* it is clear, for example, that plays treating the combat and the destruction of the Old Man were fairly common in antiquity. It frequently took the form of struggles between masters and servants and burlesque versions of legendary fights. The Silenus of the satyr play, the Pappus of the *atellanae*, and the marvelous old codgers of the *phlyax* vase paintings were apparently favorite butts of ridicule. Plays dealing with wooings leading to sexual consummation seem also to have been widespread, chiefly featuring coarse tales of adultery between slaves and their mistresses and grotesque treatments of Zeus' amours. Plays exhibiting nature's stubbornness are illustrated in the mimes of Herodes and in the fragments of similar plays which these illuminate; the third mime, the *Didaskolos*, is the first in a long tradition of schoolroom plays; the fourth, *Ascheioi Anatitheisai Kai Thueiazousai* ("The Women Making Sacrifices and Offerings to Asclepius"), indicates the probable emphasis on idle intractability.

The only unit of material from the revue plays of the Middle Ages and Renaissance difficult to place firmly in antiquity are the transformation and the machinery for generating a frenzy. That the second of these is difficult to discern in the fragments is not surprising as it can only be inferred from a total structure and cannot be very clearly recorded in paintings. That there is so little certain evidence of the transformation, however, is puzzling. As a unit of material it was abundantly anticipated in ritual ceremonies celebrating rebirth and renewal, and of course it is common in the later New Comedy and the plays of Plautus. But in the early drama, or in fragments of it, we find sporadic uses only in Aristophanes.

Moreover, our historical difficulties do not end here: whatever the relation between Plautus' work and the Greek and Roman revue plays, it is clear that he owed a profound debt to Hellenistic New Comedy. Whether that debt went beyond the borrowing of outlines of dramatic actions, what the precise nature of the New Comedies borrowed from was, what the relations were between New Comedy and the Greek and Roman revue plays — these questions have no easy answers. Classical scholars have long contended that New Comedy developed from Middle Comedy, which developed from Old Comedy, which evolved from phallic revels and dramatic exercises like the *komos* and the comic agon. Arguing from the substantial fragments of three New Comedies by Menander (ca. 342–291 B.C.) unearthed about fifty years ago and other smaller fragments and comments, they have characterized New Comedy as an urbane, rather romantic form which typically turned on the problems of lovers and frequently involved recognition scenes. The interest in romantic complications and recognition scenes, the argument goes, can be traced to Euripides. Presumably, Plautus' practice was to borrow these actions and, in the process of adapting them for Roman audiences, to make them coarser and funnier than the originals.

There was little to quarrel with in this theory until the early 1950s, when a complete play by Menander entitled *Dyskolos* ("The Bad-Tempered Man," 317 B.C.) was discovered in Egypt; its implications for New Comedy have yet to be examined carefully. It combines a standard wooing action with episodes which treat the destruction of the Old Man in the figure of Cnemnon, the grouch. Sostratos, the son of a rich farmer, loves Cnemnon's daughter, but his attempts to approach Cnemnon on the subject are repulsed. Ultimately, Sostratos wins the support of his sweetheart's half-brother, another neighbor named Gorgias, and he even goes to work in the fields to prove to Cnemnon that he is no idler, but it is not until Cnemnon accidently falls into a well and Getas, one of Sostratos' father's slaves, saves him that Sostratos begins to have hope. Deeply moved by his escape, Cnemnon puts the matter of his daughter's marriage entirely into Gorgias' hands, with the result that Gorgias quickly arranges a match with Sostratos, while Sostratos tries to reciprocate by arranging a match, which his father resists, between his sister and Gorgias. All ends happily, however, with a double marriage and a dance in which even Cnemnon joins. Indeed, the final episode is reminiscent of the ritual revival of the dead in that Cnemnon is carried in on a couch, listless, and is persuaded to rise from it and dance.

Even this sketch suggests that, though it contains romantic interest, the *Dyskolos* is actually more like a play of Plautus than like the hypothetical form extrapolated from Menander's *Epitrepontes* ("The Arbitration") and other evidence. The *Dyskolos* comes reeling into the traditional picture of New Comedy like a country cousin unexpectedly bursting in on a polite soiree. Critics like Philip Vellacott (*The Bad-Tempered Man*, pp. xiii, xvii) and Lionel Casson (*The Plays of Menander*, p. xviii) have already begun to minimize its importance by arguing that, after all, it is an early play and not a fully developed example of Menandrian New Comedy, and this explanation may be the right one, though it is not so overpowering as to obviate all others. One possibility is that New Comedy was not, as has long been thought, a single form, but embraced different, if related, kinds of plays. In addition to the urbane domestic comedy so long traced by classical scholars to Middle Comedy and Euripides, there may also have been a more raucous, coarser type which owed something to the Greek and Roman revue plays (see fig. 12). To carry this speculation one step farther, it might be claimed that Plautus drew upon New Comedies of the second type, while Terence drew upon those of the first. We can suspect, at least, that the type of vulgar comedy which I am calling "Plautine" existed earlier than Plautus and that the term is a misnomer.

Yet the work of Plautus represents the first substantial evidence of this more sophisticated type of vulgar comedy, and, whatever Plautus' actual responsibility for it, as things now stand it is convenient to trace its definition to him. Let me briefly review the picture from antiquity. We have the fragmentary evidence of the ritual revels in Greece and Rome and the dramatic rituals and dramatic exercises related to them, and the equally fragmentary evidence of what I have been calling the revue play in antiquity: the mime (including seven complete texts of recited mimes by Herodes), the satyr play (including one complete text in Euripides' *Cyclops*), the *phlyax* farces,

12. Comic actors in a New Comedy. Roman bas-relief, first century B.C.,
National Museum, Naples. Photo Alinari.

and the *atellanae*. We have, in addition to very brief fragments of the work of writers like Philemon (ca. 361–ca. 263
B.C.) and Diphilus (ca. 340–289 B.C.), three substantial
parts of plays and one complete play by Menander representing New Comedy. Finally, we have the twenty extant
plays of Plautus, our first examples (except the *Dyskolos*)
of the long, intricate structure which completes the range of
dramatic forms which *buffo* expression has taken. The
achievement of the Plautine play cannot be overestimated.
By comparison with the revue play — and we know the
revue play, it should be remembered, largely from later
evidence — it marks with its more capacious, more subtle
structure distinct technical advances. In the history of vulgar comedy it supplied the model which, once it was revived by the humanists in the early Renaissance, served for
most of the important work in vulgar comedy thereafter. The
six plays of Terence (166–160 B.C.), by contrast, add nothing
to the definition of the basic type.

◇　·◇　◇

If the revue play in antiquity was (in the matter of
materials, at least) very like the later revue play, one of
Plautus' chief accomplishments was to collapse and combine the separate units of material in actions designed to
sustain a more elaborate articulation of *buffo* than was
possible in short plays. He often overlaid a wooing action
with episodes representing the destruction of the Old Man,
with others expressing nature's stubbornness, and with
still others suggesting transformation. In the *Bacchides* (ca.
195 B.C.), for example, the central wooing action concerning the two young men and the twin courtesans named
Bacchis is supplemented (in the scenes where the twins
are confused by a strong interest in transformation and in
other scenes) by a calculated destruction of the Old Man,
in the shape of their fathers. In the *Poenulus* (ca. 200 B.C.)
the young hero's attempts to wrest his beloved from the
procurer Lycus comprise both a wooing and the destruc-

tion of the Old Man in the person of the tyrannical procurer; with the arrival of the old Carthaginian, who proves
to be both the girl's father and the hero's uncle, the world
of the play quite literally is transformed.

Moreover, Plautus not only collapsed and combined
the *materia* of the revue play but did so in such a way as to
subordinate them to the purpose of generating a frenzy,
and in the process he created a new dramatic structure, one
not only longer and more complex, but also different.
There is more of everything in the Plautine play: more
characters, more complications, a more complex orchestra-
tion of materials. Instead of a single pair of young lovers,
we frequently find two or more; instead of one Old Man,
hence one obstacle to the lovers' union, we frequently find
several; instead of a single nucleus of interest, we typically
find lovers moving through a highly circuitous intrigue
toward union, an intrigue which along the way touches on
the hunger of parasites, the amorality of cunning slaves,
repeated defeats of one or more Old Man figures, and
stunning transformations of identity in a wide variety of
recognition scenes. Plautus — though he may not have
invented it — was a master at designing and sustaining this
kind of structure; like a juggler, he outdid his predecessors
by keeping not three balls but five balls, two plates, and a
hat in the air. He not only produced a fresh amalgam of
familiar materials and skills but created something quite
new out of them.

A good part of this achievement consists of the discovery of the technical means of combining several
materia into a single action and then sustaining that action
throughout the play. Plautus' favorite devices were extended deception and mistaken identity; building from
them as from structural axes, he designed dramatic actions
which became models of *buffo* expression.

His *Mostellaria* ("The Haunted House," ca. 199
B.C.) is a representative example of his practice. The play
turns primarily on a struggle between youth and age.
Philolaches has been left in charge of his father's house

and, at the opening of the play, has been entertaining his young friends and favorite courtesans at enormous expense for three years. His father, Theopropides, early in the play returns unexpectedly. With Philolaches on the side of youth, love, freedom, and high spirits are his beloved Philematium, whom he has bought out of bondage; Tranio, his slave; Callidimates, his friend; and Delphium, Callidimates' girl friend. Allied with Theopropides on the side of age, money, property, materialistic cunning, and all that seems bent on constraining youth and love are Scapha, Philematium's maid; Simo, Theopropides' neighbor; and Misargyrides, the moneylender who has advanced the money to Philolaches with which to buy Philematium's freedom. This opposition, or combat, is tempered throughout by comic details. The father-son struggle has all the formulaic value of the ritual contention with none of the distress of real life. Philolaches, though at fault, is easily redeemable and too conventional a prodigal son to elicit anxiety; Theopropides is a standard Old Man, too greedy to be highly sympathetic, too generalized to be a source of great concern. Moreover, the struggle, echoed in various parallel oppositions and reinforced by evidence of nature's stubbornness in Philolaches' rebellious appetites and Tranio's amorality, is played out in scenes given largely to revelry, lighthearted talk about debauchery, and battles of wits. The dominant tone of the action is playful and high-spirited, like the songs and lyrical measures with which classical scholars tell us Plautus continuously brightened everything.

The play's principal comic controls, however, are built into the action's basic design, by which Tranio sustains and intensifies the tension between youth and age in a series of proliferating deceptions. With each deception Theopropides comes closer to discovering what has happened during his absence; with each threat of discovery Tranio is driven to greater ingenuity and outrageousness; with each cliff-hanging readjustment the frenzy is accelerated.

The play opens with a group of scenes which define a domesticized revel. In the first scene Grumio, the "good" country slave, quarrels with Tranio, the "bad" city slave, about the riot and dissoluteness of the past three years, anticipating, in their clear declarations against and for revelry, the later struggle between youth and age. Grumio's fulminations introduce the condition which Theopropides will oppose:

> Nunc, dum tibi lubet licetque, pota, perde rem,
>   corrumpe erilem adulescentem optumum;
> dies noctesque bibite, pergraecamini,
> amicas emite liberate, pascite
> parasitos, obsonate pollucibiliter.*   (ll. 20–24)

In the second scene in an outsized monologue Philolaches ruminates on the details of his delightful ruin, introducing the metaphor of prodigal youth as a house whose timbers are being rotted by the torrential waters of love. In the next scene Philematium fills out the image of young love as she prepares herself to receive Philolaches and, in another contrast between youth and age, rejects Scapha's counsel to take advantage of the "big harvest" already in by prudently looking for security. Additionally, Philematium extends the house metaphor by applying it to herself but insists that the rains of love which have soaked her house have been fructifying rains. It is tempting, of course, to refer all this to the idea of the "haunted" house, a house which is about to be brought to a new life but which is as much haunted by youth and love as it is by Tranio's spirits of the dead. In any event, the picture of youth and the revel world is completed with the lovers' tender meeting and Callidimates' arrival with his girl friend Delphium: Callidimates, appropriately, is reeling and singing, indeed literally falling-down drunk.

---

* "So now you've got the chance, and choose to do so, drink away, wreck the property, demoralize that fine young son of master's! Get fuddled day and night, live like Greeks, buy girls and set 'em free, feed parasites, go in for fancy catering!"

Into this scene Tranio bursts with the news that Theoproprides has just returned, and this revelation — accomplished, it should be noted, through the comment that Jupiter, the father-god, is bent on destroying them — establishes the main terms of the youth-age struggle. Theoproprides is the typical father: wily, practical, narrow, oblivious of the needs of youth, vengeful and dangerous (in appearance at least). The various wishes that he soon die anticipate his symbolic destruction, but until that occurs he poses a formidable threat to Philolaches' group. For the moment, Tranio agrees to take him on and to manipulate the confusion for a happy resolution. To this end he meets Theoproprides at the door of his house and tells him an elaborate tale of how the house has been haunted for seven months by the ghost of a man who lived there earlier.

From this point forward the play works by the mechanism of "brinkism." In successive episodes Theoproprides returns to the house, threatening with each appearance to explode the deceit, only to be put off each time by a new fabrication; each time he bullies his way as close as possible to discovery; at the last moment he is swept by Tranio's lies into a new digression. With each approach to discovery, suspense is heightened; with each escape it is released. In I, 6, for example, as Tranio tells Theoproprides for the first time that the house is haunted, someone within nearly exposes him by rattling the door and whispering. But Tranio quickly converts the threat to an advantage by recoiling in terror at the noises and pretending that they have been made by the ghost. In the same way, at the beginning of the next scene, when Theoproprides has just spoken to the former owner of the house and has disproved the ghost story, as he thinks, Misargyrides, the money-lender, appears, and discovery, threatened from two sources, seems inevitable. But again Tranio improvises brilliantly and converts both threats to his advantage by telling Theoproprides that Philolaches bought Simo's house to replace the haunted one and borrowed the money for the down-payment from Misargyrides. For the moment

Theoproprides is distracted by the thought of new property, and Misargyrides, another Old Man, is relieved to hear that Theoproprides will stand behind his son's debt. In the next scene, when Theoproprides is brought face to face with Simo, whose house he thinks he now owns, all seems lost again until Tranio gains access to Simo's house for him by telling Simo (another Old Man whose account of his struggle with his wife furnishes a parallel combat) that he wishes to look at the interior for ideas to be used in his own home. And so it goes, skirting at all points the danger that the lie will be penetrated by something said innocently, like Simo's invitation to Theoproprides to look around his house as if it were his, until finally Theoproprides learns the truth with the surprise arrival, during Tranio's momentary absence, of Callidimates' slaves.

Theoproprides' discovery of the ruse leads swiftly to his symbolic destruction and the comic denouement. He quickly reads his personal end in the facts of the deception: "Perii hercle, quid opust verbis?" ("By god, I'm dead. Why speak further?" l. 993); "Ei mihi, disperii. Vocis non habeo satis. Vicine, perii, interii" ("Death and damnation! I no longer have a voice. Oh neighbor, I'm dead and buried"; ll. 1030–31).*

But Tranio still knows nothing of this as he comes bustling in, determined to "muddle" matters farther; only his native acuteness enables him to perceive that something is amiss and at the last moment take sanctuary on the altar from the brutes whom Theoproprides has hired to beat him.

Finally, the difficulties are unravelled and Theoproprides is persuaded to accept and forgive even Tranio by the generosity of the now sober Callidimates, who offers to pay all expenses. The speed of the denouement is a final proof that Plautus' main interest here was in generating a frenzy and intensifying exhilaration: the instant the excitement begins inevitably to fall off, he hastens to the end.

---

* I have touched up Paul Nixon's translations of these speeches to make them more literal.

156

Extended deceptions like Tranio's, deceptions not merely ingenious but capable of elaboration and proliferation, constitute one of the chief technical means by which Plautus constructed the subtly orchestrated dramatic actions with which his name is identified. One of the peculiarly Plautine effects of this structure was increased confusion within the world of the play, a confusion which took the form of more comings and goings, more schemes and counterschemes, forces poised on coiled springs in such a way as to make an explosion seem inevitable. Even without literal references to rebirth or transformations of identity, this confusion frequently confers a metamorphic quality on the world of the play, a sense of a world teetering on the edge of some uncharted domestic chaos. Yet it also had other advantages, and chief among these was that it enabled Plautus to control comic excitement by structural means. Extended deception provided a way of internalizing that excitement: it placed squarely in the playwright's hands the wherewithal to generate excitement by means of an action which articulated itself in a certain way, and hence could be controlled or "tuned" as the playwright wished, rather than by means of special, "loaded" materials like the combat, the destruction of the Old Man, etc.

It is in this dynamic process that the Plautine play reveals its kinship to that last, maverick type of revue play which has as its governing purpose the generation of frenzy. In the majority of revue plays comic excitement is produced by restating in dramatic terms a familiar formula for action: the combat in its various forms, the destruction of the Old Man, etc. But in this type of revue play comic excitement is produced by treating materials — any materials — so that they generate comic suspense. Characteristically the action includes the execution of a scheme against great odds or the piling up of disasters which almost defy probability. In the Plautine play comic excitement is produced both by the use of the familiar formulas and by stimulating comic suspense repeatedly until excitement approaches frenzy. In other words, the Plautine play builds from a considerably broader base of materials and exploits the principle of generating a frenzy to a degree beyond anything attempted in the revue play.

The fertility of Plautus' invention in devising such actions is clear in his use of extended deception in the *Mostellaria;* but the full range of his ingenuity can only be gauged in the intricacy and subtlety of plays like the *Pseudolus*, (191 B.C.) and the *Epidicus* (ca. 200 B.C). In the *Pseudolus*, for example, Pseudolus' problem is to get his master's beloved out of the hands of the pimp Ballio, who has just sold her to a Captain, and the task is made more difficult by the fact that everyone knows what he is trying to do. He boasts to Simo, the father of his young master, that he will that very day get from him the money needed to buy the girl. He boasts at large that he will demolish or batter down this Ballio ("Ballionem, exballistabo"), the common foe ("inimicum communem"), and win the girl from him; moreover, Ballio is told of the boast. With everyone alert and Ballio, who was formidable enough to begin with, extremely wary, bets are made on the outcome. These obstacles, however, serve only to drive Pseudolus to a masterpiece of ingenuity. From the absent Captain's representative, Harpax, himself very cautious, he gets the Captain's letter and token by posing as Ballio's servant. With some borrowed money, the letter, and the token, he succeeds in getting the girl through the services of another slave who poses as Harpax. Having won the girl, he collects his bet from Simo, who in turn collects his bet from Ballio, who loses all around in that he must also pay back the Captain. As background to this multi-staged deception, the domestic revel which has been developing as Ballio's birthday party easily becomes a celebration for the victorious young. In the final scene Pseudolus, already drunk, leads Simo off to drink, while Ballio capitulates with the line: "Certumst mi hunc emortualem facere ex natali die" (I have decided to make this my death-day instead of my birthday") (l. 1236).

In the *Epidicus* Plautus runs two separate schemes

together so that the schemers are threatened not only by their natural enemies but also by their colliding schemes. At the beginning of the play Epidicus has just worked out an elaborate stratagem to enable his master's son to marry a girl musician. Suddenly he learns that the young man has changed his mind and now wishes to marry a captive. When a second deception is imposed on the first, the result is extraordinary confusion which only Epidicus is able to pick his way through. Both the *Epidicus* and the *Pseudolus* are bewilderingly complex, brilliant proofs of Plautus' virtuosity with this structural strategy. Moreover, both illustrate how his handling of extended deception produces domestic confusion of such magnitude and intensity to suggest a world on the threshold of chaos and, hence, on the threshold of transformation.

But Plautus' technical adroitness is no less evident in his handling of mistaken identity, which provides the second structural means by which he manages his distinctive amalgamation of materials and form. The play most richly illustrative of his skill with this device is *Menaechmi* (ca. 205 B.C.), in which the key characters are twins who have been separated as boys and have grown to manhood in Syracuse and Epidamnus, respectively. The action takes place in Epidamnus on a day when Menaechmus I is sneaking out of his house carrying one of his wife's dresses to keep a rendezvous with the courtesan Erotium. On his way he meets a parasite named Brush, whom he invites to dinner at the courtesan's house. After a brief visit, they leave while dinner is being prepared. Into all this comes Menaechmus II, who has been journeying around the Mediterranean looking for his long-lost brother, and his slave Messenio. Confusion grows, as the two Menaechmi are mistaken for each other. First, Menaechmus II is mistaken for his brother by Erotium, who, to his bewilderment but great pleasure treats him with lavish generosity; as they part, she gives him the dress given to her by Menaechmus I so that he can have it altered. Of course when Menaechmus I, accused of theft by his wife, asks

Erotium to return the dress to him, he is told that he has it. Menaechmus II, meanwhile, is seen by Menaechmus I's wife and reviled by her. Menaechmus II entrusts some money to Messenio, thinking that in this way he will keep it from the strangely friendly courtesan, but Messenio, predictably, gives it to Menaechmus I. As the two Menaechmi move through this situation but never meet each other, errors are compounded until everyone is literally at the point of distraction. Conventional social postures are taken, but they do not apply: all presumably known and understood relationships are turned upside down and inside out until the ordinary little domestic world of husband, wife, mistress, quack doctor, and father-in-law seems, as everyone in the play finally admits, to have gone mad; what had seemed safe and perhaps a little bit dull suddenly becomes unpredictable and precarious. It all ends happily, of course, when the complications are untangled, the lost brothers are reunited, and the identities which seemed for a time to have vanished into thin air are returned to their grateful claimants. As we experience the confusion, however, we begin to feel that the world is a dream or a madhouse. It is the particular happiness of *buffo* that we feel this approach to dissolution keenly and yet feel none of the anguish of the threat. Then, as the madness abates, we are made to feel that the confusion somehow confers a blessing.

In even this partial description of the action of the *Menaechmi* it is possible to see how mistaken identity served Plautus. Like extended deception, it enabled him to combine and collapse several *buffo* interests in the monumental hunger of Brush, the destruction of the Old Man in the quack doctor, and the theme of transformation in the pervasive conviction of the characters that their familiar world is no longer recognizable. Like extended deception, too, it supplies the technical means to compound complications so as to generate intense suspense and excitement. Moreover, it provides the opportunity to do all this and at the same time to extend the whole by making the world of the play, with all its confusion and increasingly frenetic pace, expressive in its vitality of the possibility of renewal — the same renewal obliquely present in its materials and achieved in the recognitions of the final scene. Mistaken identity leading to confusion, deception leading to confusion, confusion leading to coincidences, surprises, discoveries, realignments of character, re-makings of worlds: these are the prime movers of Plautine comedy, the sources of the energy and vitality which make the process of these plays as important as any of their constituent events. It is in the process of their unfolding that these plays achieve their distinctive expression of *buffo*. Thus, one way of describing Plautus' achievement in the history of vulgar comedy is to say that he perfected the form which articulates this process.

Apparently Shakespeare understood this perfectly when he turned to the *Menaechmi* as a source for *The Comedy of Errors* (ca. 1592). His most conspicuous changes in Plautus' plot are those which multiply the possibilities for mistakes in identity and for recognition, unions and reunions. Instead of one set of twins — the Antipholi, in his play — he has added a second in the twin slaves, the Dromios. Instead of an ineffectual father-in-law, he has added the Antipholi's father, Egeon, and their mother, Emilia; they, like the two sets of twins, have been separated for many years. To the Plautine wife — Adriana here — he has added a second young woman, her sister Luciana, who at the end of the play is paired with the unattached Antipholus. Further, he has added the Duke, dropped the parasite and Erotium's cook, greatly reduced the role of Erotium — here simply the "courtesan" — and replaced the doctor-pedant with the quack magician Dr. Pinch. All these modifications serve to intensify the confusion and to deepen the sense of wonder in the action, the sense that the process completed has been strangely magical.

Indeed, magic provides a convenient link between first things and last in this study, for because of Shakespeare's emphasis on it here, *The Comedy of Errors* seems closer to the folk backgrounds of vulgar comedy than do most plays by Plautus. Not only does its world seem mad to everyone in it, but it is deliberately yoked to magic by way of Dr. Pinch and the other conjurors and sorcerers rumored to inhabit it. Dr. Pinch, derived from the wonder-working doctor of the English folk play, is symptomatic of all those changes and additions which associate the human tangle of this action with magic, with an order of forces operating through nature but beyond human control or comprehension. The connection is made by various characters. Antipholus of Syracuse says, after his first meeting with the Dromio of Ephesus,

> They say this town is full of cozenage,
> As nimble jugglers that deceive the eye,
> Dark-working sorcerers that change the mind,
> Soul-killing witches that deform the body.   (I, ii, 97–100)

Then Dromio of Syracuse says toward the end of II, ii, "O for my beads; I cross me for a sinner. / This is the fairy land" (189–90). After that the charge is commonplace: "I, amazed, ran from her as a witch" (III, ii. 143); "There's none but witches do inhabit here" (III, ii, 155); "And here we wander in illusions — / Some blessed power deliver us from hence!" (IV, III, 41–42); "Thou art, as you are all, a sorceress" (IV, iii, 64). By the last act the Duke can say with authority, "I think you all have drunk of Circe's cup" (V, i, 271). The chief effect of this emphasis is that it prompts the inference that the world of the play is somehow magical, that in these extraordinary complications and strivings of spirit — though *we* can see their cause — there is something magical, that nature, embodied as it is here in a society in which every conventional and supposedly known relationship and identity is upended, is magical. It is magical because, as we ultimately see, it is capable of bringing out of unbelievable chaos a higher order of harmony than we began with; it is capable of recon-

ciling the estranged, of restoring the dead (the brothers
have been dead to each other and to their parents), of
returning those absent from their true selves to themselves, of generating love and fellow-feeling, and of recon-
stituting the world for the welfare of men. Magic — or the
metaphor of magic — is one of the chief contributors to the
marvelous sense that nature, the world, the stuff of life, is
irrepressibly creative.

In the same way, many of the other additions and
changes which multiply errors and compound confusion
intensify our sense of the abundance and energy of this
world. They lead not only to a more complex harmony at
the end — more complex in that in it more elements are
orchestrated — but also to a more complicated sense of
vitality. They serve to prime the Plautine uproar with additional charges, which broaden and deepen our sense of a
world testing its own resilience.

Yet a study of Shakespeare's changes and additions in
The Comedy of Errors reveals that he was also interested
in comic values which have little to do with *buffo;* in fact,
the play is almost as useful for illustrating what *buffo* is not as
for illustrating what it is. A good many of his changes and
additions qualify the pervasive hilarity and add a dimension
— however slight — of sentiment and poignancy. Egeon is
perhaps most important. He is a touching figure, a character
truly lost: alienated from his world, estranged from his wife
and children, under sentence of death for remote, improba-
ble causes in a distant land, he is a man all but literally dead to
all he values most. In the course of the play, of course, he is
restored to life, like the scapegoat king of the ritual, but not
until his presence has reminded us that real lives and serious
values are at stake. Egeon brings a dignity and a mellow, if
rather pathetic, resignation to the play. It is he who first
introduces the idea that this is all a dream ("If I dream not,
thou art Emilia"), and though the motif is sounded by others,
it is in him, blinking on the edge of the grave at marvels
taking place all around him, that the sense of a dream is
strongest.

Less important but part of the same pattern are characters like Emilia, the Duke, Angelo, and the Second Merchant; no one of them is prominent, yet each sounds a note rather different from those of the central frenzy. The Duke brings gravity and the world of politics and national rivalries into the play. Emilia, the Abbess, brings another touch of Egeon's poignancy but also a reminder of other societies, other rules, other systems. Angelo and the Second Merchant — still less important — with their not entirely comic embarrassment and distress support a sense of a world governed by a rhythm and sobriety not evident in the chaos of the Antipholi's confusion.

Luciana and Adriana, on the other hand, point to still other values. Created by Shakespeare from whole cloth to provide a balance for Adriana and a prospective match for Antipholus of Syracuse, Luciana helps to fill out the picture of several couples united and reunited at the end, but she is striking because she is more than just a pretty young thing ready to be married off. In his characterization of Luciana we see Shakespeare's first attempt at creating a young woman of sensibility, a young woman who is so particularized that we begin to care about her and to take a distinct pleasure in her success and in the implications of that success for the world. Likewise, Adriana, the stock wife in the Plautine play, is something more than a type: she gives evidence of intelligence, sensitivity, and a range of feeling and awareness which imply a woman whom we could care about intensely if these qualities were more pronounced. In Luciana and Adriana, in any event, we see an early experiment in one of the principal dramatic strategies of Shakespeare's later romantic comedies: he makes us admire and sympathize enough with the young people in distress so that when they marry we rejoice not only at the abstract victory of life, but also at the particular victory embodied in their voluntary engagement in life.

If all of this is rather dim in *The Comedy of Errors*, it is still sufficient to demonstrate that in this first comic effort Shakespeare was pushing out in new directions. In the history of vulgar comedy it is difficult to find a play which celebrates the marvelous unexpectedness of life with greater ebullience than *The Comedy of Errors*. Yet it is also clear that the play contains important comic values which are not comprehended by *buffo*.

The Plautine play is designed to generate in the beholder an exhilarating sense that the vulgar world of husbands and wives, prodigal sons and courtesans, fathers, pimps, parasites, and slaves can yield unions, reunions, and reassignments of power which come to nothing short of a rebirth. It is a world which combines a consciousness of great wells of vitality with a consciousness of the metamorphic potential inherent in the most familiar surfaces. In quality and meaning, therefore, the Plautine plays are very like the revue plays. Plautus did not alter the character of *buffo;* he devised a more elaborate and more intense articulation of it. The differences between the revue play and the Plautine play are a little like those between a group of loose sentences and a full-blown Ciceronian sentence. The words can be the same; the principles of syntax can be the same; even the fundamental meaning can be the same. Yet the amalgamation achieved in the Ciceronian sentence makes something new of it all, releasing secondary meanings not to be found in the loose sentences, qualifying and extending the whole without seriously changing anything. To shift the metaphor, Plautus was a little like the master fireworks-maker who designs pyrotechnic displays for holidays: he used the materials of the revue play to contrive not a simple explosion or even a simple series of explosions, but an intricate pattern of them. He supplied the tradition of *buffo* with the structural model for its greatest achievements.

◇ ◇ ◇

Since my concern here is not so much with Plautus as with the Plautine play, it will be useful to trace its later history, at least to the point in the story of vulgar comedy at which it was revived by Renaissance humanists. As we have seen, it is difficult to ascertain how original Plautus' work was because it is impossible to determine how much of his structural model was taken from the work of Menander and other writers of New Comedy or from the work of his own contemporaries. But we can gauge something of the importance of this model in the story of vulgar comedy by the fidelity with which it was appropriated by the Renaissance humanists seventeen hundred years after Plautus.

When the physician Jacques Grévin (ca. 1538–ca. 1570) was commissioned by Henry II of France to write a comedy for the wedding of the Duchess of Lorraine in 1560, he followed the lead of Étienne Jodelle (1532–1573) and the French humanists who had written and performed plays in Latin, and wrote a Plautine play entitled *Les Ébahis* ("The Astonished Ones"). In it, Josse, an old merchant whose age, incapacity, and closeness to death are much stressed, and whose wife, Agnès, has disappeared, has become engaged to Madelon, the young daughter of the wealthy Gérard. Josse's valet, Antoine, is enamoured of Marion, Madelon's laundress, while Madelon is pursued by a group of young men, including the "Gentilhomme," the "Avocat," and Panthaleone, an Italian braggart who has just brought another woman to town. The woman with Panthaleone is actually Agnès, Josse's wife, now become a high-class prostitute. Julien, the Avocat's man, and Marion conspire. While seeming to encourage Antoine, Marion tricks him into giving her a garment of Josse's, and, disguised with it, the Avocat gets into Madelon's house and ravishes her, to her delight. When the Avocat is seen leaving by Madelon's father, however, Julien says that the fleeing figure is Josse, and Gérard goes after Josse to avenge his honor. Of course Josse denies everything. Meanwhile, the Gentilhomme pays for Agnès, and they hit it off beautifully, while Panthaleone is humiliated, first when Julien faces him down, then when he is accused of having ravished Madelon while disguised as Josse. At the end Josse is confronted with Agnès, whom he ultimately forgives and accepts back, and is forced to release Madelon from her promise of marriage and to return the dowry.

There is nothing new in pointing out that the humanists of the sixteenth century imitated Plautus and Terence when they wrote comedies, yet of the many scholars and critics who have acknowledged the debt, none has ever discussed the fact that it includes not just the five-act convention and the stock characters but fundamental, if elusive, techniques of play construction. What is important about Grévin's play is that structurally it recapitulates the Plautine method of organizing units of material from the revue play around an extended deception. By the sixteenth century these materials could be traced to a great many sources: the figures of Josse and Agnès are remarkably like Carnival and Lent; the wooing of Madelon by a group of young men is distinctly reminiscent of the late medieval wooing plays; the contention between youth and age and the destruction of the Old Man in the figures of Josse and of the braggart Panthaleone were familiar materials in both ritual revels and the revue play. But the method of structuring it all and the intense, highly intricate articulation of *buffo* achieved were Plautine.

The same can be said for many other sixteenth-century plays. To take two more examples, one from Italy and one from England, *La Calandria* ("The Affairs of Calandro," 1513), by Bernardo Dovizi (1470–1520), later Cardinal Bibbiena, has an extraordinarily complex action. A brother and sister have been separated, and each has disguised himself as the other, with predictable sexual confusion. As each becomes the object of a misguided sexual scheme and they pursue counterschemes of their own, the intersecting schemes provide the framework for a running contention between youth, in the shape of the brother and sister, and age, in the figure of Calandro, the old husband who, in fact, enacts a death scene to seduce his wife's young "female" companion (actually the brother in disguise). After repeated sexual metamorphoses and protracted domestic confusion, the young people are restored to each other and to their proper selves.

For its first three acts *Ralph Roister Doister* (ca. 1553), by Nicholas Udall (1505–1556), consists of a series of schemes by which the unwanted wooer of the title tries to win Dame Custance with the help of Mathew Merygreeke, who does all for mirth. Roister Doister is part fool and part traditional braggart. "In a trance" like his braggart-brethren, he is rejected several times, mightily abused verbally, and finally routed in a pitched battle with Dame Custance and her "knightesses," or kitchenmaids. At one point — before the battle, actually — his "destruction" leads to his poetic death, a requiem, and a mock funeral. Altogether, the play is less subtle than *La Calandria* but is similar in that its power also derives from a suspenseful union of a wooing action and a sustained destruction of an Old Man. Moreover, the assault on Roister Doister is played out against a holiday background filled in by songs, the gamesome Merygreeke, and Dame Custance's playful women, a background which leads easily to the song and the supper celebrating the union of Dame Custance with Gawyn Goodluck which end the play.

Taken together, *Les Ébahis*, *La Calandria*, and *Ralph Roister Doister* are representative of the group of plays which reactivated the Plautine model in the Renaissance. As a group they differ in minor respects from Plautus' plays: they are on the whole coarser, more rowdy, and even more brutal: for example, many more actual adulteries and beatings take place in them. They reveal that, however self-consciously and deliberately these humanist-playwrights may have followed the example of Plautus, they glanced frequently and lovingly at the medieval and early Renaissance revue play as they did so, and this despite pretentious distinctions such as that made in Italy between the so-called farces and Learned Comedy. Despite these differences, however, and despite the differences among the humanistic comedies as a group, they filled the important function of reestablishing the Plautine play and laying the groundwork for the achievements in the form which was to come.

Later the Plautine play underwent many vicissitudes, not all of which are relevant to the story of vulgar comedy. It is only marginally relevant to the description of *buffo*, for example, that the Plautine play supplied the structural base for such later comic conceptions as romantic comedy, satirical comedy, and the comedy of manners. We have seen how Shakespeare extended it in *The Comedy of Errors* to include elements of gentility and sentiment, elements which would transform it totally in the romantic comedies. Ben Jonson and Molière adapted its basic framework to satire in plays like *Volpone* (1605–1606) and *L'École des Femmes* ("The School for Wives," 1662), while Molière and the English Restoration playwrights pushed it still further in the comedies of manners. In all these extremely important generic developments the Plautine play provided what we might call the syntax, the basic organization of energies which was then modified and extended according to the new comic conceptions. What we know about the Plautine play, about the materials and technical strategies which give it substance and shape and the purposes which govern it, can scarcely tell us everything about plays like *Twelfth Night, Volpone*, and *The Country Wife*, but it can tell us a great deal. For the present it is enough to see that, in addition to being appropriated to these new comic types, the Plautine play persisted in its own right. Although continually modified, it persists even now as a major vehicle for *buffo* expression.

PART III
Buffo

7

The Power of Buffo

The revue play and the Plautine play provide the chief matrices for *buffo*'s expression in drama. Moreover, the material and formal elements which constitute them provide the main evidence of continuity all up and down the line. As we pursue the further history of *buffo,* we shall see these material and formal elements become the lineaments of vulgar comedy, the basic features, so to speak, in a face which changes — ages, if you like — yet remains the same. Perhaps it is more appropriate to speak of a mask than of a face, for vulgar comedy is always stylized, bigger and bolder than life; its human contours are always exaggerated and distorted.

We must now try to describe this mask, shifting our focus from vulgar comedy to the quality fundamental to it. Our question at last becomes, what is *buffo?* How can we best describe the peculiar genius which informs both a Dorian mime and, allowing for marginal cultural differences, one of the court farces of Sir Arthur Wing Pinero; how can we isolate the quality central to plays by Plautus and the village-square comedies of sixteenth-century

France, to the commedia scenarios from seventeenth-century Italy and the afterpieces of George Colman or David Garrick?

As we shift our attention from vulgar comedy to *buffo*, from substance to quality, we should recognize that what defines the one tells us a great deal about the other. What we have seen of the material and formal elements of vulgar comedy is rich in suggestions about *buffo*. In continuing to describe vulgar comedy, accordingly, we are preparing for the moment when we shall focus on its dominant quality. Once again, we must proceed with care by acknowledging that the description of vulgar comedy, as well as the implicit elucidation of *buffo*, involves elusive problems.

Perhaps the most fundamental of these is that what I have called the lineaments of vulgar comedy also appear in works which have little if any connection with it. If we grant that certain materials like struggles between youth and age, the destruction of the Old Man, and transformation, as well as certain formal strategies like sustained deception and mistaken identity, constitute persistent features of this comedy, we must in all honesty also admit that not all works which use these materials and strategies are vulgar comedies. To take an outrageous example, *King Lear* might well be described as a play which treats the destruction of the Old Man, yet no one would mistake it for a comedy of any type. Transformation figures prominently in the *Eumenides* and *The Tempest*, but they, too, are qualitatively as different from vulgar comedy as they are from each other. *'Tis Pity She's a Whore* depends on an extended deception as a premise for its action, but it can scarcely be confused with a play by Plautus. In other words, even after we have established the importance to vulgar comedy, and ultimately to *buffo*, of the materials and strategies discussed, and have demonstrated their crucial function in particular works, that obnoxious student in the back of the room is still justified in asking: "But how do we know it's vulgar comedy?"

Most attempts to define genres or to describe qualities like the tragic or the tragicomic turn on the isolation of some element thought to be crucial to the genre or the quality. That element may be material or formal; it may be the response characteristically elicited or the meaning characteristically demonstrated. It would require no great effort to construct a theory of vulgar comedy around an element like the struggle between youth and age. Ingeniously contrived, it could account for a great deal and would have the undeniable attractions of simplicity and neatness. But it would also have the overriding disadvantage that it could not take enough of the evidence into account. More responsible is the admission that if it is impossible to think of vulgar comedy apart from the materials and formal strategies everywhere found in it, it *is* nonetheless possible to think of those materials and strategies apart from vulgar comedy.

If it is clear, then, that some selection of the material and formal elements already discussed is always present in vulgar comedy, but that by themselves they are not sufficient to establish that any specific work is a vulgar comedy, it must follow that these elements constitute but one factor indispensable to this sub-genre and that its certain identification requires the presence of at least one other, perhaps of several others simultaneously.

I propose that the identification of vulgar comedy, as well as the identification of *buffo*, demands the presence of a configuration of factors, a gestalt. Confronted with a Laurel and Hardy two-reeler, we know that we have to do with vulgar comedy because the configuration or gestalt is there. We recognize it, doubtless, as a result of a learned sensitivity. But it is easy enough to imagine someone who would not recognize it. Baudelaire was probably right when he argued that a person reared far from civilization and its terrors would respond to the grotesqueness and violence of early farce with fear rather than laughter, just as very young children respond to their first clowns and Halloween masks as often with tears as with delight. We, on the contrary, have assimilated enough in the way of clues about vulgar comedy to know that we need not fear when Oliver Hardy steps in a puddle and disappears from sight or when Charlie Chaplin is attacked by the neighborhood bully in *Easy Street*. Moreover, having seen how civilization constrains, frustrates, and torments men, how it arbitrarily asserts one rule in the face of a nature teeming with possibilities for others, we are prepared for the ugliness and brutality of civilized life as we meet them in vulgar comedy. We know when we are in the presence of *buffo* because we have been prepared to recognize the gestalt.

The gestalt is completed, I believe, by two other factors; I shall call them "distance" and "coarseness." The term "distance" refers to the beholder's relation to a theatrical image. Invariably, he sees and experiences a vulgar comedy as if at a considerable distance, a distance which prevents him from seeing very much of the human detail, from seeing anything, indeed, but a bold, general image. Surely we can take some pride in the fact that, usually, the more we know of the human detail the less we are inclined to laugh. It is easy to laugh at the fat man, snug in his tennis togs, trying to wedge himself into his sports car, until we know enough about his painful sensitivity to his condition. It is easy to laugh at the husband cuckolded by a vivacious wife, until we know as much about him as about Leopold Bloom or Raimu's baker in the film *The Baker's Wife*. Seen with enough distance, Othello is a big, black clown whose insane idea of himself is being exploded by his crafty ensign. Distance, as Brecht knew so well, is crucial to our adjustment to the theatrical image, crucial to the process of our assembling the clues which tell us what kind of work we have to do with.

But distance is not the result of a paucity of human detail alone; it is prompted and controlled by — and can be identified in — a variety of other matters. Most obvious is characterization, the principal source, usually, of human detail. It is a rule of thumb that characters in vulgar comedy are always rendered simply and boldly; like their probable predecessors in festive processions and dramatic rituals, they are types, unmistakably defined by physical appearance and role. As I have argued earlier, it is fair to suggest that the cast of characters in this sub-genre is substantially one cast, which brilliantly and conveniently achieved definition among the commedia troupes in the sixteenth century. The Pantalones, Dr. Grazianos, Capitanos, Arlecchinos, Pulcinellas, Flavios, and Columbinas are models for the feisty fathers and old husbands, authority figures, scheming servants, and lovers to be met everywhere in vulgar comedy. They are not without human interest: they are in love, they are vengeful, they are avaricious, they hunger, they lust, and they feel pain when they are beaten. But these traits are typically simplified and exaggerated so that we see virtually nothing of the complexity which usually accompanies them in human beings. The characters always retain a strange abstractness, "strange" because, though they move in a concrete, commonplace world and reflect commonplace needs, they are always notably reduced as human figures. This prompts the beholder to view the total image as if at a distance, prompts him to adjust to the whole, to focus the whole, as he has focused the characters.

This mode of characterization, moreover, is entirely congruent with other features of the dramaturgy of vulgar comedy. We note the presence of songs in Plautus, the medieval French farces, the *singspiele* and English song plays, and the serenades of the commedia scenarios; the use of frequent asides in all the plays and indeed a general tendency toward a free use of the stage; the frequent employment, in the early plays especially, of typical costumes, of masks or whitened or blackened faces, and, in the earliest examples, of prop phalluses and accentuated physical deformities (see fig. 13). All these features indicate conventions which, though they vary from period to period, impose theatrical dimensions on a dramatic surface

13. The grotesque in *buffo* figures. (*Left*) Mandacus, from the Atellan farces. Roman terracotta statuette, first century B.C., Louvre. Photo Giraudon. (*Right*) The mime fool. Roman terracotta statuette, first century B.C., British Museum. Photo Courtesy British Library Board.

already reduced in density. They also prompt a distinct detachment in the beholder and dictate a characteristic stylization.

One aspect of this stylization which calls for a slightly more extended comment is the acting style of vulgar comedy. From the earliest times to the middle of the nineteenth century it was always exaggerated and larger than life (see fig. 12). The costumes and masks (when they were worn) of the *phlyax* actors, the mime actors, the *atellanae* actors, the commedia actors, and the French *farceurs* of the early seventeenth century (see figs. 3, 13, 7, 14) clearly suggest such a style; the sixteenth-century frescoes of commedia performers in Tausnitz Castle in Bavaria (Katherine Lea, *Italian Popular Comedy*, I, 3–16) and Jacques Callot's engravings in the eighteenth century (fig. 15) provide visual evidence of the commedia actors' appearance and hints about their extravagances of movement.

Throughout much of the history of vulgar comedy its performers have been associated with dancers and acrobats. In Rome they were sometimes known as *planipes,* a term which calls attention to the fact that they were barefooted, hence ready to dance or leap. In the thirteenth century, in *Penitential,* Thomas de Cabham describes one class of minstrels as "those who wear horrible masks, or entertain by indecent dances or gestures." In the eighteenth century one of the companies at the fair of Saint Germain went by the name "Les Sauteurs établis au Jeu de Paume d'Orléans." The famous Scaramuccia and friend of Molière Tiberio Fiorilli (1608–1694) was so accomplished an acrobat and dancer that at eighty he could still tap a man's cheek with his foot. Giuseppe Domenico Biancolelli (ca. 1637–1688), his son Pietro Francesco Biancolelli (1680–1734), and Jean-Charles Deburrau (1829–1873), all famous for their variants on Harlequin as Dominique or Pierrot, were superb dancers. Will Kempe (fl. 1600), Shakespeare's colleague, who on one occasion took a month to dance from London to Norwich; Joseph Grimaldi

14. Early seventeenth-century French *farceurs*. French print by P. Mariette, Cabinet des Éstampes, Bibliothèque Nationale, Paris. Photo Giraudon.

(1778–1837), the celebrated "Joey" of the early nineteenth century; Grock (1880–1959), the music hall clown of the early twentieth century; and Charlie Chaplin, Buster Keaton, and Zero Mostel — these are some of the *buffo* performers who have mastered, if not dance, at least the grace and dexterity of dance movement, the kind of physical movement which fills out the picture of a flamboyant acting style. The peculiar physicality of this style is important to our response to *buffo* and will be discussed later. For the moment it is enough to say that the acting style of the performers of vulgar comedy, especially in the context of dramatic actions which frequently turn on repetitions and symmetries of various kinds, contributes much to the process by which the *buffo* image is "distanced."

Distance always conditions our perception of the material and the formal elements of vulgar comedy, and by that conditioning focuses these elements for *buffo*. But though it tells us much about how we perceive, it does not tell us quite enough, and it tells us too little about our response. To complete the *buffo* gestalt I will use the term "coarseness."

"Coarseness" also plays a part in the process by which the theatrical image is distanced, though it is ultimately different from distance. It not only refers to the tendencies to simplification and reduction in vulgar comedy — to what might be called a coarseness of grain in the image — but also points beyond the state of the image to the response elicited. A signal feature of our response to vulgar comedy is that it too is coarse, in the sense that, though frequently intense, it is relatively simple and uncomplicated. Vulgar comedy requires from the beholder no great range of sensitivity and no high order of intelligence. We expect no delicate sentiment, no subtle irony, no nice discrimination. The *buffo* image is painted in bold, primary colors, and our response to it involves orders of emotion and intelligence neither better nor worse than those involved in other responses, but notably simpler — like most of life, coarse.

15. The flamboyance of *buffo* actors. Jacques Callot, *Balli di Sfessania*, ca. 1625, Museum of Nancy. Photo Alinari.

Fracischina   Gian Farina

Capi Mala Gamba   Cap. Bellauita

It is, I suspect, this factor more than any other which has prejudiced critics against vulgar comedy. During the Restoration and the eighteenth century in England scarcely a good word was said for it, despite its great popularity. Dryden, Pope, Bishop Hurd, Thomas Wilkes, Dr. Johnson all held it in contempt, apparently, despite the variety of their arguments, because of the coarseness of thought and feeling characteristically elicited. In his preface to *An Evening's Love* (1668) Dryden denounces such comedy for entertaining with "grimaces" and "what is monstrous and chimerical," by which he seems to refer to its exaggeration and stylization. In his "On the Provinces of Drama" (1753) Bishop Hurd focuses on the simplicity of the materials of vulgar comedy and on its "sole aim," "which is to excite laughter" (*Works*, II, 30, 96–97). Both writers seem unable to countenance the fact that this kind of comedy has virtually none of the sophistication cultivated in other contemporary literary types.

Wycherley's *The Country Wife* (1675) is helpful here. Its action consists of materials from vulgar comedy (the male-female combat and the destruction of the Old Man), and structurally it makes use of the strategies of vulgar comedy (sustained deception and disguise); moreover, its action is viewed at a considerable distance, for the controls of exaggeration and stylization are there. But no one would call the play coarse. It may be immoral, and objectionable because its sophistication is made to serve immorality, but it is clearly designed to elicit a complicated, highly ironic, delicately shaded sense of the world. Indeed, it is principally pleasurable because it defines and celebrates our capacity to achieve this highly civilized sense. It is the refinement of thought and feeling which best distinguishes *The Country Wife* from, say, a farce by Sir Arthur Wing Pinero or Georges Feydeau, which in many respects resemble Restoration comedies of manners except that, among other things, they are grounded in coarseness.

A number of critics have commented on the peculiar physicality of the performers in vulgar comedy, usually in the context of commenting on their mastery of stylized movement. In writing of Edmund Kean, who was apparently as great a comic actor as he was a tragedian, William Hazlitt says: "to be harlequin, [an actor] should have his wits in his heels, and in his fingers' ends!" (*Works*, XVIII, 348). The actors of vulgar comedy — in Kierkegaard's suggestive phrase, "those lyrical geniuses who plunge the abyss of laughter" (*Repetition*) — communicate by way of gesture and movement at least as much as by words. What has not so far been suggested is that the actor's physicality also implies something important about our response to vulgar comedy: not only do we read the theatrical image to a large extent by way of gestures and movement, but we also apprehend *buffo* as a distinctive quality or power by way of the muscles as well as by way of the mind. This physicality is an important part of our response, and an important aspect of the coarseness of such comedy.

Coarseness, distance, and the presence of the materials and formal strategies of vulgar comedy, then, comprise the *buffo* gestalt. Although we probably retain very little of what has been called a ritual sensitivity, that is, a readiness to respond fully to ritual structures and meanings, apparently we do have a sensitivity to this gestalt and to the tradition which it implies. When the gestalt is right, we know we have to do with a particular kind of celebration, with a special way of seeing the world. Knowing this, we can ready ourselves for the peculiar process of this comedy.

◇   ◇   ◇

Most efforts to define and describe vulgar comedy as a genre or sub-genre center on farce, or a specific historical form of farce, and deal with one or at most two of the variables involved. The most ambitious descriptions of medieval French farce, for example, typically emphasize such materials as quarrels between husbands and wives or adultery, and link these materials with the modest aim of provoking simple, unreflective laughter. Such work is too narrowly based to be useful in a study of *buffo:* it does not deal with the quality crucial not only to medieval French farce but to all forms of vulgar comedy, from the Dorian mime to the present.

Much more useful here is that ambitious body of work known as "comic theory," all those reasoned arguments about comedy from Plato and Aristotle to Elder Olson in our time. This theory is treacherous to apply. It attempts to explain individual works and sub-classes of works by reference to the principles and qualities found in their parent class, but in attempting to explain all comedy and/or all laughter, it inevitably ignores distinctions and deprives a sub-species like vulgar comedy of its distinctive character. Moreover, the arguments developed by theorists as different as Aristotle, Schopenhauer, Bergson, and Freud turn on assumptions and emphases, critical languages, so different from each other that they are extraordinarily difficult to compare. Where one will argue in terms of materials — that is, in terms of the kinds of characters and situations used — another will focus on form or the ways in which surprise or incongruity are managed. The next may discuss the effect or response characteristically elicited, and that either as vision or as psychological state, and still another may link thematic materials with responses to them in an argument which scarcely acknowledges the connection.

Yet despite these difficulties, certain ideas found in general comic theory can be highly useful as we move from vulgar comedy to *buffo*. Intended to illuminate principles and qualities which are better seen in a whole class of works than in individual ones, these ideas are, to begin with, consonant with an attempt to describe a pervasive, dominant quality.

Particularly helpful is that group of ideas which D. H. Monro in his *Argument of Laughter* calls "superiority theories." They include the work of Aristotle, Hobbes, Alexander Bain, Bergson (with some slight forcing), A. M. Ludovici, James Feibleman, and most recently, Elder Olson, and they recommend themselves chiefly because they explain comedy in terms of the sense of well-being or superiority which it induces. Most of the evidence of vulgar comedy's origins, materials, and forms seen thus far suggests that this explanation is relevant. Taken as a whole, virtually everything we know of the ritual revels, of dramatic rituals and exercises, of emergent plays, and of the materials and forms of simple vulgar comedies suggests an overriding purpose of moving the participant or beholder to a state of exhilarating well-being. A little afterpiece entitled *Le Mariage de la Folie,* played with Jean-François Regnard's *Les Folies Amoureuses* (1704), makes the point succinctly: as Momus, Folie, and Carnaval come in, the latter two presumably to be married, Folie sings that they will "remplir le cerveau de quelque heureuse manie" ("fill the brain with some happy madness"). Later Momus says of the dance to be performed:

C'est se trémousser hardiment;
Et voilà des folles fringantes,
Qui pourraient mettre en mouvement
Les cervelles plus pesantes.*

The emphasis on rousing the mind to a pitch of gaiety associated with madness would seem at first glance to have little in common with Aristotle's brief comments on the pleasure which comes from contemplating harmless ugliness or Hobbes' "sudden glory," by which he means the unexpected perception of inferiority in others. But in fact what Aristotle and Hobbes have in common with Folie and Momus is that they see the comic work, or comic event, as a process which produces in the beholder a happy sense of sovereignty. *Buffo* is, of course, this happy sense. It dominates this kind of comedy; it is the genius of vulgar comedy. Although an adequate study of it requires the fullest exploration of all the variables involved and a thorough

---

* "It consists of fluttering about boldly; / And then there are sprightly fools / Who could stir up / The dullest brains."

examination of the comedic process which produces it, the organizing principle of the study should be what the superiority theories emphasize, the illumination of this happy state of being.

Since the superiority theories are the earliest comic theories, it is understandable that they have been frequently attacked. Many critics have argued that in the work of their earliest exponents — Aristotle, Hobbes, and even Bain — the idea of superiority is severely limited by the fact that the superiority described is personal. This criticism is just. For the most part these theorists see comedy as a process which turns on "degradation," to use Bain's term, the downgrading of a person or an event which has the effect of upgrading oneself. Unfortunately, this emphasis on a personal relation between the person or action perceived and the perceiver not only limits the idea of superiority but is misleading. To insist that the relation between the perceiver and the perceived is largely a matter of the perceiver's feeling that he is better than the agent perceived, or that his values are more elevated than those revealed in the event, is to argue that the perceiver is alienated by the comedic process from the world he observes. Such a description can hardly be reconciled with the evidence of vulgar comedy's origins and of particular vulgar comedies, in which the end desired, whatever there may be of elements of personal scorn, is clearly a feeling of well-being *in* the world, perhaps more precisely described as a confidence about one's world.

In his *In Praise of Comedy* James Feibleman deals with this problem by arguing that for most comedy the relation between the perceiver and the perceived is not personal at all, but a relation between the perceiver and a condition. This seems right for vulgar comedy. We are not moved to a state of happy confidence by a play like Edward Ravenscroft's *The Anatomist* (1696) because Young Gerald is so much more attractive than Old Gerald that his success and his father's failure in trying to marry Angelica is a matter of personal satisfaction resulting from the warmth we feel for the son and the animus we feel for the father. The truth is that we are never permitted to know enough about any of the characters to feel very much of anything for them personally. What we are engaged by — and it bears repeating that the engagement frequently involves great intensity — is the condition: the struggle of a young world against an old, of life and the opportunity to express life against all that is moribund, as Old Gerald is, both literally and figuratively. The combats between husbands and wives and fathers and sons, the destruction of authority figures, and the celebration of intractability and transformation do not work primarily to enable us to think well of ourselves while thinking badly of others. They confirm our confidence in forces at work in human nature and the universe at large — more precisely, in a process at work in the world which favors all that makes for life and opposes all that seeks to inhibit it.

Bergson's work is useful here because he, more than the other theorists, was committed to the view that the comic event takes place against the necessary backdrop of a state of natural plasticity with which human rigidities, though sometimes also rigidities in things, continuously collide. He traces these rigidities to a generic condition which he calls "absentmindedness," a tendency to fixity which prompts human beings and even nature itself to forget, so to speak, that nature subsists in a state of flux. Most illuminating is his discussion of the artistic means which produce the comic perception of these collisions — his examination of the "mechanical encrusted on the living" and his analysis of repetition, inversion, and what he calls the "reciprocal interference of series" as structural strategies by which a sense of "absentmindedness" is elicited. Indeed, his description of comedy as a perception of rigidities which serve to remind us of the natural plasticity of life seems reasonably consonant, if only generally so, with what we have seen of vulgar comedy.

As Bergson extends and qualifies his description, however, it becomes clear that he is interested in a quite

189

different kind of comedy. In my discussion of the materials of vulgar comedy I did not use the term "rigidities" because I think it too limited to describe what is actually at issue in the defeat of husbands, wives, fathers, and authority figures, the representations of intractability, and the other key elements in *buffo* actions. But "rigidities" is the right term for Bergson's description because in his view the comic response does not stop with the perception of rigidity at war with flux but includes a corrective action which follows from that perception. Like a good many other comic theorists, he ties comedy to a social purpose. He assumes that the beholder, though an individual, takes the point of view of society, and he concludes that the beholder's perception of rigidity, whether in agents, things, or events, serves to strengthen society by relaxing in him the tensions which society normally generates and by urging him toward less rigid social forms. Comedy is an instrument of progress and civilization for Bergson: as he says, it serves society by offering nature its revenge on it; it is civilization's way of protecting itself against itself and at the same time improving on itself. Comedy, therefore, is essentially a critical gesture for Bergson, an activity of intelligence working entirely free of feeling to promote a plasticity of mind. With Milton and many others, he was of the opinion that "smiles from reason flow, / To brute denied" (*Paradise Lost*, bk. 9, ll. 239–40).

Despite the interest of much of this argument and the many insights into *buffo* which it supplies, it is clear that Bergson did not have vulgar comedy in mind when he developed it. We have only to recall the anarchic thrust of the medieval French farces, the Elizabethan jigs, or the plays of Plautus to see that they are essentially without "social purpose" as that phrase is usually understood. Whatever we might grant them of the more general purpose of social therapy, they have virtually nothing to do with correction, or standards of intelligence, or standards of behavior. More often than not they create images of a social structure only to demolish them: in the perspective

of *buffo* the pillars of social authority are invariably
enemies whose chief crime is that they inhibit life.
Moreover, it would take great ingenuity to support, on the
evidence of vulgar comedy, Bergson's claim that our response to the comic event is exclusively an act of intelligence, a critical gesture. On the contrary, an important
dimension of *buffo* is that our response to it is non-critical
and instinctive: it consists of an exhilaration which com-
municates by way of the muscles as well as the mind.

Still another line of attack on the superiority theories
has been mounted by the group of theorists, beginning
with Kant and Schopenhauer, whom Monro calls the incongruity theorists. They believe that the superiority
theories do not effectively account for the laughter which
proceeds from observing disparities and unexpected con-
junctions; their main effort, accordingly, is to study the
materials — more often anecdotes and simple events than
dramatic actions — which produce this laughter. Altogether, their criticism of the superiority theories is useful
both in understanding some kinds of laughter and in
understanding something further about vulgar comedy.
Their focus on materials reveals a good deal about the
process of surprise in comedy and its sub-species, including vulgar comedy, explaining, for example, how the spec-
tator's expectations are upset by incongruous linkages —
how he is forced to see fresh possibilities. Their work
enables us to see that our response to the destruction of
forces which inhibit life does not consist simply of atavistic
glee at the destruction but of a perception of creativeness
prompted by the unexpected form which that destruction
has taken. In a play like the well-known *Farce de Maître
Pathelin*, for example, our pleasure does not consist simply
in the fact that the lawyer Pathelin, who has just bam-
boozled the court, is defeated by his client, but in the fact
that he is tricked by the very device which he himself
contrived. The issue here is not simply that an authority
figure is put down, but that as he is put down the world
suddenly reveals fresh possibilities.

191

Pushed a bit farther, incongruity theory suggests that part of comic perception is frequently a perspective on the mind itself. Although this phenomenon is no truer for vulgar comedy than for any other kind of comedy, it has been insufficiently noted, despite the fact that the sort of comic perception which works through incongruity — surprising linkages, unexpected connections — has as one of its dimensions a recognition of the mind's failure to establish firm categories. When Pantalone discovers that the delicious Columbina he has been pursuing is really his long-lost daughter and that his young rival Flavio, who with the help of Arlecchino has beaten him at every turn, is really his best friend's long-lost son, we sense that the walls of Pantalone's world are coming down to reveal new possibilities for life, and that he, we, everyone was, after all, mistaken about the actual state of the world observed. We laugh at the mind, therefore, for the officious, authoritarian organizer it is.

In vulgar comedy, which of course the incongruity theorists, like the others, lump together with other comic types, this pleasure which comes from seeing the mind subverted just as all other authorities are subverted is consistent with the happy confidence produced because our perception of the mind's infirmity carries with it a recognition of our capacity to recognize that infirmity. In the world of *buffo* this human talent is part of the general configuration making for creativeness.

A third group of theorists has contributed much to our understanding of the psychological processes involved in evoking well-being or a state of "happy confidence." Called by Monro the "release-from-restraint" theorists, their point of departure is, for the most part, Freud, and their basic assumption is that laughter and comedy essentially provide relief from tension. L. W. Kline, in his "The Psychology of Humor" (1907), puts the argument rather poetically by describing "release" as a delicate cutting of the "the surface tension of consciousness" (p. 438). For him the comedic process is aesthetic rather than practical, except that in the long run its effect of giving the beholder a sense of freedom has the social function of increasing the pliancy of consciousness "to the end that it may proceed on a new and strengthened basis." A few years earlier Freud, although more cautious in limiting his comments to jokes and their relation to the subconscious, had advanced essentially the same argument in rather more clinical terms. He proposed that our pleasure in hearing jokes consisted of two kinds: the pleasure of perceiving an "economy of energy" in "harmless" wit, by which he means the kind of wit which turns on surprising associations and provides shortcuts for the emotions; and, second, the pleasure of expressing socially unacceptable impulses, in what he calls "tendency" wit. His explanation of tendency wit as a mechanism which operates like a safety valve is the basis for most of the work of his followers.

Virtually all the theorists of this group see release from restraint as a sufficient end for every sort of laughter, comedy, humor, and wit. With the notable exception of Ernst Kris, they see no relation between release, or purgation, as it is sometimes described, and the happy confidence which I have been discussing. Eric Bentley, for example, is especially interesting because he applies the theory specifically to farce. "Like dreams," he says in his introduction to *Let's Get a Divorce!*, p. x, "farces show the disguised fulfillment of repressed wishes"; their wildness, their violence, their cruelty are essential parts of the psychological reality being expressed. Moreover, these theorists easily encompass the social purpose of other theories in the idea of comedy or laughter as a kind of safety valve; the principal difference is that they see it more often as a mode of social adaptation than, as Bergson does, as a mechanism for progress.

The main difficulty with these theorists is that they try to explain too much. With the single exception of Freud, who shrewdly limits himself to jokes, they typically range freely over comedy, or laughter, or humor, collapsing or ignoring distinctions between sub-types and in general homogenizing their subject so as to make anything more than very general statements impossible. It takes no great effort of imagination to see that their work has relevance for vulgar comedy and *buffo*. The release or purgation which they are unanimous in stressing is doubtless part of our response to, say, the destruction of the Old Man or the numerous forms of disguised combat in vulgar comedy. But psychic economy or the expression of unacceptable aggressions are not the only or the main issues even in these materials. Our response is not to the Old Man or to the triumphant young lover but to a condition in the world.

In the same way, sexuality as we meet it in the plays, as well as in their origins, involves more than the release from inhibition which the Freudians trace without difficulty to adulterous acts. Of adultery in vulgar comedy there is plenty, it is true, but there are also rivalries in love, marriages, and marvelous births in abundance. What is difficult to see, and what the Freudians have not seen, is that sexuality in all its forms in vulgar comedy, including adultery, is evocative of a sense of the fecundity of nature, of a world of life and vitality. Release from restraint might well be a part of this sense of fecundity, but it is only a part. Finally, what Kline and Wylie Sypher, in their refinements on the theory, describe as a kind of liberation is doubtless also a part of the response, but even that term is limited: only with great difficulty can it be related to such nuclei as intractability, transformation, and generating a frenzy.

Within the last twenty years Ernst Kris has taken this psychoanalytic argument one important step further. While accepting Freud's conclusions that our pleasure in jokes stems from psychic economy and the expression of sexual and aggressive impulses normally repressed, he applies them to the broader category of the "comic" and extends them by adding that a crucial part of our pleasure consists in our mastering or dominating anxiety ("Ego Development and the Comic," in *Psychoanalytic Explorations in Art*). Like children's games, he contends, the comic typically involves repetition, which in turn involves return and rediscovery. The effect of this process is to render harmless what had been thought dangerous by making it familiar through repetition and by recalling the past victories of the ego in adapting to danger. In his work on caricature (some of it with E. H. Gombrich) Kris explains that its exaggerated, simplified representations are perfectly adapted to prompt psychic economy and to dissipate danger.

Whatever the value of his detailed argument, Kris's work is extremely useful in demonstrating how the release-from-restraint theories, particularly the psychoanalytic ones, can be reconciled with the idea of superiority. By proposing that comic pleasure also consists of "dominating fear" or "mastering anxiety," he provides a rationale for retaining the word "superiority" as descriptive of the state of being to be explained while at the same time retaining large parts of the release-from-restraint theories and even the incongruity theories as partial explanations of how the sense of superiority, or what I have been calling "happy confidence," is produced.

In order to draw upon what seems to be useful in all these theories, one must find a term which makes it possible to see their connections. "Mastery" would seem to be perfect. By understanding the sense of superiority or happy confidence as a sense of mastery, we are in a position to see how incongruity generally works to support that sense by forcing a fresh awareness of the world's possibilities, and how the process of release from restraint also supports it by serving to disarm danger. The term "mastery" provides a new focus for the separate strands of this inquiry.

To summarize, then: *buffo* is a power inhering in situations — particularly, for our purposes, in dramatic structures; — it is activated when the beholder recognizes the peculiar gestalt of vulgar comedy. Having recognized it, and prepared by his experience of the tradition, the beholder is moved to a gaiety or exhilaration which the most pertinent comic theorists describe as superiority. A survey of comic theory conducted against the background of vulgar comedy, however, suggests that "superiority" as a descriptive term must be carefully qualified. Since the superiority experienced is directed at a condition rather than at persons or values, it is notably non-personal; it does not have the effect of alienating the beholder from his world by sealing him in self-pride but makes him feel hopeful about his world. "Superiority" as a descriptive term, accordingly, might be usefully replaced by the phrase "sense of well-being" or "happy confidence." Moreover, this happy confidence involves little of the social purpose claimed for comedy and laughter by many comic theorists, and it is not primarily a critical or intellectual state of being but is instinctive, visceral, even in part muscular. Indeed, the process of *buffo* subverts the mind almost as often as it subverts other agents of authority thought to inhibit life. Still further, we have seen that the happy confidence at issue is sometimes elicited by incongruities of various kinds, the general effect of which is to startle the beholder, to upset his expectations, and by this process to suggest fresh possibilities in the world, an unexpected potential for creativeness. In part this happy confidence consists of the beholder's having been freed from restraint, relieved of tension, by the process. Finally, a still better descriptive term than "happy confidence" for accommodating all facets of the state of being under scrutiny is "mastery," a temporary sovereignty which has as one part a sense of release and as another a fresh perception of one's condition, and which can be constructed to be as much a matter of emotional *élan* as of intelligence.

◇ ◇ ◇

Very simply, *buffo* is this sense of mastery, this feeling of temporary but triumphant security in a perilous world. We feel it in the ancient combats — between Carnival and Lent, husbands and wives, fathers and sons — and it scarcely matters who wins, or that anybody wins, because it is apparently sufficient to affirm the struggle in nature. We feel it in the destruction of the Old Man as father, husband, judge, bullying soldier, pedant, etc., as we see the walls built by human ingenuity and perversity crumble under the onslaught of all that wants life. We feel this antagonism between life-inhibiting and life-creating forces in the struggles of young lovers against their parents, in courtships which invariably end in marriage and sexual union. We meet it more elusively in actions which show the innate stubbornness of nature in the face of society's demands for morality and discipline. This stubborn anarchism is expressive of energy or vitality in its simple resistance to all that ties life down. We feel this sense of mastery perhaps most clearly of all in the transformations which metaphorically — and, by the eighteenth century, literally — represent the world's potential for metamorphosis. In the transformation of Harlequin into an ostrich or Cinderella into a princess, or in the marvelous night scene in Aphra Behn's *Emperor of the Moon* (1684), in which the world of the play actually changes before our eyes, we have the quintessential event of the *buffo* process: the world becoming a new world, in defiance of all laws. Finally, we feel this mastery in actions in which no one of these *materia* is dominant but in which the structure has been contrived to generate an exhilaration or frenzy which is itself evidence of the vitality locked in ourselves and the world of convention. Indeed, in sophisticated works on the model of Plautus, *buffo* resides both in the materials of the action and in its process, a process carefully calibrated to reinforce the power inherent in the materials.

Buffo is a kind of light-hearted hubris, a sense of riding high which is almost giddy because so intensely felt and so closely allied to abandon. While Pseudolus is able to keep all his schemes in the air, while Flavio succeeds in possessing the beautiful Isabella and cuckolding Pantalone, while Ruzzante persists in his amorality and stupidity, we feel not only the equal of our world but its master.

We no longer feel the usual dangers because we have seen them engulfed in new sources of creativity and energy, and we feel ourselves in control, invulnerable, because we have also felt that magic vitality in ourselves. *Buffo* consists of a sense of this potential for creativity, a sense that we have left the tracks of convention and logic to find new reserves of life in the nature which logic and convention ignore. It is a thrilling sense of new beginnings, of youth surging through the muscles and the blood.

Transformation might legitimately be considered the quintessential event in vulgar comedy because it depicts the revelation and discovery which is fundamental to all forms of the *buffo* process. We are not concerned here with revelation and discovery of a complex, sophisticated kind. *Buffo* contributed a good deal to the subtle comic visions of Ben Jonson or William Congreve: it provided their basis, their matrix. But unlike these visions, *buffo* is simple, direct, coarse, like a pie in the face. Complexity and subtlety are to be found not in our response or in the discovery which is a part of it, but in the ingenuity of the means, the key to which is the idea of a world revealing itself afresh.

The notion that transformation is central to *buffo* explains certain secondary characteristics of vulgar comedy. We can see it operating in the use of puns and verbal confusions, as in *La Farce de Mahuet Badin* (ca. 1500), in which Mahuet is destroyed by the variability of the phrase "au prix du marché," or in any of the plays of H. J. Byron (1834–1884), in which punning is carried to sometimes tedious lengths. We see it in the extravagant exploitation of a single metaphor, as in *La Farce des femmes et le chaud-ronnier* (ca. 1510–20), in which the tinker's efforts to serve the women by filling the holes in their pots are entirely sexual, or in *La Farce d'un ramonneur* (ca. 1520), in which chimney-sweeping takes on the same meaning. We see it in the fondness of Plautus and Molière for equivocation and argument-bending, which have the effect of creating fugitive worlds of words, or in the use made of hybrid languages like the Italian-Latin of Judge Messer Malingo in Niccolò Campani's *Strascino* (ca. 1519). In all these examples the language itself suggests instability and variability: words become confused with other words like them; they take on new meanings; they suggest a different reality from that which they normally indicate; they help to create a special universe. When put to these uses, language in vulgar comedy functions much as it often does in the work of Rabelais, Joyce, or Lewis Carroll, all of whom play with the metamorphic potential of words to support a pervasive sense of an amorphous, yet creative, world. However, in the work of Joyce amorphousness and the threat of dissolution are often as strong as a sense of creativity and the promise of renewal, while in *buffo*, as in Rabelais, the emphasis is on a potential for transformation in language which is consonant with creativity.

The idea of transformation is also helpful in explaining the persistent prominence of improvisation in vulgar comedy. The commedia dell'arte, of course, was essentially improvised: the actors, all specialists in their characters, embroidered on the scenario selected for the performance, both inventing and introducing favorite set speeches and comic turns or *lazzi* as they went. But improvisation has been a conspicuous aspect of *buffo* from the time of the comic devils who frisked among the spectators at medieval mystery plays and the Elizabethan plays whose texts, despite Hamlet's complaints, have blanks left to indicate improvisation, to the Marx Brothers and the ad-libbing actors and comics of our time. (In the contemporary theater and on television, to their disgrace, improvisation or "breaks" are frequently rehearsed.) Improvisation in the theater has a peculiar excitement of its own, a small element of which may be the suspense as to whether the actor will succeed or fail, but which mostly centers on the happy delight we feel at almost anything he manages to do under these circumstances. The pleasure of improvisation consists, first, in seeing broken down the conventions which held the actor to a limited space or to a predetermined text, and, second, in seeing him invent — "wing it," as they say in the American theater. In this exercise we have a small model of transformation, a paradigm of convention yielding to creativity.

Finally, the idea of transformation helps us to understand the frequent dimension of peril in vulgar comedy. A world in which an inexhaustible creativity is unpredictably revealed is also, because of the unpredictability, perilous. The makers of vulgar comedy have always known this, from the earliest mime in which the thieving slave was surprised and beaten by his master to the innocent-looking street corner puddle which proves to be a pit for Oliver Hardy. The world of *buffo* is a world seething with potential for disaster: simple flirtations have a way of ending with the would-be seducer hiding in a chest or pretending to be a spirit from the deep; the preparation of a meal can easily lead to the destruction of a house; a game of golf may well result in a riot. Yet this peril is somehow not a source of distress. Harold Lloyd, though he dangles from the flagpole and the hand of the clock for what seems an interminable period, never falls; if Oliver Hardy does fall from the airplane, he always lands in an obliging haystack. The *buffo* gestalt in part assures us that there is no real danger; the conventions of the form will not allow it. But we are moved to exhilaration by these perils for an even better reason. In vulgar comedy we understand, I believe, that if the world is infinitely variable it is also infinitely perilous. Accordingly, the representation of unpredictable peril in vulgar comedy implies the broader power of inexhaustible creativity. In the one we find the other, and in this way peril becomes yet another variant on the theme of transformation.

The fact of peril, however, is symptomatic of yet one other important feature of *buffo* in that its presence, like the presence — in the earliest work, especially — of ugliness, grotesqueness, violence, and cruelty, serves in some measure to temper what could otherwise be a soft, facile picture of the world. *Buffo* prompts us to a sense of mas-

tery, but grounds this sense in a series of casual, unpreten-
tious contrasts between agents for and against life, attractive and unattractive. The presence of peril enables us to
see clearly what was implicit in the ugliness and violence
touched on earlier: though *buffo* always resides in simplified, stylized, and hence somewhat sentimental images
of the world, it also has a peculiar tough-mindedness. In
the earliest work, especially, it accommodates a good deal
of the gritty reality of life in monstrous masks, deformity,
beatings, and pain; two extreme examples are Antonio Bar-
zizza's *La Cauteriaria* (ca. 1450), in which Scintilla's genitals are actually branded, and Angelo Beolco's *Bilora* (ca.
1527), in which the old seducer is not just beaten but is
killed. Usually, however, the grotesque masks of the commedia actors, the hunchbacks and blind men of medieval
farce (fig. 13), and the beatings met everywhere until the
eighteenth century are not sufficient to disturb the process
of celebration: rather, they ballast what might otherwise be
too insubstantial, give authority to what might easily seem
arbitrary. Buffo's intensity would be impossible without
this authority.

The authority of literature and drama proceeds
largely from what we accept as an honest and faithful
rendering of the facts of experience as we know them, the
version of the world which the writer has given us. As a
result, we acquiesce in the process of his work: we think
and feel about his world largely as he wants us to think and
feel. This authority has little to do with mathematical or
scientific proofs and even less with revealed religion. As in
mathematics or science, we must see before we believe,
but to believe we need not see the sort of evidence we see
in mathematics or science. Literature and drama serve
their creators. They present assertions about human life
which might be called "truths," though they are in no way
susceptible to the tests of truth usual in science or logic.
They are, rather, assertions about human life which have
been deeply felt to be true, but which also have the undeniable effect of consoling the very writers who feel them

deeply and who have invented a means of expressing them.

Recent criticism has tended to lose sight of the many ways in which literature and drama please. In its determination to explain how books "mean" — that is, how they teach, solve social problems, and render every novelty of thought and feeling which has floated up through the chaos of modern sensibility, it has severely limited the idea of pleasure, reducing it to what in the eighteenth century were called "graces" in a work — artfulness and technical skill. So narrow a view is clearly inadequate to explain that substantial part of our literary and dramatic heritage which, in addition to teaching and pleasing through its formal graces, also pleases because it is reassuring and consoling.

Hegel says of tragedy that it reconciles the individual sufferer to his condition by referring him to the general structure of life, which is itself affirmative or hopeful. I would revise this to say that tragedy presents images of the fundamental, irremediable insecurity of human life in such a way as to show that this insecurity is in some measure good because it is indispensable to the creation of values which give human life grandeur. Viewed in this way, tragedy is more than a vision of life: it is a kind of exercise in reconciliation, a celebration of what men have long felt to be a crucial "truth" about the structure or process of human experience. It is pleasurable because it brings us face to face with the grimmest facts — pain, failure, death — and then, without distorting them, empties them of bitterness. It does involve a profound statement about the relation between suffering and certain of the values we prize most in human experience, and in particular places, at particular times, for particular people, this is a true statement in the sense that it withstands the test of experience. But it would surely be wrong to say that it is true for all people at all times. If suffering sometimes produces courage, perseverance, or greatness of spirit, it sometimes produces meanness, cowardice, and dehumanizing despair. Tragedy celebrates the first "truth" but ignores the second. It has been highly valued by so many generations because it satisfies a deep need, but it can also be seen as an exercise in consolation, a consolation which may involve self-deception.

Generic descriptions of both tragedy and comedy have been severely hampered because, at least since Plato's *Symposium,* they have usually been viewed either as opposites, obverse sides of the same coin, or as complementary modes existing on a single scale and inevitably shading into each other at some point. These metaphors rest on the doubtful assumption that, beneath all the accidentals, tragic and comic works are enough like each other to illuminate each other through comparison and contrast. It is just as likely, it seems to me, that tragedy and comedy are quite separate creations, highly valued because they fill deeply felt needs, but sharing no more with each other than they share with epic, satire, tragicomedy, and melodrama. Each might be thought of as existing on a scale or plane of its own, operating by its own laws and processes, a peculiar exercise in its own right. Viewed this way, they resemble each other to the extent that they are all literary or dramatic modes of expression governed by the general purpose of teaching and pleasing; they differ in that they use different literary and dramatic means and teach and please in different ways. The characteristic form of each genre treats a special "truth" or "truths" and provides a distinctive reassurance or consolation.

If we can say, then, that the pleasure of tragedy lies in its power to affirm the value of suffering, to reconcile us to life for a brief time by celebrating a positive feature of the structure of painful experience, we might say that the pleasure of comedy consists in its power to affirm the sufficiency of the individual in the world. Hegel is again useful here as a point of departure: in his *Philosophy of Fine Art* (IV, 301–2) he argues that comedy characteristically moves us to a sense of "infinite self-assuredness," "infinite geniality and confidence." The phrases are very general, it is true, and, in fact, comedy, unlike tragedy, is probably too various to be usefully described in any single phrase: its sub-types have been so fully articulated that they resist a single category. Yet surely self-assurance is a notable part of our response to a satirical comedy, which indicts and ridicules, but which chiefly celebrates the quality of mind which indicts and ridicules — the critical intelligence which stands aloof, analyzing, judging, and enjoying the spectacle of human folly. And just as surely self-assurance is a part of our response to a comedy of manners, which holds society up to view, in part to define its standards and to ridicule and criticize its failures, but chiefly to celebrate the highly sophisticated sensibility which enjoys the comedy of human attempts to create value through social conventions. In both these comic sub-types the sufficiency of the individual — the sufficiency of personal resources for confronting the menaces of the world — is affirmed, though to stress the affirmation too strenuously is to lose sight of the important differences between the two.

Certainly a description of comedy which subsumes its many pleasures in the general pleasure of self-assurance will easily accommodate vulgar comedy. *Buffo*, the dominant quality of vulgar comedy, as noted earlier, consists in a sense of mastery, a tonic intuition that we are in control, invulnerable, because we have been led to perceive, in the world and in ourselves, fresh, unexpected sources of creativity and vitality. It has none of the poise, complexity, or ironic self-awareness of our responses to satirical comedy or comedies of manners, or, for that matter, to Romantic or festive comedy or sentimental comedy; its sense of mastery is not primarily the product of intelligence or sensibility. But what it lacks in subtlety and delicacy, it makes up in intensity. Further, it has in common with other comic sub-genres, and indeed with all literary and dramatic genres, major and minor, that the articulation of its "truth," the generation of its peculiar pleasure, is also, finally, an exercise in consolation. It has lasted so long, survived so many cultural revolutions, because it has so long supplied what men wanted and desperately needed. Its intensity is the correlative of the depth of the need filled, and there has probably always been a strain of hysteria in it because of the "cheekiness" of its affirmation. Superiority! Confidence! Sovereignty! Self-assurance! Mastery! As Baudelaire says of laughter, it is satanic and a little bit mad because, like many unfortunates in asylums, it is a little bit drunk on pride and delusion.

Finally, even *buffo*'s peculiarly optimistic view of creativity and fecundity is arbitrary. As Santayana has argued in his beautiful essay "Carnival" (*Soliloquies in England, and Later Soliloquies*, pp. 418–23), to become aware of the infinite creativity of existence is to become aware of the absurdity underlying this life which matters so much to us. It is to become aware that whatever form or situation has come into being could just as easily have been any of a million others, that it is the result of a principle so remote from human control as to be virtually an accident. It insists that a particular life is, in the profoundest sense of the term, a dream, a dream which has happened but which has no better excuse for being than the infinite number of other dreams that might have been formed in the chaos of our existential night. To be aware of this, to know only that, despite the odds against it, this particular dream of a life *has* happened should stimulate great compassion for the life which surrounds us. Yet *buffo*, though it is grounded in this sense, insists on a good deal that runs counter to it. Infinite creativity and fecundity are operating in a frame which is absurd, but operating to man's advantage. Existence is a fount of creativity, *and* (and the addition is crucial) that creativity will save us. *Buffo* struggles to promote all that is healthful and joyful; it opposes and ultimately suppresses all that stands against human life.

8

Buffo *Forever!*

The value of *buffo* to Western man is to
be seen most simply and clearly in the fact that it is found
virtually everywhere in European drama. From the first
impersonations of which we have records down to this very
week on Broadway or in the West End of London, in times
of theatrical flowering and of decay — wherever there is
theater, there is vulgar comedy. Of course historians of
drama have frequently viewed its popularity as a sign of
dramatic decadence, and, in fact, even at moments of the
greatest cultural trauma, when apathy has overtaken the
other theatrical genres, it has flourished. But surely its
resilience can just as easily be interpreted as a proof of its
health. Like a robust country cousin, vulgar comedy simply
survives all plagues. Its dramatic and theatrical forms and
materials have undergone progressive modification, but its
essential power and vision persist with very little change.

A thorough survey of this long, complicated story
would be impossible within the limits of this study. Indeed, I have largely restricted my attention to Italy, England, and France because to try to do more would be a

little like trying to write a short history of the world. Yet even within these limits the sheer number of vulgar comedies is sufficient to discourage the most industrious encyclopedist. My purpose, accordingly, will be to see what can be learned about *buffo* from a synoptic history of its expressive means in the three countries.

In Italy, as we have seen, vulgar comedy made its initial appearance in ancient Rome, where it flourished in the mime, the *atellanae,* and the work of Plautus and Terence. It then disappeared until the high Middle Ages, when it reappeared first in primitive farces, *mariazi,* and *bruscelli,* then in the work of the humanists of the fifteenth century. The period of greatest fecundity in Italy followed in the next century, both in short, popular plays and in the longer, so-called Learned Comedies. The short, popular pieces were for the most part the work of writers like Angelo Beolco of Padua, Antonio Caracciolo of Naples, Anton Francesco Grazzini of Florence, Giovan Giorgio Alione of Asti, and Andrea Calmo of Venice. Much of it was performed either by local semi-professional troupes (as in Siena and Padua) or by the so-called societies of youth (as in Asti), typically on carnival occasions. The Learned Comedy of such late humanists as Machiavelli, Aretino, and Ariosto, on the other hand, was rarely performed. In the last three decades of the sixteenth century the first commedia troupes emerged, performing virtually everything everywhere. The only texts which survive from this period, unfortunately, are the scenarios preserved in Flaminio Scala's *Teatro delle Favole Rappresentative* (1611) and a dozen or so manuscript collections.

Following this extensive production, vulgar comedy has had an unbroken history in Italy, largely in the dialect traditions still in evidence today, but there has been little to compare with the sustained richness of the Renaissance. Seventeenth-century taste was limited to Spanish comedy, especially in Naples, and to further work by the commedia companies, which were by then performing as often in France as in Italy; the eighteenth century produced little more except for the outstanding achievement of Carlo Goldoni. Apart from the substantial portion of Goldoni's work which can be described as vulgar comedy (much of it in Venetian dialect) and the work of such nineteenth-century imitators as Paolo Ferrari, the story from then on is chiefly to be found in the recent dialect traditions.

By contrast, vulgar comedy in England began rather slowly and unimpressively. It emerged during the sixteenth century in the work of John Heywood, the anonymous writers of the jigs, and Plautine imitators like Nicholas Udall and persisted into the next century in the jigs and drolls and as subsidiary actions in full-scale plays. It did not make its way to England's main stages, however, until the end of that century, when Restoration imitations of French and Italian farces suddenly became popular. Thereafter, its history is rich and unbroken. In the eighteenth century examples range from full-length, five-act farces to short afterpieces, and include much of the work of David Garrick, Samuel Foote, Henry Carey, George Colman, and Arthur Murphy, as well as burlesques and the pantomimes of John Rich and his competitors. In the nineteenth century it continued to be abundant, if not so distinguished; the most notable work is that of H. J. Byron in the middle decades, the highly important plays of A. W. Pinero and H. A. Jones later, and the pantomimes, soon to become the Christmas pantomimes.

In France the picture is different. An important body of vulgar comedy developed very early in the medieval farces, and the current of *buffo* has run broad and deep since then. By the fifteenth century the production and probably most of the writing of the farces was undertaken by the *sociétés joyeuses,* usually performing on mystery stages not in use or on booth stages during the period before Lent or at the summer festivals (see fig. 16). By the mid-sixteenth century touring professional entertainers began to appear, and students became prominent in the experiments in humanistic comedy led by Marc-Antoine Muret and George Buchanan at the College of Boncourt and

16. Farce on a booth stage. Detail of *A Village Fête*, attributed to Pieter Breugel the Younger, Fitzwilliam Museum, Cambridge.

Étienne Jodelle and Jacques Grévin at the College of Beauvais. Although the total production of these academic writers probably did not exceed a dozen plays, the plays proved to be highly important in France, as their analogues did elsewhere, because they fed the work of Plautus and of the so-called Learned Comedy of Italy into the popular stream and because, by the end of the century, they became the models for professional playwrights like Alexandre Hardy. By 1600 this largely literary stream of influence complemented the continued production of farces by the *sociétés* and small professional troupes, and after 1620 the popular vein was sustained at the Hôtel de Bourgogne by the famous *farceurs* Turlupin, Gros-Guillaume, Gaultier Garguille, and Bruscambille (see fig. 14), and on the Pont Neuf by Tabarin. Tabarin was succeeded by the equally famous Jodelet, who was finally hired by Molière and cast in *Les Précieuses Ridicules* ("The Affected Ladies," 1658).

We can gather from an early Molière play like *La Jalousie du barbouillé* ("The Jealousy of Flour-Face," ca. 1650) — despite the problem of authorship — something of the state of vulgar comedy as he inherited it, and from a play like *Le Mariage forcé* (1664) something of his mastery of the form. Certainly the best work of the seventeenth century can be traced to those parts of Molière's production which can fairly be described as vulgar comedy, though the visiting Italian companies were solidly established in Paris during the middle decades of the century and their plays also represented much of the best to be seen. Indeed, upon Molière's death the tradition of *buffo* was largely sustained by the Italians (until their companies disbanded in 1697) and by the short Crispin plays of Raymond Poisson. There followed several decades of confusion in which *buffo* survived chiefly in diluted form in the plays of Jean-François Regnard (1655–1709), Alain-René Lesage (1668–1747), and Florent Carton Dancourt (1661–1725). It reappeared only with the establishment of Luigi Riccoboni's Nouvelle Troupe Italienne in 1716.

The drift of vulgar comedy away from France's main stages in the late seventeenth century was completed about 1750, when the fairs at Saint-Germain and Saint-Laurent became the centers for its production. Bitterly resented by the Comédie Française, the performers at the fairs and Riccoboni's Italians flourished for a time, but finally, under steady pressure, they were either absorbed by the new Opéra Comique (founded in 1762) or driven to the new theaters on the boulevards. In the early nineteenth-century boulevard theaters the partly musical *comédies à vaudeville* and *comédies à ariettes,* both staples at the fairs, yielded to the form known simply as *vaudevilles,* ultimately modified by Eugène Scribe and Eugène Labiche to *comédie-vaudeville.* This became the definitive form of the important boulevard comedy of the second half of the nineteenth and the twentieth centuries and comprehends, to name only the most important, the production of Georges Feydeau and Georges Courteline. It continued in the plays of Sacha Guitry and Marcel Achard. Moreover, the rowdier comedy of the fairs has never disappeared: a collection like Jean Variot's *Théâtre de tradition populaire* (1942) attests to its continued survival, until recently at any rate, on French provincial stages.

◇ ◇ ◇

The main defect of this historical outline is that important features of *buffo* cannot be accommodated to a scheme of dramatic continuities. I have omitted to mention, for example, those great entertainers who were not so much actors associated with theaters and plays as clowns and comics. Yet performers like the celebrated carnival entertainers Zan Polo and Cimador of sixteenth-century Venice, the English pantomimists John Rich in the eighteenth century and the famous Joseph Grimaldi in the nineteenth, music hall comics like Grock, and circus clowns like the Fratellini brothers in the present century are solidly in the tradition of *buffo.* Though their ephem-

eral skits and *lazzi* come down to us largely through reports, what we know of them accords perfectly with *buffo*
principles.

But the defects of the simplicity of the outline are
outweighed by the fact that we can range freely over the
details of this picture and trace in its highlighted contours
the main variations on the norms. Like everything else,
buffo was tempered and conditioned by time and cultural
shifts and was tinkered with and modified by successive
generations of writers and actors. Ultimately, of course,
these modifications, however marginal, create important
alterations in its power and vision.

A good many of the changes were technical, the result of the efforts of writers and actors to refine upon and
extend the expressive means which they had inherited.
Mistaken identity, deception, and disguise persisted as
the axes, or bases, for the structure of episodes designed to
present the standard materials. These structures comprise
a body of technical and material resources which writers
still draw upon. A play like Feydeau's *La Puce à l'oreille*,
with its look-alikes Poche and Chandebise, provides an
excellent, relatively recent example of mistaken identity;
Eugène Labiche and Alfred Delacour's *Célimare, le bien
aimé* ("Célimare the Beloved," 1863) and Feydeau's
Occupe-toi d'Amélie ("Keep an Eye on Emily," 1908) are
superior examples of ingeniously sustained deceptions.

Since the Renaissance, disguise has been handled
with increased sophistication. In Dovizi's *La Calandria*, a
brother and sister are disguised as each other to suggest
through the resulting sexual ambiguity a world on the
threshold of metamorphosis. Both Odet de Turnèbre's *Les
Contents* ("The Happy Ones," ca. 1577) and Garrick's *The
Irish Widow* (1772) bristle with disguises and confusion.
But by all odds the most ingenious and imaginative uses of
disguise are to be met in the work of Molière. To take two
brief examples: there are few moments in drama to compare with Sganarelle's scene in *Le Médecin volant* ("The
Flying Doctor," 1659) in which, pretending to be his own

twin brother, he manages first to play out a reconciliation with his "brother" to satisfy Gorgibus and then succeeds in kissing him/himself as Gorgibus looks on. Moreover, there is little to approach the quality of comic nightmare in the third act of *M. de Pourceaugnac* (1667), where Pourceaugnac, disguised as a woman, is, after many other losses, finally deprived of even his sex and identity. Among highly effective recent uses of disguise are that classic of the summer stock circuits *Charley's Aunt* (1892) and the film *Some Like It Hot* (1959).

However, playwrights did more than merely refine traditional techniques; they discovered new ones. As transformation became more popular, new ways of handling it were invented. Some time in the sixteenth century the use of magicians and magic in plays like Ariosto's *Il Negromante* (1520) brought forth the magic garden, a magical locale which might also be a grotto or a den or a wood and in which everything became subject to a law of miraculous change. Perhaps in part inspired by the pastoral, our best examples are commedia scenarios like *L'Arbore incantato* ("The Magic Wood," ca. 1600), *L'Arcadia incantata* ("The Enchanted Arcadia," ca. 1630), and *Il Creduto Principe* ("The Impostor Prince," ca. 1630). The first abounds in enchanted apples and metamorphoses of all kinds; in the second the entire world of the play is magical: trees burst into flames and Pollicinella becomes, with the help of a magician, the king of Arcadia. In *Il Creduto Principe* a wood near the prince's palace is inhabited by a magician who transforms the individuals who pass through it, most notably Trivellino, into the absent prince.

But the magic garden is probably less important in its own right than as the probable point of departure for a long series of related developments. Its suitability for scrambling and unscrambling identities and relationships makes it but a short step to scenes at night, usually in gardens, in which everyone gets lost and relationships get tangled and then untangled in a way almost magical. These night scenes, so popular in seventeenth-century drama, are much in evidence in the commedia scenarios and continued to be popular — as the magic garden did not — into the eighteenth and nineteenth centuries. A scenario like *Le Burle d'Isabella* ("The Ruses of Isabella," ca. 1600) is fairly typical: it contains three young women and a full complement of lovers and rivals. In the concluding night scene Isabella works a trick which, helped by darkness, so confuses matters that everyone seems about to marry the wrong person, though in fact both the confusion and darkness prove fortunate in that they lead to the matings desired. In *La Commedia in commedia* ("A Play within a Play," ca. 1610) and *Il Finto Marito* ("The Imposter Husband," ca. 1615), extraordinary complications are sorted out under the metamorphic auspices of night. Among later plays, the final act of Molière's *Georges Dandin* (1668) is notable because it does not use the confusion created by darkness to lead to new sexual pairings but to defeat the Old Man (the rustic husband, Dandin) and thus to confirm the pairings set up at the beginning. The scene from Aphra Behn's *Emperor of the Moon* (1684) in which Harlequin and Scaramouche grope about in the dark, each mistaking the other for an object, does not provide a resolution at all but a kind of metamorphic grace note in an action steeped in other evidences of magic. For the most part, however, the night scenes in eighteenth-century plays and especially in English pantomines of the eighteenth and nineteenth centuries serve chiefly to intensify confusion and then supply a magical resolution: to reorder the life of the play and thus suggest a world in the throes of transformation.

Moreover, the magic garden and, more particularly, the physical changes worked by the presiding magician seem to foreshadow the mechanical transformations met everywhere in the English pantomines. Consisting largely of ingenious uses of stage machinery and trick costumes, these tours de force date, at the latest, from the final, highly spectacular scene of *Emperor of the Moon* and probably owe a good deal to certain *lazzi* of commedia actors, but they did not become important until the first half of the eighteenth century, when the competition between the English companies giving pantomines reached extremes of mechanical absurdity. The action of *Harlequin Sorcerer* (1725), John Rich's most famous pantomine, consists simply of Harlequin's efforts to elope with Columbine in the face of the obstacles created by her father, Pantaloon, and the scenes turn for the most part on Harlequin's successive transformations. At one point he comes in as an ostrich, then reverts to himself and runs off with Columbine; in another scene he turns into a washerwoman and douses his pursuers with suds; in still another he is the horseman on an equestrian statue which is being unveiled. With its prolonged contention between young and old and its scene toward the end in which Harlequin is carried off by devils, the work is a clear example of the familiar ritual contents taking the new form of literal, mechanically contrived metamorphoses.

But other examples are no less clear and interesting. *Harlequin, Doctor Faustus* (1733), the most successful work of Rich's competitors at Drury Lane, lacks the usual wooing action as the frame but embraces a series of spectacular marvels. *Harlequin and Mother Goose* (1805), perhaps the most successful pantomine of all time and long the vehicle of the great Joseph Grimaldi, and *The House That Jack Built* (1824), another very successful work, illustrate the structural strategy which became standard in the nineteenth century, that of placing a harlequinade within the main action and then carrying that action forward in terms of commedia surrogates for its characters. In *The House That Jack Built* Jack has to build a house in the forest by sunset in order to win his beloved. He succeeds, but when he claims Rosebud from her father, Gaffer Gandy refuses to give her up because he has determined to marry her to Squire Sap. During that wedding, however, Venus sends Cupid to cast a spell over everything, and Jack is changed into Harlequin, Rosebud into Columbine, Gaffer into Pantaloon, Squire Sap into the lover, and the priest into the clown. Then follows a series of dream-like scenes: a winter skating scene in Hyde Park, a scene in Kew Gardens on a May morning, and a scene featuring an excursion to Paris in a balloon. Finally, of course, the dream world is returned to the reality of Jack and Rosebud, and they are united.

The predilection of the writers of pantomine for such loosely orchestrated, rather abstract actions is easy to understand: to create situations which would support tours de force of mechanical transformation they were driven to the loose probabilities of fantasy and then back, by a kind of reverse principle of concretization, to the ritual-like combats, paradigmatic wooings, and archetypal cast. The pantomines reveal with unusual clarity the relevance of these ostensibly trivial marvels to the dramatic actions which frame them and, more broadly, the essential consonance between transformation, whether literal or figurative, and the unexpected fecundity emphasized by *buffo*.

The final development of the magic garden was the use made in the eighteenth century and later of the inn or hotel as a kind of carnival fun house in which identities and relationships become so mixed up that the world seems dominated by a diabolical law of disorder. On the face of it, the magic garden or its variants appear to have little to do with inns or hotels, yet by the middle of the eighteenth century, at about the time of Carlo Goldoni's *L'Osteria della posta* ("The Post Inn," 1761), inns become, as the magic garden and its variants had earlier, a setting for metamorphic confusion and a reordering of the world of the play. Although the transformation is always figurative, in this hurly-burly of rapid comings and goings and atmosphere of compounded error the sense that the world has been cut loose from its moorings can be acute. In the short and relatively simple *L'Osteria della posta,* for example, a young woman engaged to marry a young man she has never met flees the city and stops at an inn. There, by chance, she meets her fiancé, who is equally frightened of the match, traveling in the opposite direction. The young man withholds his identity, and when another suitor unexpectedly arrives, mistakes and confusions multiply, but in the end the almost magical result is resolution of all difficulties and the wedding which the two young people had feared. Goldoni used this strategy frequently, and his full-length plays, like *Il Servitore di due padroni* ("The Servant of Two Masters," 1745), show its potential.

For the most skillful uses of the inn or hotel as magic garden, however, we must look to the boulevard comedy of late nineteenth-century France. In the work of Labiche, Feydeau, and their confreres — particularly in that of Feydeau — the hotel setting is used as a kind of alembic which brings confusion to a rolling boil and then distills a resolution. In *L'Hôtel du libre échange* ("The Hotel of Free Exchange," 1894), written with Maurice Desvallières, or *La Puce á l'oreille*, or *Le Dindon* ("The Dupe," 1896), everything moves toward a long, climactic scene in which all the characters find themselves in the same hotel, some by chance, some by assignation, and some in pursuit of the others. Feydeau's inventiveness and skill in creating intricate, frenzied complication and generating a pressurized state of hilarity in such scenes is unequaled. The Hôtel Ultimus, the Hôtel Minet Galant, the Hôtel du Libre Échange, or, to move to the court farces of the same period in England, the Hotel des Princes in Pinero's *The Magistrate* (1885) or the deanery in his *Dandy Dick* seem remote from the magic wood of *Il Creduto Principe,* but they are essentially the same place and they are put to essentially the same use: a state of metamorphic confusion is created by concentrating a cluster of intrigues in a single locale and then, as everyone scrambles to escape, effecting a mass "discovery."

Many benchmarks of the earlier and simpler vulgar comedy persist in these sophisticated elaborations. Some or all members of the archetypal cast can be recognized in the contending husbands, wives, and lovers and especially in such Pantalone figures as Putzeboum from *Occupe-toi d'Amélie* or Célimare from *Célimare, le bien aimé* or Pos-

ket from *The Magistrate*. There is a surprising recurrence
of physical deformity in Camille's serious speech defect in
La Puce à l'oreille and Mme Pinchard's deafness in *Le
Dindon*. Perhaps the most useful play from the period for
illustrating survivals and continuities is one of those anonymous works put on by traveling companies at the turn of
the century in France and preserved in Variot's collection,
entitled *Gonsalve, ou l'auberge plein* ("Gonsalve, or the
Inn with the Full House"). Here, in addition to the strategy
of the magic inn, we find a marvelous use of disguise by the
wife, who, pursuing Gonsalve in the manner of Lent pursuing Carnival, successively persuades him that she is a
tyrannical male traveler, the King, the Queen, and last a
woman about to give birth. Like the best of the plays
which use transformation, this work conveys a sense
not only that the world is teetering on the brink of
metamorphosis, but that life is fundamentally a rather
grotesque, zany dream which will somehow turn out well.
This quality is also strong in plays like Charles Johnson's
The Cobbler of Preston (1716) — a version of the Christ-
opher Sly story from *The Taming of the Shrew* — and
L'Herbe d'erreur ("The Magic Greenery") and *Les Ren-
contres imprévus* ("Unexpected Encounters"), both plays
from Variot's collection. *L'Herbe d'erreur,* in fact, combines a magic wood and numerous literal transformations
with an ingenious elaboration of the combat between a
husband-Carnival figure and a tyrannical wife-Lent.

Altogether, the enlarged repertory of techniques for
handling transformation accounts for the majority of purely
technical changes in vulgar comedy from the Renaissance
to the present, almost as if the writers and actors had
agreed that transformation was, after all, the basic issue,
and hence the most fruitful for experimentation. Other
traditional materials were not neglected, however. Human
nature's stubbornness and unresponsiveness to discipline
and training was a favorite subject in antiquity and was
brilliantly portrayed, in the shape of hungry slaves, amoral
parasites, doltish students, and lustful old men. By the late

Renaissance the stupid Bucco of the *atellanae* had become the Gros-Guillaume of the Hôtel de Bourgogne and Robert Cox as Simpleton eating away slowly and silently at his very large piece of bread. The hungry Dossenus had taken the form of insatiable servants like Leccardo of Andrea Calmo's *Il Saltuzza* ("The Jumper," ca. 1540) and, later, Truffaldino of *Il Servitore di due padroni* and Galopin of *La Farce de l'aiguille* ("The Farce of the Needle," another Variot text). The unteachable students of Herodes' third mime had become the rebellious cut-ups of Braca's *Della Scola* and *De la Maestra* (ca. 1585); the old wooers of the *phlyax* farces had become the old Amerigo of Anton Francesco Grazzini's *Il Frate* (1540) and the old Josse of Grévin's *Les Ébahis*. All the variations on physical deformity and grotesqueness — blindness, deafness, gout, and obesity — represent ingenious, sometimes brilliant developments of the traditional material.

The one clear innovation in handling this aspect of human nature was the use made of objects to express it. Perhaps the best illustration of this relatively recent technique is the well-known *lazzo* in which the comic tries to free himself from a piece of flypaper. But by the late nineteenth century the malice of the object was evident in a variety of actions emphasizing things: scenes built around drawers which will not pull out or motors which will not start resonate with a sense of an inveterate perversity in things, the profound indifference of the physical world to the needs and aims of men. American film comedies of the twenties and thirties abound in the technique, in all the ladders and scaffolds which inevitably bring Laurel and Hardy down into fresh cement, all the banana peels, errant cakes of soap, and tricky window ledges which enable gravity to prevail or threaten to prevail over Chaplin or Harold Lloyd. My favorite example is the Variot text entitled *Le Mariage de Pantalon,* in which the furniture in the play, like Grock's famous piano stool, simply keeps collapsing for no reason other than to suggest that the world is like that.

Only one of the technical innovations unrelated to either transformation or intractability is important enough to deserve mention; it is the use made of monomania. We see something of monomania as a spring for action in earlier plays which turn on miserliness, where it is always inextricable from the figure of the Old Man ripe for destruction. It does not occur with any frequency, however, until the eighteenth and nineteenth centuries in plays like Johann Nestroy's *Der Zerrissene* ("A Man Full of Nothing," 1844), in which Lips' Byronic apathy works like a tyranny. By this time the monomania is not always found in an Old Man, yet the operative principle continues unchanged: it is a kind of artificial authority, like the Old Man, and like him, according to the logic of *buffo*, it is destroyed.

Taken together, at any rate, these modifications in the materials are largely technical and can best be explained as efforts made by writers and actors to extend and refine upon the expressive means which they inherited.

◇　◇　◇

The remaining changes in the traditional materials are better explained in cultural terms, though inevitably they too have a technical dimension. The defeat of the Old Man, which, over all, seems closest to the oldest ritual paradigm, continues to be prominent in those limp television family comedies which regularly scale the father down to the level of a grateful moron, like William Bendix's Riley in *The Life of Riley*, or Dagwood Bumstead, but the distance between this figure and the crusty, often dangerous Senex of Plautus or the Pantalone of the commedia plays is a measure of the gradual softening which has occurred not only here but in all these materials. In Rome, the Middle Ages, and the Renaissance the Old Man was an active figure, a canny schemer like Plautus' pimp Lycus in the *Poenulus,* or a frisky wooer like Lysidimus, who spends much of the *Casina* trying to lay hands on a sixteen-year-old slave girl; moreover, he was vindictive and could be cruel. By the eighteenth century he had lost not only his aggressiveness but also his toughmindedness and vitality. Rarely a wooer (and if he was, he was seldom prompted to the role by lust), he became a father or an uncle who created obstacles for the young because he disagreed with them but who had their best interests, not his own, at heart. He was troublesome but harmless, like Old Whittle, Mrs. Brady's docile old wooer in Garrick's *The Irish Widow,* or old Goodall in Fielding's *The Intriguing Chambermaid* (1734), an eighteenth-century version of the *Mostellaria.* By the nineteenth century this god of the dying year and king of carnival had become an amusing eccentric, like Posket in Pinero's *The Magistrate* or M. Perrichon in Labiche and Edouard Martin's *Le Voyage de M. Perrichon* (1860). It is this figure which largely survives into the present century, though there is one striking exception: Sheridan Whiteside of George S. Kaufman and Moss Hart's *The Man Who Came to Dinner* (1939). Whiteside is not only old, or at any rate not young, but formidable in intelligence and withal fairly vicious; moreover, like his ritual ancestor, he has been disabled and then cured (only to be disabled again at the end), appropriately at Christmas time.

The gradual softening of *buffo* in the late seventeenth, eighteenth, and nineteenth centuries probably reflects the principal cultural movements in the West during those centuries: the Age of Reason with its humanitarianism and sentimentalism, the Romantic revolution with its implications for individual sensitivity and political egalitarianism, all the sense and sensibility and *sturm und drang* of these centuries. The tendency was to soften, to eliminate, or to conceal the violence, brutality, and ugliness of earlier comedies in favor of a more polite exterior. The Old Man and other authority figures were made more genteel and less menacing, and their defeats were gradually altered to look less like defeats than reasonable compromises. Where the old husband Messer Nicia of Machiavelli's *Mandragola* (ca. 1515) is actually beaten and cuckolded, his nineteenth-century counterparts, Charles Moore in Benjamin Nottingham Webster's *A Novel Expedient* (1852) or M. Vatelin from *Le Dindon*, are merely embarrassed. Where the dramatic metaphors for the death and restoration of the Old Man retain some vestige of their violent origins in Dovizi's *La Calandria* or Edward Ravencroft's *The Anatomist* (1696), in both of which the old men pose as corpses, by the nineteenth century — except for curious survivals like the girls in Pinero's *Dandy Dick* who refer to their father as "the waxworks" or the later reprise already noted in *The Man Who Came to Dinner* — even the metaphors had largely disappeared.

During these centuries vulgar comedy, to revert to a convenient metaphor, gradually lost the harsh, rather terrifying features of the early demonic masks — longest retained in the commedia dell'arte — and acquired the snowy beard and plump cheeks of a kindly Santa Claus. The wily Harlequin becomes the will o'the wisp Pierrot; the funny but frequently unpleasant Capitano Spavento dell'Vall'Inferno becomes the docile Captain Kootoo of H. J. Byron's *The Old Story* (1861); the lovers who, in earlier versions, were often determined on adultery become young innocents with nothing more serious than marriage in mind. The combats which earlier involved elements of violence and danger and which were always in deadly earnest become increasingly harmless as the opposition between male and female or youth and age pits innocent wives against stern but kindly husbands, as in Pinero's *The Cabinet Minister* (1890) or mischievous children against officious but malleable parents, as in H. A. Jones' *The Maneuvers of Jane* (1898).

The wooing actions, though they gain in intensity as they become more and more technically complex, are tempered by sentimental values. In the very popular play by H. J. Byron, *Our Boys* (1875), the complication grows out of the fact that the boys choose girls of whom their fathers do not approve and then defy them, not with machinations and deceits, as a Roman or Renaissance youth would have done, but by moving out and attempting to support themselves. After a good many misunderstandings, in which it seems to the fathers that their sons are living in sin in London, it is explained that the boys harbor only honorable intentions toward the girls and have the deepest affection for their fathers. However insipid it may be, *Our Boys* illustrates the ground that has been covered since Argante and Géronte were used and abused by Scapin in the name of youth and love: its ingredients are essentially those of *Les Fourberies de Scapin* ("The Rogueries of Scapin," 1671), but here roguery has been replaced by innocent misunderstanding, aggressive wiliness and even vindictiveness by idealistic stubbornness. The play is scarcely typical of the best work to be found at the end of the nineteenth century, and clearly it has none of the brilliance of Feydeau, Labiche, or Pinero, but it exemplifies, as better plays do not, the extent to which *buffo* by that time had been tempered by sentimentality.

But sentimentality is merely the most conspicuous of the modifications worked in *buffo* by the changing cultural ambience. As *buffo* became softer and tamer, it also became more moral. With the exception of French boulevard farce of the late nineteenth century, very little work after the early eighteenth century deals with adultery or with deceptions which result in anybody's being permanently deceived. Instead of actions designed primarily to generate an uncritical exhilaration, we find actions which serve satiric and didactic purposes. In a play like Garrick's *Bon-Ton, or High Life above Stairs* (1775), we find adultery, but only as the principal vice into which the corrupt sophisticates of the play have fallen. Sir John Trotely, a country squire who describes himself at the end as "a knight-errant [dedicated] to [rescuing] distressed damsels from those monsters, foreign vices and *Bon-ton*, as they call it," spends the whole play surprising Lord and Lady Minikin,

Miss Tittup, and Colonel Tivy in a variety of depravities, practiced in part under cover of those standard features of *buffo* a masquerade and a night scene; at the end Sir John drives the men away and whisks the women off to the country with him. Despite its resemblances to vulgar comedy, the bulk of the content here is shaped by a satiric purpose, and the whole becomes almost a parody of the heroic folk model. This King of May does battle not with an anti-life monster but with false sophistication, and not for the sake of marriage or sexual union or any of the usual signs of fecundity but for the sake of social probity. In other words, morality, which had been largely irrelevant to a happy outcome in earlier work, has now become a sign of health. To take one further example: in George Colman's *The Deuce Is in Him* (1763) there is a male-female combat in Colonel Tamper's attempt to test Emily's affection and Emily's strategy for revenge, and there is a quite elaborate deception in Emily's assumption of a disguise with which to taunt Tamper with a rival, but all this is intended not to generate a sense of mastery but primarily to teach a lesson. Tamper is "wounded" and "cured," it is true, but only in the sense that he learns not to trifle with Emily's affections or to doubt her.

For all their glorification of critical intelligence and their dedication to man as he is, the sons of the Age of Reason and the Romantic revolution were not inclined to celebrate a healthy grossness in the world. They understood *buffo* and valued it, but apparently felt that it should be more civilized than it had been — more decorous, more respectful of father, family, country, and money.

One of the most interesting culturally related modifications in *buffo*, in fact, is the sudden appearance of money as a decisive social factor in the work of the late seventeenth century. Plautus was the first to make money an issue in vulgar comedy: his characters want it and need it to live, and in his plays it becomes a sign of health, of what must be possessed if life is to proceed as it should. In the Middle Ages and the Renaissance, however, the issues of sex, food, supremacy, intractability, and transformation took its place as dominant themes. In the seventeenth century it reappeared in vulgar comedy — it had been a serious issue for some time, of course, in the satirical comedy of Jonson and Middleton — and became an important sign of power, perhaps the clearest indication that its possessor was adequately endowed with the means of life. It is such a sign in Molière, notably in *Les Fourberies de Scapin* and in *L'Avare,* his version of Plautus' *Aulularia* ("The Pot of Gold"); by the eighteenth century, and especially in England, it had become an unquestioned good, the object of infinite scheming and the crowning reward for being young, virtuous, and in love. Henry Carey's *The Contrivances* (1715) turns on a standard wooing action which sets Arethusa and Rovewell, whose problem is that he appears to be penniless, against her father, Argus, who wants to marry her to the wealthy Squire Cuckoo, and it contains the usual collection of deceptions and disguises, a scene in which Argus, the Old Man, is beaten, bound, and gagged, and even a scene of "miraculous" revelations. The one new element is the prominence given to money, first the obstacle to the lovers and then their glorious legacy: in the world of the play youth, love, and health are proved to be in the ascendant in part by the fact that the young lovers ultimately have money in abundance.

Artistically, *The Contrivances* is no better or worse than dozens of other plays which reflect an unconscious acceptance of money as both *primum mobile* and symbol of success, plays like Henry Fielding's *The Intriguing Chambermaid* and *The Lottery,* Garrick's *The Irish Widow* and *The Lying Valet* (1741), or, in the nineteenth century, H. J. Byron's *Not Such a Fool as He Looks* (1869) and Pinero's *The Cabinet Minister.* In all these plays vitality, fertility, and health are affirmed by financial settlements and the social position and security which they make possible. Money does not replace success in love, the defeat of the Old Man, or the celebration of a nature which is apparently fecund because it is intractable or is seething with a potential for metamorphosis. These materials and the cognate structural principle of generating a frenzy continue to dominate, but money as a sign of health enters the picture during the seventeenth century and remains into the twentieth.

What is remarkable is that while money persisted as an unquestioned good in the work of this period, the society responsible for it was more and more often characterized as an enemy. Society as an abstract force was simply not an issue in the plays of the Middle Ages and Renaissance, nor, for that matter, in Plautus. Even in the seventeenth, eighteenth, and nineteenth centuries it was never as important in vulgar comedy as in comedies of manners or satirical comedies. But by the time of Arthur Murphy's *The Apprentice* (1756) it had taken a place in vulgar comedy alongside the crusty old fathers and obnoxious suitors as a notable inhibitor of life. Despite the fun made of stage-struck youngsters in *The Apprentice,* the dramatic interest centers chiefly on Dick Wingate's struggles against society in the form of the apprentice system and the sacred cow of filial duty. By the time of Pinero's *The Cabinet Minister,* society as a collection of empty forms and shallow observances had virtually become a menace to life. It gradually came to be seen as a source of authority distinct from the authority figures which had long opposed vitality and creativeness. Often, of course, the combat is extremely civil, as in *The Cabinet Minister;* deeper brutalities and deeper joys, if they exist, are decorously concealed by drawing room conventions.

The story of *buffo* in the centuries following the Renaissance, then, presents a curious commentary on Western culture; compared with histories and studies of scientific progress, political movements, the rise and fall of ideas, and the intricate picture of changing sensibility, it is remarkably simple, almost a child's commentary. As a cultural critique it emphasizes that Western society since the Renaissance has tended to conceal from itself what had earlier been felt to be the basic issues in life. The Old Man, who had been a specific husband, father, or old wooer — a difficult, resilient, frequently ugly and even dangerous figure who had to be fought and sometimes even destroyed — gradually became a well-intentioned, rather foolish benefactor or even disappeared altogether. In earlier work the basic condition of life had been conflict — combat between husband and wife, young and old, strong and weak — but now it took on the appearance of a romantic escapade, a flight from unpleasantness into the airy remoteness of a harlequinade or the thrilling confusion of a magic garden, inn, or hotel. In earlier work ugliness, grotesqueness, violence, and pain were facts to be faced and assimilated into a vision of the world renewing itself, but now they disappeared or became so encrusted with polite metaphors as to be scarcely noticeable. The signs of success had been food, sex, supremacy, or the many proofs that nature was fermenting according to principles of its own, prompting combats, resisting preordained forms; now it increasingly took the form of compromises, agreements, acquiescences, financial settlements when the problem was, as it increasingly was, financial, slight adjustments in judgment when the conflict proceeded from conflicts of interest. *Buffo* had changed: the grotesque, rather terrifying demonic mask of the carnival rites and commedia actors had come to resemble a living human face, both more ambiguous and less alive.

◇   ◇   ◇

Yet despite these changes, the mask has persisted, and the differences between early *buffo* and *buffo* after the Renaissance are less important than the similarities. For all its surface politeness the boulevard comedy of late nineteenth-century France and plays from England, America, and Italy like Brandon Thomas' *Charley's Aunt* (1892), Joseph Kesselring's *Arsenic and Old Lace* (1941), and Aldo de Benedetti's *Due Dozzine di rose scarlatte*

("Two Dozen Red Roses," 1936) are also dizzying exercises in exhilaration. Although they have touches of the softness discussed above, they retain still more of the characteristic vitality of *buffo*.

Perhaps the most striking fact in the long history of *buffo* is that the social, political, and artistic revolutions of the last centuries have touched it very little. It has been qualified by them, but only as the act of making love has been qualified by them. History has made marginal differences in the great needs which lead men and women to it and marginal differences in the solace which they take from it; but at bottom it has changed nothing.

The American film comedies of the twenties and thirties furnish a case in point. After centuries during which the tradition of *buffo* in its pure form was left largely to clowns, Punch and Judy, and provincial troupes so obscure that we can now scarcely find any trace of them, the archetypal cast and the standard materials of vulgar comedy reappeared suddenly and brilliantly in the silent films of Chaplin, Buster Keaton, Harry Langdon, Charlie Chase, Laurel and Hardy, and the Keystone Cops, almost as if to demonstrate that they had really been there all along. In the extensive production of these masters, the whole repertory of *buffo* again came into play: the Old Man was real and nasty, the combats were fierce, the perils were many, and the world was perpetually young and seething with energy. In an age of unparalleled materialism, they added a new antagonist to those which the hero traditionally faces. Cars, furniture, houses, logs arranged in mountainous piles, goods of any kind in abundance and arranged neatly — all these they destroyed with an unconscious, almost innocent dedication. One of the classics in this vein is the short film with Laurel and Hardy entitled *Big Business* (1929), in which, as Christmas tree salesmen, the two run afoul of a hostile customer and systematically destroy his house and grounds as he, in turn, destroys their automobile. That is all there is to the film: a simple, straightforward combat of an order of purity which recalls the medieval French farces, but with the difference that it is things which are now the objects of the destructive frenzy. The particular fondness for demolishing cars — in virtually all the Keystone Cops films, in Laurel and Hardy's *Two Tars* (1928) (see fig. 17), and in Chaplin's *The Floorwalker* (1916) — was prophetic of the monstrous importance which they would take on in the postwar world.

Still more recently in the theater of Samuel Beckett, Eugène Ionesco, Michel de Ghelderode, and their followers there have been what some critics describe as deliberate attempts to reconstitute *buffo* traditions in serious dramatic forms. According to Jan Kott in his *Shakespeare Our Contemporary,* who is perhaps the most influential of these critics, the combination of ugliness, grotesqueness, and absurdity found in what he calls "buffoonery" became in Beckett's hands the basis for a tragicomic vision of life, an irrational "philosophy of the viscera" made up, in essence, of contempt. In this work a revolutionary fusion has been effected, these critics believe, between the exuberance of *buffo* and the bitterness and despair of the middle of the twentieth century.

The whole question is extremely complicated. It is true that much of this drama uses elements from vulgar comedy; we need only recall Beckett's clown-like characters and their music hall *lazzi* in *Waiting for Godot* and Ionesco's treatment of intractability in *La Leçon* ("The Lesson"), the male-female combat in *Délire à deux* ("Frenzy for Two"), and the transformation in *La Cantatrice chauve* ("The Bald Soprano"), *Amédée,* and *Rhinoceros.* Yet it is also not difficult to see that in this work the traditional materials are handled in a different way. Certainly the world of *Rhinoceros* seethes with a potential for transformation, and it is funny, exhilarating, grotesque, *and* rather terrifying. But if the metamorphic power of "rhinoceritis" is the hope of the future, the solution to the narrow, dishonest, sloppy bourgeois world of Bérenger, its values are limited and it demands barbaric conformity. In other words, transformation is an ambiguous

17. The modern contention with things. Scene from Stan Laurel and Oliver Hardy, *Two Tars*, 1929.

issue in this play, as it is not in the countless *buffo* vehicles where it flourishes simply as something in nature which will save us.

None of this work, in fact, is shaped by the artistic principles which govern *buffo*. Despite Kott's claims for the viscera, these playwrights and their followers are all highly sophisticated craftsmen committed to the familiar route of artistic innovation through a rediscovery of primitive forms. As Cleanth Brooks explained some years ago in his *Modern Poetry and the Tradition* (pp. 69–109), this style of literary revolution returns to early, elementary, ostensibly naive forms on the assumption that in them there is health and vigor. This particular theatrical revolution fixes on the primitive materials and forms of the *buffo* tradition; indeed, in some of the extreme experiments of the free-form enthusiasts — in some of the work of the Open Theatre in New York City, for example — it fixes on the folk models which lie behind that tradition. But the use of these materials and forms is studied, almost dilettantish; the plays tell us nothing of *buffo* except by showing us what it is not.

Jean-Claude Van Itallie's *Motel*, from *America Hurrah* (1966), for example, is in most outward respects a conventional *buffo* exercise in the destruction of the Old Man, in this case the Old Woman. It is set in a tawdry motel room into which a grotesquely padded young man and young woman, both wearing outsized masks, are ushered by a sweet old proprietor, also masked and heavily padded. As the landlady rehearses the advantages of her motel, the young couple brutally destroy everything in the bedroom and the adjoining bathroom, then finally turn on the proprietor and dismember her, revealing a dummy.

All this could be fun: it recalls the ritual destruction of the carnival dummy for Lent, and it has such supportive elements as masks, the assault on things, and the victory of youth over age. But of course it is not fun at all; *Motel* is a terrifying play, and it is intended to be. Van Itallie has recapitulated a *buffo* paradigm, but in a key so gratingly

discordant that whatever it retains of traditional meanings
and qualities can only reverberate distantly and ironically
in this atmosphere of horror. Despite its debt to the *buffo*
tradition, *Motel*, like most of the work of this highly important movement, is neither primitive, nor coarse, in my
sense of that word, nor endowed with the simple vigor
usually associated with literary and theatrical beginnings.
It is a self-conscious exercise in desperation, a bitter celebration of age and exhaustion.

Most of modern drama, like most of modern literature, has sought to discover new ways to push out the
frontiers of self-awareness. Modern playwrights are no
longer interested in the consolations of tragedy or the re-
invigorations of comedy or the self-improvement which
comes of testing scrupulously articulated moralities —
at any rate, these are not their main interests. Modern
drama attempts to generate in the beholder an increased
sense of the self and of the conditions of its life, a
heightened consciousness of what it is to be human now, to
ask questions and fail to find final answers, to seek unity
and find only fragments, and to contemplate one's self in a
chaotic arrangement of mirrors. The most characteristic,
most pervasive effect of modern drama is to enrich self-
consciousness and, as it enriches it, to celebrate it as the
main asset left to us — perhaps the only one. Just as earlier
times sanctified heroism and love and social elegance and
moral sensibility, our century has canonized self-
consciousness, and literature, as usual, provides the
liturgy.

In the story of *buffo* this effort has produced the kind
of adaptation that we find in Beckett and Ionesco and
earlier in Alfred Jarry and even in Chekhov. It consists,
very generally, of an attempt to assimilate the resources of
buffo in a wider experience of the self. The results may
well be applauded by sympathetic critics; they are often
quite magnificent. But all this has nothing to do with *buffo:*
it marks neither a revival nor a reconstitution. Where modern drama celebrates self-consciousness, *buffo* celebrates

instinctive vitality. Where modern drama emphasizes ambiguity, irony, and complexity, *buffo* stresses tonic exhilaration. Where modern drama moves toward philosophical and intellectual values, *buffo* focuses on gut-level reactions. Finally, these modern plays are in the fullest and perhaps even the best sense of the term sophisticated, while *buffo* is vulgar.

Primitive, instinctual arts survive even in this age of increasing self-consciousness — in music, in poetry, in fiction, in the plastic arts, and in drama. *Buffo* lives on — in the continued production of the classics of vulgar comedy, in occasional new plays on Broadway, in the boulevard theaters of Paris, or in the West End of London, in the dialect traditions still encountered in Italy, and in films — good ones, like *Some Like It Hot* or *Les Vacances de M. Hulot* ("M. Hulot's Holiday"), and mediocre ones, like the Totò films in Italy and others elsewhere. It requires, as always, a willingness to submit to what, to take the most cynical view of it, is probably an elaborate exercise in somewhat delusory consolation. In its long history it has probably had no discernible effect on the large contours of culture. But why not a little self-deception? Why not a little delusory consolation? The tradition of *buffo* is like a window through which we can look back on some part of the extremely rich human legacy of joy. And perhaps the most important discovery about that legacy is that a large part of it depends on a capacity to find joy whether the facts of life justify it or not. In this sense *buffo* is a gift, a gift from man to himself.

Appendix: Stages in the Development of Vulgar Comedy

Ritual Revels	Dramatic Rituals
Seasonal revels:	
DIONYSIAC FESTIVALS Lenaea (Jan.–Feb.), Anthesteria (Feb.–Mar.), City Dionysia (Mar.–Apr.), Rural Dionysia (Dec.–Jan.), etc.	processions (dances and games) lampoons *(ithyphalloi, phallophoroi, autokabdoloi,* etc.)
FESTIVALS TO ARTEMIS Elaphebolia (Mar.–Apr.)	
FESTIVALS TO APOLLO e.g., Thargelia (May–June)	
CALENDS OF JANUARY (Jan. 1–3)	processions (dances and games)
BACCHANALIA (dates unknown)	
FLORALIA (Apr. 28–May 3)	
SATURNALIA (Dec. 17–19 under Augustus; longer earlier and later)	scenario for *libertas decembris (rex saturnalis)*
ROMAN HARVEST AND PLANTING FESTIVALS	Fescennine verses
Carnivals:	
EPIPHANY (Jan. 6)	
PLOUGH MONDAY (Monday after Epiphany)	processions (dances and games); scenario for the festive king and/or queen
NEW YEAR'S (Mar. 25 until 16th–18th century)	
"CARNIVAL" (from Epiphany to Ash Wednesday, the first day of Lent, or 40 days before Easter, but especially the final Sunday, Monday, and Tuesday, the *jours gras*)	
MAY DAY (May 1)	
PENTECOST (Whitsuntide: 50 days after Easter)	
MIDSUMMER'S DAY (June 24; in southern Europe the Feast of St. John the Baptist)	scenario for the Feast of Fools; scenario for the Feast of the Boy Bishop
ST. NICHOLAS' DAY (Dec. 6, often until Christmas) or Holy Innocents' Day (Dec. 28)	
	processions (dances and games); serenades; *Armeggerie;* "Aller voir Mars"
Nuptial revels:	
especially at Epiphany, Valentine's Day (Feb. 14), New Year's Day, March 1, and May Day	

Dramatic Exercises	Emergent Plays	Fully Developed Comic Forms
comic agon *komos* beast mummeries	carnival plays	Dorian mime, *phlyakes*, satyr play Old Comedy (Middle Comedy and New Comedy)
saturae	(some part of Italian car- nival plays)	Roman mime (pan- tomime), *atellanae*, Plautine farce
monologs *contrasti; débats* soties Easter smacks *causes grasses* revue forms (Germany) sword dances morris dances	Italian carnival plays Plough Monday plays *Maggio;* St. George plays Robin Hood plays mummers' plays Bruscelli Maggio-mariazo English wooing play	Italian farce of the late 15th and 16th centuries (commedia dell'arte) interlude farces in Eng- land French farce of the 15th and 16th centuries, *Fastnachtspiele*

Bibliographical Commentary

Full publication information for works cited is given in the Selected Bibliography following this section.

Chapter 1

The key works for both the ritual backgrounds in antiquity and for the detail of what I have called the multi-staged evolution through dramatic ritual, dramatic exercise, emergent plays, and free-standing vulgar comedies are A. W. Pickard-Cambridge's *Dithyramb, Tragedy and Comedy* and *The Dramatic Festivals of Athens* and Allardyce Nicoll's *Masks, Mimes, and Miracles*. These books effectively assimilate the work of previous scholars and theorists. For other important accounts of the theory tracing drama to seasonal ritual, see also Gilbert Murray, *Five Stages of Greek Religion*; Jane Ellen Harrison, *Themis, a Study of the Social Origins of Greek Religion*; F. M. Cornford, *The Origins of Attic Comedy*; and Theodore Gaster, *Thespis; Ritual, Myth and Drama in the Ancient Near East*; as well as the monumental work of Sir James Frazer. For additional detail concerning the pre-dramatic and primitive dramatic evidence leading to the Dorian mime, the satyr play, the *phlyax* farces, Atellan farces, etc., see also Margarete Bieber's *The History of the Greek and Roman Theatre*; *Harper's Dictionary of Classical Literature and Antiquities*, edited by H. T. Peck; the three-volume *Dictionary of Greek and Roman Biography and Mythology*, edited by William Smith; M. Willson Disher's rather eccentric but useful *Clowns and Pantomimes*; and George E. Duckworth's *The Nature of Roman Comedy*. The best and almost the only source of evidence for the carnival drama in Greece is still the largely unassimilated work of the anthropologists R. M. Dawkins ("The Modern Carnival in Thrace") and A. J. B. Wace ("North Greek Festivals and the Worship of Dionysos" and "Mumming Plays in the Southern Balkans").

236

Chapters 2 and 3

Because of the wide divergences in custom and practice, assembling a complete calendar of rituals, rites, and ceremonies for the Middle Ages is probably impossible, but a reliable outline fixed on major feasts and major ritual observances can be constructed from handbooks and encyclopedias. For a general calendar I found the three-volume *British Calendar Customs*, edited by A. R. Wright and T. E. Lones, George Long's *The Folklore Calendar*, and Francis Xavier Weiser's *Handbook of Christian Feasts and Customs* very helpful.

Specialized works are indispensable for the study of a given locality. For Italy the key sources are the works of Paolo Toschi, most especially his *Le Origini del Teatro Italiano*. This work furnishes the clearest and most complete account of the basic scenario of carnival, the May festival, wooing rituals, and other ritual observances germane to this story. As support, Pietro Gori's *Le Feste Fiorentine attraverso i Secoli*, Alessandro d'Ancona's *Origini del Teatro Italiano*, and Vincenzo de Bartholomaeis' *Le Origini della Poesia Drammatica Italiana* are helpful. For references, discussions, and sometimes brief summaries of pre-dramatic and primitive dramatic pieces Toschi is again indispensable, but the works themselves, though rare, can be consulted in "Drammi Rusticali," volume 10 of *Teatro Italiano Antico*, edited by Giulio Ferrario; in d'Ancona, *Origini*; in Luigi Manzoni, *Il Libro di Carnevale dei Secoli XV e XVI* (for *contrasti*); in Curzio Mazzi, *La Congrega dei Rozzi di Siena*; in late nineteenth-century reprints edited by Giovanni Giannini, Knisella Farsetti, Nicola Zingarelli and Michele Vocino, Michele Scherillo, Vittorio Cian, Alfredo Bonaccorsi, Maria Azara, Bianca Maria Galanti, Luigi Manzoni; and in the originals mentioned in the text. The originals, like the reprints, are very rare, but all are in the Biblioteca Nazionale in Florence.

For France, Arnold van Gennep's *Manuel de folklore français contemporain* serves much the function of Toschi's work, providing extensive discussions of general and local festive customs and important references to and sometimes brief summaries of pre-dramatic evidence. Less helpful but occasionally useful are Louis Morin's *Carnavals parisiens*; Gustave Cohen's *Le Théâtre en France au Moyen Âge: Le Théâtre profane*; Victor Fournel's *Tableau du vieux Paris: Les Spectacles populaires et les artistes des rues*; Louis Petit de Julleville's *Histoire du théâtre en France: Les Comédiens en France au Moyen Âge*; and Joachim Rolland's *Théâtre comique en France avant le XVe siècle*. Texts of pre-dramatic and primitive pieces are scarce for France, but in addition to summaries in Van Gennep, they are found in *Ancien théâtre français*, edited by M. Viollet le Duc; in *Choix de farces, soties, et moralités des XVe et XVIe siècles*, edited by Émile Mabille; in *Recueil de farces, moralités et sermons joyeux*, edited by Le Roux de Lincy and Francisque Michel; in *Recueil de poésies françaises des XVe et XVIe siècles*, edited by Anatole de Montaiglon and James de Rothschild; in *Le Recueil Trepperel*, edited by Halina Lewicka; in *Le Théâtre français avant la Renaissance*, edited by Edouard Fournier; and in *Recueil des pièces rares et facétieuses, anciennes et modernes . . .* , edited by Charles Brunet.

For accounts of the ritual backgrounds in England, the key works are E. K. Chambers' *The Medieval Stage* and *The English Folk-Play* and Charles Reade Baskervill's "Dramatic Aspects of Medieval Folk Festivals in England." Texts of pre-dramatic and emergent pieces are chiefly to be found in *The English Folk-Play*, Baskervill's *The Elizabethan Jig* and "Mummers' Wooing Plays in England," R. J. E. Tiddy's *The Mummer's Plays*, and Disher's *Clowns and Pantomimes*. For further detail concerning backgrounds and continuity in England, the books by Nicoll and Disher, already mentioned, are especially useful.

For Germany no comprehensive work which pulls the backgrounds together is known to me. Most useful are the work of Walter French, *Medieval Civilization as Illustrated by the Fastnachtspiele of Hans Sachs*; Eckehard Catholy, *Das Fastnachtspiel des Spätmittelalters*; George Lussky, "The Structure of Hans Sachs' Fastnachtspiele in Relation to Their Place of Performance"; M. J. Rudwin, *The Origin of German Carnival Comedy*; and S. L. Sumberg, *Nuremberg Schembart Carnival*. The chief source of early plays and playlets is Adelbert von Keller's four-volume collection of *Fastnachtspiele*.

The best accounts of the companies of fools in Italy and France are to be found in Toschi, *Origini*, and H. G. Harvey's *The Theatre of the Basoche*; texts of French pieces can be found in Harvey and in Martial d'Auvergne's *Les Arrêts d'amour*.

Chapter 4

Tangential support for the theory advanced here can be found in the works of Pickard-Cambridge, Nicoll, and Toschi already cited. Fragmentary analogous treatments of the transition of materials from ritual to dramatic status can be found in Toschi, *Origini*, in his discussions of the progression of carnival figures into the commedia dell'arte; in Maurice Sand, *Les Masques et bouffons de la comédie italienne*, the source for the theory that the commedia characters derived from the Atellan farces; and in Harvey's *Theatre of the Basoche*, which takes up the development of the work of that company of fools. Especially useful on the progress of commedia materials in England, a later phase in the transitions at issue, is M. Willson Disher's rather uneven *Clowns and Pantomimes* and Leo Hughes' *A Century of English Farce*.

Chapter 5

Most of the theory and attempted classification in this chapter is original, as far as I know, but similar, if unrelated, attempts to classify the components of vulgar comedy, or some part of it, are to be found in Alan E. Knight, "The Medieval Theater of the Absurd"; Pietro Toldo, "Études sur le théâtre comique français du Moyen Age"; Eugène François Lintilhac, *Histoire générale du théâtre en France*; Barbara Bowen, *Les Characteristiques essentielles de la farce française et leur survivance dans les années 1550–1620*; Ian Maxwell, *French Farce and John Heywood*; and Eckehard Catholy, *Das Fastnachtspiel des Spätmittelalters*. Highly useful on the subject of transformation is the chapter on that subject in Disher's *Clowns and Pantomimes*.

Chapter 6

On the backgrounds of Plautine comedy see Nicoll, Bieber, and Duckworth, as well as Alfred Körte's *Hellenistic Poetry*, translated by Jacob Hammer and Moses Hadas. These backgrounds are taken up with particular attention to Plautus in Gilbert Norwood's *Plautus and Terence* and Erich Segal's *Roman Laughter*. Also useful as criticism of Plautus are Ettore Paratore's "L'Arte Plautina," Raffaelle Perna's *L'Originalità di Plauto*, and Barthélémy Taladoire's *Essai sur le comique de Plaute*.

238

Chapter 7

The theorists important here are explicitly cited within the text of the chapter. For earlier and different attempts to circumscribe this kind of comedy, see Gustave Lanson, "Molière et la farce"; Barbara Bowen, *Les Characteristiques essentielles de la farce française et leur survivance dans les années 1550–1620*; G. K. Chesterton, "A Defense of Farce"; Barbara Cannings, "Toward a Definition of Farce as a Literary 'Genre' "; Robert Metcalf Smith, *Types of Farce-Comedy*; Robert C. Stephenson, "Farce as Method"; and V. Meyerhold, "Farce."

Chapter 8

A more detailed picture of the history of vulgar comedy in the countries studied in this chapter can be obtained from a variety of general and specialized studies. For Italy I have found the following most helpful: Douglas Radcliff-Umstead, *The Birth of Modern Comedy in Renaissance Italy*; Carlo Grabher, *Ruzzante*; Anton Giulio Bragaglia, *Storia del Teatro Popolare Romano*; Katherine M. Lea, *Italian Popular Comedy*; Vito Pandolfi, *La Commedia dell'Arte*; Alessandro d'Ancona, *Origini del Teatro Italiano*; Vincenzo de Bartholomaeis, *Le Origini della Poesia Drammatica Italiana*; and Joseph Kennard, *The Italian Theatre*.

For France, the following studies are useful: Barbara Bowen, *Les Characteristiques essentielles de la farce française et leur survivance dans les années 1550–1620*; Gustave Cohen, *Le Théâtre en France au Moyen Âge: Le théâtre profane*; G. Doutrepont, *Les Acteurs masqués et enfarinés du XVIe siècle au XVIIe siècle en France*; Edmond Faral, *Les Jongleurs en France*; Victor Fournel, *Tableau du vieux Paris: Les spectacles populaires et les artistes des rues*; Grace Frank, *Medieval French Drama*; Brian Jeffrey, *French Renaissance Comedy, 1552–1630*; H. C. Lancaster, *A History of French Dramatic Literature in the Seventeenth Century*; Ian Maxwell, *French Farce and John Heywood*; A. P. Moore, *The Genre Poissard and the French Stage of the Eighteenth Century*; Louis Petit de Julleville, *Histoire du théâtre en France: Les comédiens en France au Moyen Âge*; Joachim Rolland, *Théâtre comique en France avant le XVe siècle*; and Pierre Voltz, *La Comédie*.

For England, see C. L. Barber, *Shakespeare's Festive Comedy*; Charles Reade Baskervill, *The Elizabethan Jig*; E. K. Chambers, *The English Folk-Play*; M. Willson Disher, *Clowns and Pantomimes*; Ian Maxwell, *French Farce and John Heywood*; Allardyce Nicoll, *Masks, Mimes, and Miracles*; John Weaver, *The History of Mimes and Pantomimes*; and Enid Welsford, *The Fool: His Social and Literary History*.

Unfortunately, there is little on the technical history of vulgar comedy and nothing worth mentioning on disguise, mistaken identity, the magic garden, night scenes, and magic inns. By contrast, M. Willson Disher, in *Clowns and Pantomimes*, gives a good deal of attention to transformation. As far as I know there is nothing on the relations between vulgar comedy and culture.

Selected Bibliography

Texts

England

Beckett, Samuel. *Waiting for Godot*. New York, 1954.

Behn, Aphra. *Emperor of the Moon*. In *The Works of Aphra Behn*, vol. 3. Edited by Montague Summers. 6 vols. London, 1915.

Byron, Henry James. *Not Such a Fool As He Looks*. London, 1896.

———. *The Old Story*. London, 1861.

———. *Our Boys*. London, 1875.

Carey, Henry. *The Contrivances*. In *Supplement to Bell's British Theatre*, vol. 4. Edited by John Bell. 4 vols. London, 1784.

Churchill, Charles. *Rosciad*. In *The Poems of Charles Churchill*, vol. 1. Edited by James Laver. 2 vols. London, 1933.

Colman, George. *The Deuce Is in Him*. London, 1763.

de Cabham, Thomas. "Extract" from his *Penitential*. In E. K. Chambers, *The Medieval Stage*, vol. 2. 2 vols. London, 1903.

Fielding, Henry. *The Intriguing Chambermaid*. In *The Works of Henry Fielding*, vol. 3. Edited by J. P. Browne. 10 vols. London, 1871.

———. *The Lottery*. In *The Works of Henry Fielding*, vol. 2. Edited by J. P. Browne. 10 vols. London, 1871.

Garrick, David. *Bon-ton; or High Life above Stairs*. London, 1775.

———. *The Irish Widow*. London, 1772.

Heywood, John. *The Dramatic Writings of John Heywood*. London, 1905.

The Interlude of Jack Juggler. In *Anonymous Plays*, 3d ser. Edited by J. S. Farmer. London, 1906.

Johnson, Charles. *The Cobbler of Preston.* London, 1969.

Jones, Henry Arthur. *The Manuevers of Jane.* New York and London, 1905.

Jonson, Ben. *Ben Jonson.* Edited by C. H. Herford; Percy Simpson; and Evelyn Simpson. 11 vols. Oxford, 1925–52.

Manly, J. M., ed. *Specimens of the Pre-Shakesperean Drama.* 2 vols. Boston and London, 1900.

Marston, John. *The Works of John Marston.* Edited by A. H. Bullen. 3 vols. London, 1887.

Murphy, Arthur. *The Apprentice.* London, 1756.

Pinero, Sir Arthur Wing. *The Cabinet Minister.* London, 1892.

———. *Dandy Dick.* Boston, 1893.

———. *The Magistrate.* New York, 1892.

Ravenscroft, Edward. *The Anatomist.* London, 1807.

Shakespeare, William. *The Comedy of Errors.* Edited by R. A. Foakes. Cambridge, Mass., 1962.

Thersites. In *Six Anonymous Plays*, 1st ser. Edited by J. S. Farmer. London, 1905.

Thomas, Brandon. *Charley's Aunt.* New York and London, 1935.

Tom Tyler and His Wife. In *Six Anonymous Plays*, 2d ser. Edited by J. S. Farmer. London, 1906.

Udall, Nicholas. *Ralph Roister Doister.* Edited by Clarence Griffin Child. Boston, 1912.

Vitalis, Odericus. *The Ecclesiastical History of England and Normandy.* Bohn's Antiquarian Library, edited and translated by T. Forester. London, 1847.

Webster, Benjamin Nottingham. *A Novel Expedient.* In *Webster's Acting National Drama*, no. 189, vol. 17. London, 1837-ca. 1866.

Wycherly, William. *The Country Wife.* In *Complete Plays.* Edited by Gerald Weales. Garden City, N.Y., 1966.

Note: the following works contain rare texts and useful summaries of rare texts and/or of practices for which there are no fixed texts.

Baskervill, Charles Reade. *The Elizabethan Jig.* Chicago, 1929. (Contains texts of sixteenth- and seventeenth-century jigs.)

———. "Mummers' Wooing Plays in England." *Modern Philology* 21 (1924):225–72. (Contains texts of wooing plays.)

Chambers, E. K. *The English Folk-Play.* Oxford, 1933.

Disher, M. Willson. *Clowns and Pantomimes.* Boston and New York, 1925. (Contains summaries of eighteenth and nineteenth century pantomimes and *lazzi*.)

Tiddy, R. J. E. *The Mummers' Plays.* Oxford, 1923. (Contains texts of mummers' plays.)

Selected Bibliography

France

Ancien théâtre français. Edited by M. Viollet le Duc. 10 vols. Paris, 1854.

Choix de farces, soties, et moralités des XVe et XVIe siècles. Edited by Émile Mabille. 2 vols. Nice, 1872.

d'Auvergne, Martial. *Les Arrêts d'amour.* Anciens Textes Français, edited by Jean Rychner. Paris, 1951.

de Turnèbe, Odet. *Les Contents.* In *Ancien théâtre français*, vol. 7. Edited by M. Viollet le Duc. 10 vols. Paris, 1854.

du Bellay, Joachim. *Les Regrets.* Edited by Pierre Grimal. Paris, 1948.

Feydeau, Georges. *Théâtre complet.* 6 vols. Paris, 1948–52.

Gherardi, Evaristo, comp. *Le Théâtre italien de Gherardi, ou le recueil général de toutes les comédies et scènes françaises jouées par les comédiens italiens.* 6 vols. Amsterdam, 1701.

Grévin, Jacques. *Jacques Grévin: Théâtre complet.* Paris, 1922.

Ionesco, Eugène. *Amédée.* New York, 1958.

———. *La Cantatrice chauve.* Paris, 1954.

———. *Délire à deux.* Paris, 1966.

———. *La Leçon.* New York, 1958.

Jodelle, Étienne. *Eugène.* Edited by E. H. Balmas. Milan, 1955.

Labiche, Eugène. *Théâtre complet.* 10 vols. Paris, 1893–95.

Molière [Jean-Baptiste Poquelin]. *Oeuvres complètes.* Edited by Maurice Ray. 2 vols. Paris, 1956.

Recueil de farces, moralités et sermons joyeux. Edited by Antoine Jean Victor Le Roux de Lincy and Francisque Michel. 4 vols. Paris, 1837.

Recueil de pièces rares et facétieuses, anciennes et modernes. . . . Edited by Charles Brunet. 4 vols. Paris, 1872–73.

Recueil de poésies françaises des XVe et XVIe siècles. Edited by Anatole de Montaiglon and James de Rothschild. 13 vols. Paris, 1878.

Le Recueil Trepperel. Edited by Halina Lewicka. 2 vols. Paris, 1935.

Regnard, Jean-François. *Les Folies amoureuses.* In *Oeuvres complètes,* vol. 3. 6 vols. Paris, 1823.

Tabarin [Jean Salomon]. *Oeuvres complètes de Tabarin.* Edited by Gustave Aventin. 2 vols. Paris, 1858.

Le Théâtre français avant la Renaissance. Edited by Edouard Fournier. Paris, 1872.

Variot, Jean, ed. *Théâtre de tradition populaire.* Marseilles, 1942.

Note: the following works contain rare texts and useful summaries of rare texts and/or of practices for which there are no fixed texts.

Gennep, Arnold van. *Manuel de folklore français contemporain.* 8 vols. in 3. Paris, 1937–53.

Harvey, Howard Graham. *The Theatre of the Basoche.* Cambridge, Mass., 1941.

Selected Bibliography

Italy

Alighieri, Dante. *La Divina Commedia.* Introduction by A. Chiari, notes by G. G. Robuschi. Milan, 1965.

Alione, Giovan Giorgio. *Giovan Giorgio Alione: L'Opera Piacevole.* Edited by Enzo Bottasso. Bologna, 1953.

Andreini, Francesco. *Le Bravure del Capitano Spavento.* Venice, 1609.

Gli Amori di Belinda e Milene. Edited by Giovanni Giannini. Lucca, 1892.

Un' Antica Farsa Fiorentina. Edited by Fortunato Pintor. Florence, 1901.

Aretino, Pietro. *Teatro di Pietro Aretino.* Lanciano, 1914.

Barbi, Michele, comp. "Maggi della Montagna Pistoiese." *Archivo per lo Studio delle Tradizioni Popolari* 7 (1888):97–113.

Bartoli, Adolfo, comp. *Scenari Inediti della Commedia dell'Arte.* Florence, 1880.

Befanata Drammatica Profana: Scherzo Campagnolo, in *Befanate del Contado Toscano.* Edited by Knisella Farsetti. Florence, 1900.

Beolco, Angelo [Ruzzante]. *Teatro.* Edited by Ludovico Zorzi. Turin, 1967.

Boccaccio, Giovanni. *The Decameron.* Translated by Frances Winwar. New York, 1955.

Braca, Vincenzo. *Della Scola.* In *Il Teatro Italiano dei XIII, XIV, e XV Secoli.* Edited by Francesco Torraca. Florence, 1885.

Bruscello sulla Caccia. In *Quattro Bruscelli Senesi.* Edited by Knisella Farsetti. Florence, 1887.

Calmo, Andrea. *Il Saltuzza.* In *Commedie del Cinquecento,* vol. 2. Edited by Aldo Borlenghi. 2 vols. Milan, 1959.

Campani, Niccolò [Strascino]. *Il Coltellino.* In *Teatro Italiano Antico,* vol. 10. Edited by Giulio Ferrario. 10 vols. Milan, 1808–9.

———. *Strascino.* In *Commedie del Cinquecento,* vol. 2. Edited by Aldo Borlenghi. 2 vols. Milan, 1959.

La Canzone della Zeza. In *La Commedia dell'Arte in Italia.* Edited by Michele Scherillo. Turin, 1884.

Caro, Annibale. *Gli Straccioni.* In *Commedie del Cinquecento,* vol. 2. Edited by Nino Borsellino. 2 vols. Milan, 1967.

Cartaio, Silvestro [Fumoso]. *Batecchio, Commedia di Maggio.* Siena, n.d.

———. *Capotondo.* In *Commedie del Cinquecento,* vol. 2. Edited by Aldo Borlenghi. 2 vols. Milan, 1959.

———. *Panecchio, Commedia Nuova di Maggio.* Siena, n.d.

La Commedia de Più Frati. In *Le Rime di Bartolomeo Cavanico.* Edited by Vittorio Cian. Bologna, 1893.

La Condanna della Vecchiacia. In "Il Teatro delle Campagne Toscane." Edited by Alfredo Bonaccorsi. *Musica d'Oggi* 16, no. 2 (1934):52–54.

Il Contrasto di Brighinol e Tonin. Edited by Bruno Cotronei. *Giornale Storico della Letteratura Italiana* 36 (1900):315–24.

de Benedetti, Aldo. *Due Dozzine di Rose Scarlate.* Florence, 1969.

Selected Bibliography

Dovizi, Bernardo. *La Calandria*. In *Commedie del Cinquecento*, vol. 2. Edited by Nino Borsellino. 2 vols. Milan, 1967.

Farsetti, Knisella, comp. and ed. *Tutti i Trionfi, Carri, Mascherate e Canti Carnascialeschi Andati per Firenze*. Florence, 1900. (Originally published 1559.)

Goldoni, Carlo. *Tutte le Opere*. Edited by Giuseppe Ortolani. 14 vols. Milan, 1935–56.

Grazzini, Anton Francesco [Il Lasca]. *Commedie*. Florence, 1859.

Liberatione d'Amore: Commedia Pastorale di Maggio. Siena, 1606.

Lipparini, Giuseppe, ed. "Maggi e Nozze." *Primavera*, pp. 293–304. Milan, 1912.

Machiavelli, Niccolò. *Opere*. 8 vols. Milan, 1965.

Pandolfi, Vito, and Artese, Erminia, eds. *Teatro Goliardico dell'Umanesimo*. Milan, 1965.

"La Pricunta." In *Tradizioni Popolari della Gallura*. Edited by Maria Azara. Rome, 1943.

Il Processo e la Condanna d'Arlecchino. In Bianca Maria Galanti, *La Danza della Spada in Italia*. Rome, 1942.

La Ragazza Canzonata. In *Quattro Bruscelli Senesi*. Edited by Knisella Farsetti. Florence, 1887.

La Rappresentazione e Festa di Carnasciale et della Quaresima. In *Libro di Carnevale dei Secoli XV e XVI*. Edited by Luigi Manzoni. Bologna, 1881.

La Ricevuta dell'Imperatore alla Cava. In Francesco Torraca, *Studi di Storia Letteraria Napoletana*. Livorno, 1884.

Roncaglia da Sarteano, Marcello. *Commedia Nuova: Pietà d'Amore*. Siena, 1606.

———. *Il Mogliazzo tra Borgo e Lisa, Commedia Nova Rusticale*. Siena, 1514.

Rondone e Rosalba. In *Teatro Popolare Lucchese*. Edited by Giovanni Giannini. Turin and Palermo, 1895.

Scala, Flaminio. *Il Teatro delle Favole Rappresentative overo la Ricreatione Comica, Boscareccia e Tragica, Divisa in Cinquanta Giornate Composte da Flaminio Scala detto Flavio Comico*. Translated by Henry F. Salerno. New York, 1967. (First edition, Venice, 1611.)

Trinci, Francesco Mariano [Maniscalco]. *Comedia Bellissima contro Avaritia Intitolata Il Bichiere*. Siena, n.d.

Il Vignarolo e l'Ortolano. In *Apulia Fidelis*. Edited by Nicola Zingarelli and Michele Vocino. Milan, n.d.

Villani, Giovanni. *Cronica*. Compiled by F. G. Dragomanni. 4 vols. Florence, 1844–45.

Note: the following works contain rare texts and useful summaries of rare texts and/or of practices for which there are no fixed texts.

d'Ancona, Alessandro. *Origini del Teatro Italiano*. 2 vols. Turin, 1891.

"Drammi Rusticali." In *Teatro Italiano Antico*, vol. 10. Edited by Giulio Ferrario. 10 vols. Milan, 1808–9.

Herrick, Marvin. *Italian Comedy in the Renaissance*. Urbana, Ill., 1960.

Selected Bibliography

Lea, Katherine M. *Italian Popular Comedy: A Study in the Commedia dell'Arte, 1560–1620.* 2 vols. New York, 1934.

Manzoni, Luigi, comp. *Il Libro di Carnevale nei Secoli XV e XVI.* Bologna, 1881. (Contains texts of *contrasti.*)

Mazzi, Curzio. *La Congrega dei Rozzi di Siena.* Florence, 1882.

Pandolfi, Vito. *La Commedia dell'Arte.* 6 vols. Florence, 1957–61.

Sanesi, Ireneo. *La Commedia.* 2 vols. Milan, 1911–35.

Toschi, Paolo. *Le Origini del Teatro Italiano.* Turin, 1955.

Greece, Rome, Germany, and the United States

Aristophanes. *Complete Plays.* Edited and translated by Moses Hadas. New York, 1962.

Callot, Jacques. *I Balli di Sfessania.* In *Des Gesamte Werk*, vol. 1. Edited by Thomas Schröder. 2 vols. Munich, 1971.

Comedia Bile. In Ernst Beutler, "Die Comedia Bile, ein antiker Mimus bei dem Gauklern des 15 Jahrhundert." *Germanisch-Romanische Monatsschrift* 14 (1926):3–4.

Euripides. *Cyclops.* In *Three Greek Plays for the Theatre.* Edited and translated by Peter D. Arnott. Bloomington, Ind., 1961.

Fastnachtspiele aus dem Fünfzehnten Jahrhundert. Bibliotek des Litterarischen vereins in Stuttgart, vols. 28–30, 46. XLVI. Edited by Adelbert von Keller, 4 vols. Stuttgart, 1853–58.

Herodes. *Herodes, Cercidas and the Greek Choliambic Poets.* Loeb Classical Library. Edited and translated by A. D. Knox. London, 1929.

Horatius Flaccus, Quintus. *Satires, Epistles and Ars Poetica.* Loeb Classical Library. Translated by H. Rushton Fairclough. London, 1929.

Juvenal, Junius. *Juvenal and Persius.* Rev. ed. Loeb Classical Library. Translated by G. G. Ramsay. Cambridge, Mass., 1950.

Kaufman, George S., and Hart, Moss. *The Man Who Came to Dinner.* In *Six Plays by Kaufman and Hart.* New York, 1942.

Kesselring, Joseph. *Arsenic and Old Lace.* New York, 1941.

Livius, Titus. *Titus Livius: Works.* Loeb Classical Library. Translated by B. O. Foster. 14 vols. London, 1919–59.

Menander. *The Bad-Tempered Man (Dyskolos).* Translated by Philip Vellacott. New York and London, 1960.

———. *The Principal Fragments.* Loeb Classical Library. Translated by Francis G. Allinson. London, 1921.

Murray, John, and Boretz, Allen. *Room Service.* New York, 1937.

Plautus, Titus Maccius. *Plautus: Works.* Loeb Classical Library. Translated by Paul Nixon. 5 vols. New York and London, 1916–38.

Sachs, Hans. *Hans Sachs.* Bibliotek des Litterarischen vereins in Stuttgart. Edited by Adelbert von Keller and A. Goetz. Vols. 125, 159, 173, 181, 188, 195. Tübingen, 1870–1908.

Selected Bibliography

Sophocles. *Ichneutae*. Edited and translated by Richard Johnson Walker. London, 1919.

Tacitus, Cornelius. *Cornelius Tacitus: Works*. Loeb Classical Library. Translated by Maurice Hutton. Cambridge, Mass., 1932.

Van Itallie, Jean-Claude. *America Hurrah*. New York, 1967.

Vergilius Maro, Publius. *Georgics*. In *Vergilius Maro: Works*. Loeb Classical Library. Translated by H. Rushton Fairclough. 2 vols. Cambridge, Mass., 1934–35.

General and Specialized Studies

Allen, P. S. "The Medieval Mimus." *Modern Philology* 5 (1908):436–44; 7 (1910):328–44; 8 (1910):1–60.

Apollonio, Mario. *Storia della Commedia dell'Arte*. Rome and Milan, 1930.

Aristotle. *The Poetics*. In *Aristotle's Theory of Poetry and Fine Arts*. Translated by S. H. Butcher (1894), edited by John Gassner. New York, 1951.

Bain, Alexander. *The Emotions and the Will*. London, 1888.

———. *The Senses and the Intellect*. London, 1868.

Barber, C. L. *Shakespeare's Festive Comedy*. Princeton, N.J., 1959.

Baskervill, Charles Reade. "Dramatic Aspects of Medieval Folk Festivals in England." *Studies in Philology* 17 (1920): 19–92.

———. *The Elizabethan Jig*. Chicago, 1929.

———. "Mummers' Wooing Plays in England." *Modern Philology* 21 (1924):225–72.

Baudelaire, Charles. "On the Essence of Laughter." In *The Mirror of Art*. Edited and translated by Jonathan Mayne. London, 1955. (Originally published 1885.)

Beerbohm, Max, "Laughter." *And Even Now*. New York, 1921.

Bentley, Eric. "The Psychology of Farce." In *Let's Get a Divorce! and Other Plays*. Edited by Eric Bentley. New York, 1958.

Bergson, Henri. *Le Rire, essai sur la signification du comique*. Paris, 1904.

Bieber, Margarete. *The History of the Greek and Roman Theatre*. Princeton, N.J., 1939.

Bowen, Barbara. *Les Characteristiques essentielles de la farce française et leur survivance dans les années 1550–1620*. Illinois Studies in Language and Literature. Urbana, Ill., 1964.

Bragaglia, Anton Giulio. *Storia del Teatro Popolare Romano*. Rome, 1958.

British Calendar Customs. Edited by A. R. Wright and T. E. Lones. 3 vols. London, 1936.

Broadbent, R. J. *A History of Pantomime*. London, 1901.

Brooks, Cleanth. *Modern Poetry and the Tradition*. Chapel Hill, N.C., 1939.

Bullough, Edward. "Psychical Distance as a Factor in Art and an Aesthetic Principle." *British Journal of Psychology* 5 (1912):87–98.

Cannings, Barbara. "Toward a Definition of Farce as a Literary 'Genre.' " *Modern Language Review* 56 (1961):558–60.

Casson, Lionel. Introduction. *The Plays of Menander*. New York, 1971.

Catholy, Eckehard. *Das Fastnachtspiel des Spätmittelalters*. Tübingen, 1961.

Chambers, E. K. *The English Folk-Play*. Oxford, 1933.

———. *The Medieval Stage*. 2 vols. London, 1903.

Chesterton, G. K. "A Defense of Farce." *The Defendant*. London, 1901.

Cohen, Gustave. *Le Théâtre en France au Moyen Âge: Le Théâtre profane*. Paris, 1931.

Conacher, D. J. *Euripidean Drama: Myth, Theme and Structure*. Toronto, 1967.

Congreve, William. "Concerning Humour in Comedy." In *William Congreve: Letters and Documents*. Edited by John C. Hodges. New York, 1964.

Cornford, Francis M. *The Origins of Attic Comedy*. London, 1914.

Croce, Benedetto. *Poesia Popolare e Poesia d'Arte*. Bari, 1957.

d'Ancona, Alessandro. *Origini del Teatro Italiano*. 2 vols. Turin, 1891.

Dawkins, R. M. "The Modern Carnival in Thrace." *Journal of Hellenic Studies* 26 (1906):191–206.

de Bartholomaeis, Vincenzo. *Le Origini della Poesia Drammatica Italiana*. Bologna, 1924.

Dictionary of Greek and Roman Biography and Mythology. Edited by William Smith. 3 vols. London, 1844–49.

Disher, M. Willson. *Clowns and Pantomimes*. Boston and New York, 1925.

Doutrepont, G. *Les Acteurs masqués et enfarinés du XVIe siècle au XVIIe siècle en France*. Brussels, 1928.

Dryden, John. Preface. *An Evening's Love*. In *Dryden: The Dramatic Works*, vol. 2. Edited by Montague Summers. 6 vols. London, 1931–32. (Originally published 1668.)

Duckworth, George E. *The Nature of Roman Comedy*. Princeton, N.J., 1952.

Faral, Edmond. *Les Jongleurs en France*. Paris, 1910.

Feibleman, James. *In Praise of Comedy*. New York, 1939.

Flögel, K. F. *Geschichte des Grotesk-komischen*. 2 vols. Munich, 1914.

Fournel, Victor. *Tableau du vieux Paris: Les spectacles populaires et les artistes des rues*. Paris, 1863.

Frank, Grace. *Medieval French Drama*. Oxford, 1954.

Frazer, Sir James G. *The Golden Bough, A Study in Magic and Religion*. 12 vols. London, 1911–15.

French, Walter. "Medieval Civilization as Illustrated by the Fastnachtspiele of Hans Sachs." *Hesperia*, no. 15. Baltimore, 1925.

Freud, Sigmund. *Wit and Its Relations to the Unconscious*. In *The Basic Writings of Sigmund Freud*. Edited and translated by A. A. Brill. New York, 1938.

Galanti, Bianca Maria. *La Danza della Spada in Italia*. Rome, 1942.

Selected Bibliography

Gaster, Theodor Herzl. *Thespis; Ritual, Myth and Drama in the Ancient Near East.* New York, 1950.

Gennep, Arnold van. *Manuel de folklore français contemporain.* 8 vols. in 3. Paris, 1937–53.

————. *Les Rites de Passage.* Paris, 1909.

Gori, Pietro. *Le Feste Fiorentine attraverso i Secoli.* Florence, 1926.

Grabher, Carlo. *Ruzzante.* Milan, 1955.

Grant, Mary A. *The Ancient Rhetorical Theories of the Laughable.* Madison, Wis., 1924.

Grotjahn, Martin. *Beyond Laughter.* New York, 1957.

Harper's Dictionary of Classical Literature and Antiquities. Edited by H. T. Peck. New York, 1962.

Harrison, Jane Ellen. *Themis, A Study of the Social Origins of Greek Religion.* Cambridge, 1912.

Harvey, Howard Graham. *The Theatre of the Basoche.* Cambridge, Mass., 1941.

Hazlitt, William. *The Complete Works of William Hazlitt.* Edited by P. P. Howe, after the edition of A. R. Waller and Arnold Glover. 21 vols. London, 1930–34.

Hegel, G. W. F. *The Philosophy of Fine Art.* Translated by F. P. B. Osmaston. 4 vols. London, 1920.

Herrick, Marvin. *Italian Comedy in the Renaissance.* Urbana, Ill., 1960.

Hobbes, Thomas. "Leviathan" and "Tripos." In *English Works of Thomas Hobbes.* Edited by Sir William Molesworth. Vols. 3 and 4. 11 vols. London, 1838–45.

Hughes, Leo. *A Century of English Farce.* Princeton, N.J., 1956.

————. "The Early Career of 'Farce' in the Theatrical Vocabulary." *University of Texas Studies in English* 20 (1940):82–95.

Hurd, Richard. *On the Provinces of Drama.* In *The Works of Richard Hurd, Lord Bishop of Worcester*, vol. 2. 8 vols. New York, 1967. (Originally published 1763.)

Jeffrey, Brian. *French Renaissance Comedy, 1552–1630.* Oxford, 1970.

Kennard, Joseph S. *The Italian Theatre.* 2 vols. New York, 1932.

————. *Masks and Marionettes.* New York, 1935.

Kierkegaard, Soren. *Repetition.* Translated by Walter Lowrie. Princeton, N.J., 1941.

Kline, L. W. "The Psychology of Humor." *American Journal of Psychology* 18 (1907):421–41.

Knight, Alan E. "The Medieval Theater of the Absurd." *PMLA* 86 (1971):183–89.

Körte, Alfred. *Hellenistic Poetry.* Translated by Jacob Hammer and Moses Hadas. New York, 1929.

Kott, Jan. *Shakespeare Our Contemporary.* New York, 1966.

Kris, Ernst. *Psychoanalytic Explorations in Art.* New York, 1952.

Kronenberger, Louis. *The Thread of Laughter.* New York, 1952.

Lancaster, H. C. *A History of French Dramatic Literature in the Seventeenth Century*. 9 vols. Baltimore, 1929–42.

Langer, Susanne K. *Feeling and Form*. New York, 1953.

Lanson, Gustave. "Molière et la Farce." *Revue de Paris* 3 (1901):129–53.

Lea, Katherine M. *Italian Popular Comedy: A Study in the Commedia dell'Arte, 1560–1620*. 2 vols. New York, 1934.

Lewicka, Halina. *La Langue et le style du théâtre comique français des XVe et XVIe siècles*. Warsaw, 1960.

Lintilhac, Eugène François, *Histoire générale du théâtre en France*. 5 vols. Paris, 1904–10.

Long, George. *The Folklore Calendar*. London, 1930.

Ludovici, A. M. *The Secret of Laughter*. London, 1932.

Lumini, Apollo. *Le Farse di Carnevale in Calabria e Sicilia*. Nicastro, 1888.

Lussky, George F. "The Structure of Hans Sachs' Fastnachtspiele in Relation to Their Place of Performance." *Journal of English and Germanic Philology* 26 (1927):521–63.

Maggi, Vincenzo. "On the Ridiculous." In *Theories of Comedy*. Edited by Paul Lauter, translated by George Miltz. Garden City, N.Y., 1964. (Originally published 1550.)

Manzoni, Luigi. *Il Libro di Carnevale dei Secoli XV e XVI*. Bologna, 1881.

Maxwell, Ian. *French Farce and John Heywood*. Melbourne and London, 1946.

Mazzi, Curzio. *La Congrega dei Rozzi di Siena*. Florence, 1882.

McLean, Albert F., Jr. *American Vaudeville as Ritual*. Lexington, Ky., 1965.

Meredith, George. "An Essay on Comedy." In *Comedy*. Edited by Wylie Sypher. Garden City, N.Y., 1956.

Meyerhold, Vsevolod. "Farce," *Tulane Drama Review* 4 (1959):139–49.

Moellenhof, Fritz. "Remarks on the Popularity of Mickey Mouse." *American Imago* 1 (1940):19–32.

Monro, D. H. *Argument of Laughter*. Melbourne, 1951.

Moore, Alexander Parks. *The Genre Poissard and the French Stage of the Eighteenth Century*. New York, 1935.

Morin, Louis. *Carnavals Parisiens*. Paris, 1898.

Murray, Gilbert. *Five Stages of Greek Religion*. Boston, 1951.

Nichols, J. G. *London Pageants*. London, 1837.

Nicoll, Allardyce. *Masks, Mimes, and Miracles*. London, 1931.

———. *The Theatre and Dramatic Theory*. London, 1962.

Nietzsche, Friedrich. *The Birth of Tragedy and the Genealogy of Morals*. Translated by Francis Golffing. Garden City, N.Y., 1956.

Norwood, Gilbert. *Plautus and Terence*. New York, 1932.

Olson, Elder. *The Theory of Comedy*. Bloomington, Ind., 1968.

Pandolfi, Vito. *La Commedia dell'Arte*. 6 vols. Florence, 1957–61.

Selected Bibliography

Paratore, Ettore. "L'Arte Plautina." In *Alla Scoperta di Plauto*. Edited by Achille Fioco. Rome, 1964.

Perna, Raffaelle. *L'Originalità di Plauto*. Bari, 1955.

Perucci, Andrea. *Dell'Arte Rappresentativa Premeditata ed all'Improviso*. Naples, 1699.

Petit de Julleville, Louis. *Histoire du théâtre en France: Les comédiens en France au Moyen Âge*. Paris, 1885.

———. *Répétoire du théâtre comique*. Paris, 1886.

Pickard-Cambridge, A. W. *Dithyramb, Tragedy and Comedy*. Oxford, 1927.

———. *The Dramatic Festivals of Athens*. Oxford, 1953.

Radcliff-Umstead, Douglas. *The Birth of Modern Comedy in Renaissance Italy*. Chicago, 1969.

Rasi, Luigi. *I Comici Italiani*. 3 vols. Florence, 1897–1905.

Reich, Annie. "The Structure of the Grotesque-Comic Sublimation." *Yearbook of Psychoanalysis* 6 (1950):194–207.

Reich, Hermann. *Der Mimus. Ein Litterar-entwickelungsgeschichtlicker Versuch*. 2 vols. Berlin, 1903.

Riccoboni, Luigi. *Histoire du théâtre italien*. 2 vols. Paris, 1730–31.

Richter, Gisela M. A. "Grotesques and the Mime." *American Journal of Archeology* 17, 2d ser. (1913), 149–56.

Rigal, Eugène, P. M. *Le Théâtre avant la période classique*. Paris, 1901.

Rolland, Joachim. *Théâtre comique en France avant le XVe siècle*. Paris, 1926.

Rudwin, Maximilian Josef. *The Origin of German Carnival Comedy*. New York, 1920.

Sand, Maurice. *Les Masques et bouffons de la comédie italienne*. 2 vols. Paris, 1859.

Sanesi, Ireneo. *La Commedia*. 2 vols. Milan, 1911–35.

Santayana, George. "The Comic Mask" and "Carnival." In *Soliloquies in England, and Later Soliloquies*. New York, 1923.

Schilling, Bernard N. *The Comic Spirit: Boccaccio to Thomas Mann*. Detroit, 1965.

Schopenhauer, Arthur. *The World as Will and Idea*. Translated by R. B. Haldane and J. Kemp. London, 1891.

Segal, Erich. *Roman Laughter*. Cambridge, Mass., 1968.

Smith, Robert Metcalf. *Types of Farce-Comedy*. New York, 1928.

Smith, Winifred. *The Commedia dell'Arte*. New York, 1912.

Stephenson, Robert C. "Farce as Method." In *Comedy: Meaning and Form*. Edited by R. W. Corrigan. San Francisco, 1965.

Sumberg, Samuel Leslie. *Nuremberg Schembart Carnival*. New York, 1941.

Sypher, Wylie. "The Meanings of Comedy." In *Comedy*. Edited by Wylie Sypher. Garden City, N.Y., 1956.

Taladoire, Barthélémy A. *Essai sur le comique de Plaute*. Monaco, 1956.

Tiddy, R. J. E. *The Mummers' Plays*. Oxford, 1923.

Toldo, Pietro. "Études sur le théâtre comique français du Moyen Âge." *Studi di Filologia Romanza* 9 (1903):181–369.

Toschi, Paolo. *Drammatica Popolare Italiana*. Rome, 1940.

———. *Forme Drammatiche Popolari*. Rome, 1953.

———. *Guida allo Studio delle Tradizioni Popolari*. Rome, 1941.

———. *Le Origini del Teatro Italiano*. Turin, 1955.

Turner, Victor Witter. *The Ritual Process: Structure and Anti-Structure*. Chicago, 1969.

Voltz, Pierre. *La Comédie*. Paris, 1964.

Wace, A. J. B. "Mumming Plays in the Southern Balkans." *Annual of the British School at Athens* 19 (1912–13): 248–65.

———. "North Greek Festivals and the Worship of Dionysos." *Annual of the British School at Athens* 16 (1909–10): 232–53.

Weaver, John. *The History of Mimes and Pantomimes*. London, 1728.

Weiser, Francis Xavier. *Handbook of Christian Feasts and Customs*. New York, 1958.

Welsford, Enid. *The Fool: His Social and Literary History*. London, 1935.

Zeidman, Irving. *The American Burlesque Show*. New York, 1967.

Index

Index

Index

Index

Index

Anthony Caputi received the Ph.D. degree from Cornell University. He is professor of English at Cornell.

The manuscript was prepared for publication by Jean Owen. The book was designed by Donald R. Ross. The type face for the text is Mergenthaler's Caledonia, designed by W. A. Dwiggins in 1937. The display face is Ultra Bodoni, designed by American Type Founders in 1928. The text is printed on Warren's 1854 Text paper and the book is bound in Holliston Mills' Roxite cloth and Process Materials' Elephant Hide paper. Manufactured in the United States of America.